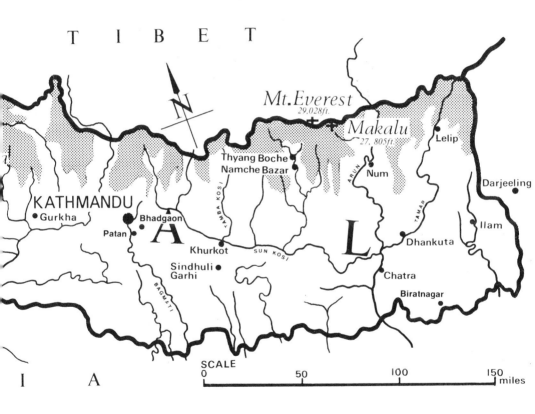

T I B E T

Mt.Everest
29.028ft.

Makalu
27, 805ft.

Lelip

Thyang Boche
Namche Bazar

Darjeeling

Num

KATHMANDU

Gurkha
Bhadgaon
Patan

A

Khurkot

SUN KOSI

TAMBA KOSI

ARUN

TAMAR

Ilam

Dhankuta

L

Sindhuli
Garhi

BAGMATI

Chatra

Biratnagar

I   A

SCALE
0   50   100   150
miles

HIMALAYAN SOLO

Also by Elizabeth Forster

THE WANDERING TATTLER

Himalayan Solo

Elizabeth Forster

Anthony Nelson

England

First Published in 1982
by Anthony Nelson Ltd.

ISBN 0 904614 03 4

Anthony Nelson Ltd.
7 St. John's Hill, Shrewsbury, England.

Printed by Livesey Limited, Shrewsbury, England.

Contents

Introduction

The First Trek   9

Towards Everest   23

Annapurna   41

Everest — The Base Camp   68

East Nepal and Kala Pattar   101

The Rough and the Smooth   152

Appendix I
    A Word About Nepal   184

Appendix II
    Useful Hints for a Trek   190

List of Birds mentioned in the Text   195

To the three Flemings, the late Dr. Bethel, Dr. Robert L., Snr.
and Dr. Robert L., Jnr. who all helped me so greatly over a very
long period.

List of Illustrations

Following Page

The party for my first trek, Pasang in centre with my camera.   30
Mingma with the dhal tree which she cut for me.   30
Itinerant Nepalese flute seller.   30
View from the pass above Takhsindu monastery.   30
Pomori with Lindgren behind.   30

Pasang's beautiful wife, Namdo, with two daughters and a friend   62
'The Fighting Men'.   62
Rhododendrons in front of Dhaulagiri.   62

Bare footprints, Chinese shoes and climbing boots all going to and
    from Namche.   94
Pasang looking for birds.   94
Chorten in Bhandar.   94
Pasang and Mingma preparing 'Sir's' lunch.   94
Inching across the Khumbu Khola.   94
Ice melting on Gokyo lake at almost 17,000 ft.   94
The Author on lower slope of Kala Pattar with Khumbu Glacier in
    the background.   94
Thyang Boche monastery.   94
Sukrabir entertaining an admiring audience.   94
Base Camp.   94
My trekking companions, Sanila on far left and Lobsang far right.   94
Small helpers bringing in their baskets of leaves.   94
Namche Bazar.   94
Cool lunch site in a hot valley.   94
Porters really resting.   94
Peaks in the Gokyo valley.   94

Machha Puchhare from above Pokhara.   126
Buying bracelets in Khasindu market.   126
Tule making makai.   126
Tibetan snowcocks feeding at Gorakshep.   126

The summit of Everest.   158
Bringing in fresh food for cattle.   158
Tule supervising cauliflower weighing in Ilam market.   158
Icy mountains on the way to Chukhkung look like accordian
    pleating.   158

Introduction

How it all began

I have been an enthusiastic walker and lover of the countryside since my early childhood and as soon as I saw my first mountains in my late teens I became even more enthusiastic at the prospect of walking among them. The Lake District, Scotland, Wales, Austria, Switzerland, and later on the Rockies, seemed to be my lot: although I had read everything I could lay my hands on about the expeditions attempting to conquer Mount Everest I never even dreamed that I should go there myself.

Then one day I heard that Nepal, for so long a closed country, had decided to open its frontiers to visitors. I resolved to go, cost what it might, and as I had been planning to take my first trip to Asia in 1964 Nepal was obviously one of the places to visit.

I was immediately captivated by the country, its people, its buildings, those incredible mountains and also the rich bird life. I knew nothing about Asian birds then but I had bought Sálim Ali's *Book of Indian Birds* and Whistler's *Birds of India,* and Sálim Ali had given me a letter of introduction to Dr. Bob Fleming. Dr. Fleming was an American missionary who had been living and working in Kathmandu since 1953, studying the birds in every spare minute in conjunction with his son, also Dr. Bob, who was a professional ornithologist. When I rang both men were away on a birding trip. 'But', said a sweet and kind voice at the other end of the telephone, 'do come here to see if I can help you'.

I went and that was how I met Dr. Bethel Fleming, who was a doctor of medicine. She was one of the most remarkable women I have ever known. Very tall and heavily built she stood magnificently upright, her head crowned with a thick plait of snow-white hair. She welcomed me with a warm and friendly smile which grew ever warmer and friendlier in later years when I knew her better. She was very sorry that her husband and son were away but would it help me at all to go with her to the clinics she held in outlying villages? I could look for birds round about while she treated her patients. This seemed too good to be true and I accepted at once, riding to her house in Patan on an ancient bicycle that I hired in the bazaar.

We went to Chapagaon on the first occasion and there I saw my first scarlet minivets, a paradise flycatcher, a mountain thrush, and many others that took hours of searching through the books to identify. On our second trip, this time to Godaveri, I saw fewer birds near her clinic but on the way back a steppe eagle flew over her car and remained nearby long enough for me to see it really well. I was enormously elated at seeing my first Asian eagle so close at hand.

During the course of our drive Dr. Bethel said that as I was so keen on walking and bird-watching she wondered why I didn't contact Jimmy Roberts. This was Colonel Roberts, a retired army officer who had been attached to the British Embassy in Kathmandu and was now starting a trekking agency. It was to be called Mountain Travel and would take parties of trekkers walking through the valleys to the snowy heights above.

My ten-week Asian trip was all planned, including visits to many parts of India and a trip to Thailand, but I decided at once that if Colonel Roberts could be induced to include me in one of his trekking parties all or any of my proposed trip could be abandoned for absolutely nothing could be better than walking and camping throughout Nepal.

But where to find Colonel Roberts? Dr. Bethel's enquiries in many directions produced nothing definite but on my last day, when I was to fly to Pokhara, I heard that he was there. I couldn't find him but eventually I found someone who thought he could take a letter to the colonel. In it I asked to be included in a trek if it could possibly be arranged and gave the address of my hotel in Darjeeling. Later in the week a cable came to me which said 'Sorry, no treks available at present'.

So began a long correspondence with Colonel Roberts until we finally arranged that I should join a party going to Everest in the early spring of 1967 when I would reach Nepal on the last leg of a trip round the world.

This was not to be. I had to come home in the autumn of 1966, after only a month, in order to have a major operation. It was successful and I soon began to plan once more, arranging that I would get to Kathmandu at the end of March 1968 and would then set off to Everest.

And that was how my love affair with Nepal began.

The First Trek

The great day came when I was to fly from Calcutta to Kathmandu to begin my first Himalayan trek.

This time I knew what to expect and took a right-hand tail seat with a clear view. An hour later I saw a distant whiteness which looked too solid for cloud and whipped out my binoculars for a first sight of the enchanted range that I was soon to see more closely. As we drew nearer the captain told us over the intercom which peak was which and a few minutes later said that anyone who was interested was welcome to come into the cockpit.

It was too beautiful to believe and my hands shook as I took a few pictures to look at when I was calmer, pictures that would confirm the reality of what I had seen.

We landed about half an hour later, a vertiginous descent amongst spiky smaller peaks, many of them terraced and cultivated right to the top. It looked to be exceedingly difficult terrain for walking.

Next day I met Colonel Roberts, a tall, loosely jointed man with a slight limp and the brightest of blue eyes. He said, to my great regret, that he thought it rather rash to go on a solo trek to the Everest region only a few months after a major operation so he had arranged a fortnight's trek to the Gosainkund lakes, a kind of circular tour up one ridge and down another. If the lakes were not open, and they might well not be as there had been a lot of snow, I could go at least to Tharepati which was 12,000 feet.

The district I was going to was Helambu, a good introduction to the greater heights, and within it were two Sherpa villages, although most Sherpas lived in the higher areas of Khumbu, Solu and thereabouts.

Colonel Roberts gave me a lot of good advice, talked about the birds to be seen at various altitudes, and warned me not to go too far too fast, to give myself ample time to acclimatise. He introduced me to my Sherpa, a very serious and well-mannered young man called Pasang Kami.

I was to have five porters and a cook as well as Pasang. It seemed an awful lot for one woman and I wondered what they would all do. Colonel Roberts said that the weather should be good but as there had been quite a lot of rain recently it might be prudent to take an umbrella. This would certainly solve the problem of rain-splashed spectacles and binoculars but what should I do with it in fine weather? Could I hand it to one of the five porters?

I was to lay my kit out on my hotel bed and Colonel Roberts or Pasang would come to inspect it to see if I had all the things I needed. It was comforting to think that Mountain Travel would be looking after me so well.

Next day I was invited to dinner with the Flemings and was very happy to meet Dr. Bethel again and to be introduced to her husband, Dr. Bob, Snr. Their son, Dr. Bob, Jnr., told me enticing stories of the wonderful birds I should see on my trek. The trip sounded complicated enough with these two experts at hand so what would it be like when I was quite alone?

The day before the trek began Pasang was in and out of my hotel throughout the day, bringing rope, headbands and parcels and packages of this and that, visitations that the hotel receptionists took in their stride even though the entrance hall was littered with impedimenta.

Departure was set for 8 o'clock next morning. I was instructed to have had breakfast and to bring a packed lunch.

I couldn't sleep for excitement and had breakfasted and collected the lunch box long before eight. Pasang did not appear until 8.45, distraught beyond anything that the occasion warranted for the jeep had broken down just as they were driving it out of the yard and had to be repaired before they could start. He packed everything in with lightning speed and off we set.

Just outside the King's Palace, its gateway flanked by two custard-coloured pillars with white running down the sides and a red knob on top exactly like a cherry on a sundae, I saw a group of young people sitting on the kerb. We stopped and took them aboard and I was told that these were our porters and the cook, four men and two women. I was unprepared for women porters to carry heavy loads, although I was to find later that they were every bit as tough as men. Looking at this somewhat scruffy bunch I had no idea that by the end of the fortnight I should be almost in tears when leaving them, so devoted had we all become.

We jolted along a dusty road to a village called Sunderijal, the site of a pumping station. Here we shook out the porters who had been so precariously perched on a mountain of gear and Pasang began to get everything in order, a task at which he was adept.

The amount of baggage looked enormous. Colonel Roberts had

said that my personal luggage should be limited to thirty pounds so what on earth was all this? It proved to be tents and groundsheets, sleeping bags, cooking utensils and lots and lots of food. I watched with great interest as the bamboo baskets were packed up, about 60 pounds to each. There were no smaller loads for the girls who sat down in front of them, slipped over their foreheads a headband attached by rope to the basket and stood up, with difficulty. We were off, Pasang and I in front and the porters plodding behind. Our way lay up a steep path by the side of a stream bordered by an unsightly pipe bringing water to Kathmandu. I was eager to see what birds were about and only hoped that at least some of them would be in Sálim Ali's *The Birds of Sikkim*, for there was then no book on the birds of Nepal.

I peered over the wall below which the stream lay and there was my first white-capped river chat, a black bird with tomato red breast and long, flicking tail and a white cap on its head which looked to be angled like a French sailor's. It flew from rock to rock, quivering that long red tail as it alighted. It was enchanting and this enchantment has never dimmed as I have watched it on almost every Nepalese river or stream that I have passed. Nearby was the plumbeous redstart. The male, a trifle smaller and stubbier that the white-capped, was a beautiful dark Air Force blue with the same trembling red tail. The female was totally different with a finely scalloped pattern on her breast, a white triangle at the base of her tail and no red 'start' to announce her status.

Soon after came a rather piercing call and a dark blue, thrush-like bird catapulted downhill. It had a bright yellow bill, a broad tail and was covered with small, lighter blue spots. It was the Himalayan whistling thrush. This was a good beginning and I kept ploughing on with plenty of energy.

Pasang walked by my side, serious and earnest. I don't think he had had a solitary female client before and he called me 'Sir' throughout. His first question was unexpected.

'How old are you, Sir?' he asked.

I said, without any hesitation, 'Fifty-nine'.

He drew a long, whistling breath. I deduced that few Sherpas or Nepalis lived to such a great age. I wondered if he felt anxious that this antique Englishwoman would become a terrible responsibility.

At length Pasang said that lunch would be a good thing. He and the porters set about preparing something for themselves and I sat under a tree with my lunchbox, tearing at a piece of rather tough chicken and trying to cope with a hard-boiled egg that wasn't. Some time later Pasang roused me for, contrary to all former procedure, I had fallen asleep; the combination of the early start and great excitement had sapped my energies. Refreshed, we walked on through the forest of rather weedy trees, some being scarlet rhododendrons which gave me a thrill. There were bushes that looked rather like St. John's wort, others were similar to viburnum; it was clear that there would be problems of identification.

The path was full as a busy city street with tramping porters, all bent under great loads. My own, apparently unconscious of their 60 pound plus burdens were laughing, joking and obviously enjoying every minute of the day.

That night we camped inside the forest just off the path, a new and wonderful experience for me. Birds were everywhere and I was particularly attracted by the red-headed tits, charming little morsels with a kind of rusty beret on their heads, a little black 'beard' and distinctive black face markings, but so small and volatile that identification was difficult and photography impossible.

I saw many kinds of tits on this trek, the most confusing being the grey tit. This, the Indian race of the European great tit, is grey, black and white, whereas another bird that looks very much like our great tit, being green, yellow, black and white in roughly the same places, is called the green-backed tit. Very difficult.

For good measure there was also the yellow-cheeked tit, a delightful, bouncy little creature with a black crest and rows of blackish-blue spots casually distributed about its plumage. There were pied woodpeckers with brown breasts, white-cheeked bulbuls with beautiful black crests that curled forwards over their foreheads and black bulbuls, grey and black with coral-pink bills, legs and feet, raucous voices and contumacious behaviour. There was a falconet, a fierce hunter of only 7 inches sitting right on top of a tree, white-tailed nuthatches, more and more new species, all beautiful, all interesting, and all, till then, unknown. I spent every spare minute looking through the books in an effort to identify what I saw. I found that Pasang had the sharpest of eyes and saw a bird clearly before I even noticed it was there. This was a great help. He walked with me most of the time but also kept a very keen watch on the porters whom he ruled with great firmness. He referred to himself as 'an old man of twenty-nine'. He was an old man of great experience for he had been on Everest expeditions as well as others of lesser magnitude and had carried oxygen cylinders, no mean weight, to well above 20,000 feet.

His camp rules were strict. I was segregated from the porters, a tubular steel chair was put out for me when we stopped for a meal, although later on I preferred to have my Dunlopillo pad laid out instead. Hot water was brought to my tent twice a day and my meals were served nicely on a tin tray.

Next morning we continued upwards, I was to find in many

different treks that my most constant poetic memory was Christina Rossetti's 'And does the road wind uphill *all* the way?' On the brow of the hill I saw an enchanting sight at the forest edge, half a dozen yellow-bellied fantail flycatchers. This ponderous name gives no indication of the charm and distinction of these thistle-down acrobats which plunge, ascend, perch and fly off again within seconds, fluttering and swooping, flicking out their beautiful fan tails and retracting them in endless succession.

I tore my eyes away from them at last and looked beyond the forest to behold an almost endless vista of distant Himalayas, the diamond necklace of mountains first seen from the plane; this time I was in the same element and not hanging unbelievably above them.

We swung out of the trees on to open, over-grazed grassland covered with tiny flowers in varying shades of blue. I learned later that these were minute gentians. I was entranced with everything I saw, particularly the rhododendrons. I knew them well as garden shrubs at home but to see tall trees blazing with clusters of scarlet bloom was almost beyond my comprehension.

There were orchids, too, great white orchids which flowed down north facing rocks and down the trunks of mossy trees, snowy blooms with golden throats. I found later that these were called *Coleogyne cristata*. Mingma, the cook, a fat boy of about eighteen, immediately shinned up to a giddy height and tore some down for me. This shocked my conservationist mind but I couldn't say anything as he had done it out of sweetness and to please Sir. And Sir, trudging onwards clutching a mixed handful of white orchids and scarlet rhododendrons, was in a blissfully happy state.

We were all pretty happy. All but one of the porters were Sherpas and they made a jolly family party, joking and laughing the entire time. Peals of merry laughter were the first sounds I heard in the morning and the last at night. The only exception to the universal jollity was a rather depressed little Tamang porter who walked by himself, cooked different food on a special fire and was definitely odd man out.

That day we had walked from 7 o'clock, with about one and a half hours for lunch, and I began to feel tired. I asked Pasang when we were going to stop and he said to my great relief that it wasn't far. I believed him then.

As we struggled up yet another hill a man passed us carrying a large sheet of corrugated iron, shining with an almost blinding brilliance. This unwieldy load was some eight to nine feet long, carried lengthwise, supported by a little bamboo contrivance suspended from his shoulders. I found on closer inspection that it was not one sheet of iron but four and later men came by, carrying as many as six sheets. The weight was far greater than the ordinary porter's load and very tricky to manipulate on any narrow path or round corners, for then the porters had to turn sideways to shuffle past. Pasang told me that in the village of Tarke Ghyang they were building a new Buddhist temple and the corrugated iron was for the roof. I thought that it must be a very big temple for relays of staggering porters bearing their unyielding metal burdens passed us every day.

I began to feel very tired indeed and asked again how far we had to go. 'Not far', repeated Pasang. 'If you look you can see the porters making fire for tea'.

I looked and saw, perhaps a couple of miles away, a wisp of smoke. By the time I reached it I was all in and that night I was very sick (in the British, not the American, sense) and realised that I had done too much too soon and that the only thing to do now was nothing.

I rested for the whole of the following day and recovered completely but wisely realised that such mammoth stages were not for Sir at fifty-nine. What had Colonel Roberts said? 'Don't go too far or too fast-at first'. Staying put on that day was no hardship for we were camped on a little cliff above a river which was full of birds, both redstarts, grey wagtails, even longer in the tail than ours it seemed, blue whistling thrushes and occasional dippers. There were white-breasted kingfishers too, spectacular birds of iridescent blue which in some lights looked jade green, the rich brown of their breasts enhanced by a snowy dickey, their brown heads terminating in a long, thick red beak.

Our camping place next day was at the junction of two rivers and here we met another Mountain Travel party, the Harrops, an English family living in Kathmandu. I made friends with them and they are my friends still.

They were all far younger than I, had very long legs and went at what seemed to me to be Olympic speed. They trotted off next morning at the double while I followed more soberly, stopping for every bird I saw, and there were a lot. The best of all, which appeared at about 8,000 feet, was another redstart, this time the blue-fronted. It was an exquisite creature of a beautiful deep blue and across its forehead and above its eyes ran a thin line of shining paler blue. Its breast and tail were tomato red like the white-capped redstart, now called the river chat, and it was lovely beyond words. I was very anxious to photograph it but this proved to be unexpectedly difficult. To take a colour slide at that time cost about one rupee and every time I tried and failed another rupee was wasted. By the time the blue-fronted redstart had been satisfactorily photographed it had come to be known as the fourteen-rupee bird.

As time passed the porter's personalities became more evident.

Pasang, the sirdar, was blazingly efficient and his word was law; not suprisingly, either, as he could do everything quicker and better than anyone else. Mingma was the cook and this was, I think, his first trip. He knew very little but he was immensely willing, good-hearted and boisterous, a large, rather fubsy individual whom one could not view with anything but an indulgent smile.

The two other men were Lagpa and Sonam and neither could have been more than eighteen. They carried their great packs without any sign of fatigue and directly they took their loads off they began to fight. This was their relaxation, to wrestle, struggle and tangle, rolling all over the ground to rid themselves of the superabundant energy which welled up in them eternally. Before and after every meal and even when we merely stopped to rest on the way these two, whom I soon christened The Fighting Men, were perpetually engaged in friendly combat.

The two girls, one pretty, one plain, were both lovable. They wore long, sleeveless, black dresses, with crossover bodices topping a long-sleeved blouse, striped Sherpa aprons and an old cardigan when it was very cold. Their big bamboo baskets had a rope on each side that was attached to a woven headband, and this was worn either high or low on the forehead according to individual preference. The two girls placed a piece of towelling folded several times on top of their heads and this, going beneath the headband, lessened the strain on their foreheads. Sometimes they bent their hands back over their shoulders and held these side ropes which again gave them relief as they plodded tirelessly on. No Sherpas ever seem to tire, or if they do they don't admit it.

In many parts of Nepal stone walls have a built-in shelf at the height of the porters' baskets. The porters back on to this, set the basket down securely and then ease off their headbands to have a few minutes' rest. If the pause is only a short one they merely sit the basket on the ledge and stand by it, relieved of the weight.

These ledges, which I always called porters' chairs, are a great blessing and a good excuse to sit down for a cigarette or a sweet. Boiled sweets are a great help on trek and one can now buy quite good ones in Kathmandu in one-pound bags. They come in mixed flavours but the pink ones were my favourites and the porters used to pick them out for me. I found that an issue of sweets, the porters called them chocolate, was an institution that was greatly appreciated, and Sir was welcome to the pink sweets if she gave each porter one of another colour three times a day.

That morning I had my first sight of red-billed blue magpies. These are the sort of birds that are often drawn on Christmas cards, bird-shaped creatures that look quite unreal. They were large and blue-grey with a hint of subdued violet in their plumage, pillar-box red beaks and long, long tails that trailed behind them like ribbons from a kite. They floated through the air in small parties and three birds flying in uneven line occupied some ten feet of air space, a kind of avian Nessie.

We tramped on and on in the uplands and then I felt an ominous tiredness coming over me. Remembering my previous collapse I said firmly to Pasang that we must camp as soon as possible. Mingma soon found a beautiful site looking into a group of snow mountains and I recovered after tea and 'a nice lie down'.

Our next stop was Tarke Ghyang. It did not seem particularly beautiful but I may have been mistaken because it was misty when we arrived. After supper Pasang and I went for a short walk before bed and what should we discover but the temple that was being built and at the side of it a huge shining pile of corrugated iron. The building was lavishly, and rather garishly, decorated with a seething mass of menacing dragons and was growing visibly under the hands of the toiling men who were building it freely to the glory of the Buddha. To Western eyes it was not a lovely sight but the spirit that created it was lovely indeed.

On about the sixth day we came to Shermarthang, a beautiful village some 9,000 feet up, with forest and open ground alternating and views of stupendous mountains all round. I grew more and more elated. This was what I had long been waiting for and I was not disappointed.

Shermarthang was lovely but tinged with sadness for me by the sight of the Tibetan mastiff at a house near our camp. This unhappy beast was closely chained and seemed never to be let loose. I threw him some biscuits which he ate ravenously but I saw no evidence of food. He must have had some or he would have died on his chain but I saw nothing all the while we were there. He and the other canine captives in the vicinity kept me from my usual sound sleep as they barked a dolorous, syncopated chorus throughout the starlit frosty night.

When it grew light we saw that the ground was white with rime. Pasang said that it would be some time before we could move on as the frost must be shaken off the tents. These would then have to be partially dried or they would be far too heavy for the porters to carry. I was glad of the delay because the field where we had camped was terraced and had little bushes and plants at intervals and among these was a flock of small birds flitting to and fro. I had no idea what they were and stalked them as quietly as I could, my footsteps crunching slightly on the crusted grass. At last I managed to see that they had chestnut cheeks outlined in cream and chestnut striped heads. There was no doubt that they were little buntings, something I had vainly searched for in Finland in 1958 and now here were about thirty of them, close at hand. Close at hand, too, was the fourteen-rupee bird and it was here that I managed to photograph him successfully.

While we were waiting to go a flock of large birds zoomed out of the mist and settled on the ground in front of us. They had dark grey heads, white bodies, wings that were a mixture of black, brown and grey, and smart red feet. They pecked about on the ground and then took off, showing a flashy banded tail-pattern of black and white. I discovered later that I had seen my first snow pigeons.

At 8.30 Pasang said that we could go and we began a steep descent of 2,000 feet that led to a river. We were on an open hillside backed by forest when a purple-blue bird flew by. I pursued it into the forest and found it sitting high up on a bare tree stump. It was a chestnut-bellied rock thrush, one of the most beautiful of Nepal's many lovely birds, its brilliant blue offset by a chestnut breast that held a hint of crimson.

We stopped to lunch by the river and every Nepalese member of the party, both male and female, washed their hair and their clothes. One of my abiding memories of Nepal is of Mingma kneeling by this river washing Sir's bra and panties. All the time as we trekked steadily on I was impressed by the sheer joy of life expressed by the Sherpas. They had very little money, no amenities and no artificial amusements yet they seemed to my uncultivated eye to be happier than any other young people I had ever met, laughing and playing as skittishly as lambs and bending to all their tasks with expedition and good humour. And as they climbed they frequently sang loudly and rather raucously, striding forwards beneath their loads at a speed that far exceeded my pack-free pace. To counter this Pasang insisted that the Sherpas' life was hard, nothing but carrying for ever and ever, with no education and no comforts.

This pattern is changing and since the British Everest Expedition first climbed the world's highest mountain in 1953 one of the first two conquerors of this formidable peak, Sir Edmund Hillary, has come back at least every two years, to climb again in Nepal and also to do something for the Sherpas who made his world-famous ascent possible. Everyone admits that without the aid of these brave, indomitable and delightful people few climbers would ever reach the summit of any really high Himalayan peak. Realising this and grateful for it, Hillary comes back with a team of New Zealand helpers and, with money raised by co-operation with World Books, has built schools in all kinds of Sherpa villages and a complete hospital at Kunde; in 1975, when his wife and daughter were killed in an air crash in Kathmandu, he was in Paphlu engaged in building a second hospital.

Pasang, like most other Sherpas, had no schooling at all and learnt to read and write later in life, but his children and all the others in Namche Bazar and many other villages now go to school and are being educated by Nepalese teachers, whose salaries are paid by New Zealand. The Hillary parties have also constructed bridges which are vitally necessary for getting about in what was until very recently virtually roadless Nepal. These bridges have to be built high above the mountain rivers to avoid the pressure of the monsoon floods. Some are swept away each year and then new ones have to be made.

I met my first Nepalese bridge over the Melemche river and I was shaken by it. It stood high above the rock-filled torrent, was rather wobbly and had no handrail. Crossing it was a salutary and most unpleasant experience and I was very glad that we were to return by another route. I heard later from the Harrops that when they reached Melemchigaon they looked back across the river to Tarke Ghyang and saw a leopard. Why couldn't that sort of thing happen to me?

I thought when climbing in Nepal that if I went to a 12,000 feet peak from Kathmandu, which was about 4,500 feet, that I should have to climb only 7,500 feet. What an idiotic misconception that was! We had already been up to 8,000 and down to 3,000 and up again for another 5,000 or so, and from Tarke Ghyang at 9,000 we were descending for at least 2,000 and then were to camp at 10,000 and still we had to get up to Tharepati.

We camped at Melemchigaon and it was cold. It was nearly a week since we had left Kathmandu and the little Tamang, with only a thin cotton garment and no shoes, huddled over his fire, talked to nobody and was thoroughly miserable in this closed shop of Sherpas. That night he told Pasang that he wanted to go home. I didn't blame him.

He left early next morning and so did we but in the opposite direction with the sun coming up as we walked and the birds singing at the top of their varied voices. The forest was the loveliest we had seen so far: first scarlet rhododendrons in profusion and then tall conifers of an unfamiliar kind; beneath these magnificent trees grew dhal.

Dhal, a wonderfully fragrant bush, grows abundantly in Nepal. It is a slightly different form of the shrub that we call daphne in Britain and I had never visualised it as a forest species. I have a daphne bush in my garden which blooms and scents the air exquisitely at a time of year when any flower seems an unexpected present. Here it was spilling all over the forest floor, bringing a touch of pure magic to this Asian forest. Its scent was so pervasive that I sensed its presence long before I saw it. As we climbed we came to the flowering bush type of rhododendron. The flowers were still scarlet but the form and habit were different. Instead of being a big tree this had a number of thin branches springing from a central point, all of them peeling like a plane tree. The flowers were smaller, brighter and not bunched in such big clusters and beneath these spreading scarlet rhododendrons grew masses of little orchid-pink primroses, their petals deeply toothed at the top and their thick dark-green leaves dentated too. In this enchanted grove, as if the flowers and trees were not enough, were yellow-bellied fantail flycatchers, excitable as ever, black-faced flycatcher warblers, brown-crested tits, spot-winged black tits and many more.

Ang Rita, one of the Sherpa girls, came to tell me that lunch was ready and returning to our camp I found another new flower, a rhododendron cluster specially made for me by the porters with a primrose head embedded in each floret, the whole tied to the top of a stick and stuck into the ground by the side of my pad. Everyone watched closely to see my reception of their little ruse and I exclaimed with great pleasure and laughed loudly, while my reception of their jest gave an equal amount of pleasure to my little gang.

After lunch the porters took one route and Pasang, Mingma and I took another, finding a few patches of snow, the first of the trip. We clambered up a rocky slope patched with snow among thick rhododendrons and I heard a piping noise just like a bullfinch. It came again and again and suddenly Pasang spotted an orange-red face with a black area round the bill, which was being stuffed to bursting point with rhododendron buds. Both voice and appetite corresponded to those possessed by the European bullfinch, bane of British fruit growers for its predation of their apple buds. I had no difficulty in identifying this bird as the red-headed bullfinch of Asia, although I wish that I had seen more than its head and shoulders. After more breathless climbing the ground flattened and we came out on to a slope almost entirely filled with deep maroon-coloured berberis, the same type of bush that I cherish in my garden, here growing like gorse on a heath. This little summit was about 10,000 feet up, topped with a small grassy plateau from which the snow had only just cleared. It was perishingly cold, ringed by mountains and forest, loud with bird song and so enchanting that I said at once that we would stay two nights so that I could explore the surroundings next day.

On the plateau was a convenient, commodious, wooden-roofed shed that was very picturesque in appearance and would serve as shelter for the porters. Snow was piled against one side of it and Mingma immediately melted this for tea.

The only thing that marred the idyllic evening was that one of the poor girls had toothache. It must have been an abscess for her face was swollen to an unpleasant degree and I felt that the aspirin which was all I was able to give her would not have much effect. Her own remedy was to put two crossed strips of sticking plaster on her cheek which I feared would be even less helpful.

I had a bad cough and cold on this section of the trek and did not sleep well. I didn't know then of the help that sleeping pills provided at altitude. As I lay coughing in my cosy tent I heard tremendous cat noises. So far as I know leopards only cough and this was like the most vocal of tom cats making ready for the fray. Snow leopard? I saw no tracks next day but then there was little snow left.

When dawn came I looked forward to a rewarding day on this serene and secret plateau, but unhappily it was misty. At last it cleared in some measure and Pasang and I went exploring, finding on a shoulder of the mountain a splendid animal that looked rather like a chamois. I made to look at it through my binoculars but Pasang, in true Sherpa fashion, made loud noises and in a flash it had gone. I was told later that it was a goral.

There was no sign of any cat to match the yowling of the preceding night but I did hear what I thought to be a growl in the undergrowth. I felt that this might be a bear and having heard of the ferocity of these creatures I was eager to be gone for I am a terrible coward at heart. Pasang pooh-poohed my fears but I knew that there were bears in Nepal and this was a fairly unfrequented thick forest.

We spent some time in this lovely place which was an almost solid mass of scarlet rhododendrons. We were looking for pheasants as Bob Fleming had said we ought surely to find some. Not a pheasant of any species did we see, but we did find a sizeable black and gold bird high in a rhododendron tree. It had a wonderful golden body with black wings and tail and its accompanying female was all olive green. We watched them building their nest but unfortunately it was very high up in the tree so we could not get really close views of them. I found from *The Birds of Sikkim* that they were without doubt allied grosbeaks, said to be not too common.

Just as dusk was falling I heard the vocal pussy again and again. It sounded very near at hand but neither I nor any of the extremely sharp-eyed Sherpas could pick out a shadowy form.

After dark the fresh wind that had blown off the morning mist became so strong and aggressive that I was apprehensive. The hurricane lamp hanging from the centre of the tent swung so violently that I had to blow it out and then the flysheet over the tent was whipped off. I visualised being blown down the mountainside and called to Pasang to say that I must move into the cowshed with the rest of them. Pasang found this to be rather an alarming prospect but agreed that it might be wise, insisting that I should sit by their fire on my tubular steel chair while he and the others struck my tent and re-erected it inside, as it was unthinkable that my segregation should not be maintained. This task achieved I slept in peace with the rest of them.

Next morning was hot and brilliant and we went to Tharepati, some 2,000 feet above, first having to descend considerably which made the climb longer. It had been very cold indeed on the previous night but when we reached the 12,000 feet ridge and had lunch, looking out over a wide and glorious prospect, the sun was so hot that I would have been happy in a bathing suit.

To reach our camp site, high spot of the trip in every way, we had to go along the ridge, masked with deep, sun-softened snow in which we sank. Although my feet sank my spirits soared for we could see high, inspiring peaks in every direction. But, as Colonel Roberts had foretold, we were not able to reach the Gosainkund lakes which lay at 15,000 feet because the snow was far too deep. I don't think I would have had the energy for a further climb to 15,000 feet and the return journey and I was very happy to stay where I was, high on my ridge. Below us, at the bottom of a deepish slope, lay a long shed half buried in snow and I remarked to Pasang that any cows there would have a cold and damp time.

'Cows?' said Pasang, in a slightly offended voice. 'That isn't a cowshed, it's a guest house!'

That night in Tharepati was extremely cold, with snow everywhere and for good measure a heavy storm with thunder and lightning which, though terrifying, was most impressive.

In the brilliant morning that followed we went down, still with no pheasants or snow leopards on my list. What did make those obviously feline noises? I found some tracks which I photographed but they were not very distinct and could have been made by almost anything, and I also found some red feathers which had obviously been moulted by or probably plucked from a satyr tragopan, the scarlet, pearl-spotted pheasant that I so badly wanted to see.

The porters raced ahead with undiminished energy. To be a nineteen-year-old Sherpa on a downhill slope is a speedy combination of circumstances and when Pasang and I arrived at the lunch site it was to find that my Dunlopillo pad had been laid out on the roof of a flat shed with a neat pile of stones beside it so that I could climb up without difficulty and enjoy the view from a better vantage point. This was the sort of thing that my little team did every day, some charming, unusual and kindly gesture to make the trip memorable.

On the way down we had our pheasants at last but not really in the way that I would have wished. As they scampered by, some of the porters had seen the monal, the beautiful turquoise-blue Impeyan pheasant which is Nepal's national bird. When we came to a wood great stones were thrown down which flushed the birds out. I strongly disapprove of throwing stones at birds, especially when the stones are so large that they have to be rolled downhill, but sure enough the monal shot out in alarm, a magnificent turquoise spectacle, glinting in the sun, and showing a snowy rump and fanned coral tail.

At tea-time we reached a little clearing near a small precipice. There was a nick in the surrounding forest through which I could see snow peaks, something that I wanted at every camp site wherever possible. It was a lovely place and while I was drinking my tea in peace a crossbill came and perched on a nearby tree. Later on we had yet another fierce thunderstorm which seemed to be the inevitable, though hardly soothing, lullaby in this area.

And so we tramped down from our lovely heights, still logging new birds as we went. At the end of it, tired as I had never been before, I was determined that this trek was to be the first of many.

On the very last lap of the journey a neat and nimble little Gurkha joined me on the path; it was very hot and I was staggering along under my man-sized umbrella and looking rather the worse for wear. I hadn't realised how much worse until he said, 'Where you been, Mummy?'

I have always dreaded the moment when a bus conductor, noting my antique appearance, would call me 'Ma' — and really this was it.

It was lovely to get back to Kathmandu with the immediate prospect of a bath but the crystalline atmosphere of the Helambu heights contrasted unpleasantly with the late spring dust in the Kathmandu Valley. It felt rather like being in the dustbag while the Hoover was working.

Parting from the porters and Pasang was very painful. The scruffy bunch that I had looked on with some distaste when we picked them up had by the end of an idyllic fortnight become people I loved dearly and I hated leaving them. The scenery, the birds and the flowers had all been wonderful but Pasang and his little band had equalled them.

How soon could I go trekking again?

Towards Everest

My first Everest trek, again under the auspices of Mountain Travel, started on 28th January, 1970, and I was lucky enough to have Pasang again. He had by then become a head sirdar who led large parties and had just returned from taking twenty-five Westerners and innumerable porters on a long trek. He was dispirited after coping with their endless problems and was very happy to set off slowly with only one client whom he already knew.

He and I and five Sherpas were packed into a Land Rover and driven along the fine, well-engineered road with a tarred surface which the Chinese have built from the Tibetan border to Kathmandu. We got out at Dolalghat and made camp on the dark grey sand which bordered the Sun Kosi river.

Pasang set the women — Pemba, Mingma and Pasang Doma — and the men — Gyalzen and Kyak Tsering — to work, while I went to look for the first birds of the trip. These were hen harriers (they may have been pale harriers but it was too late in the day to see clearly) spur-winged plovers, red-wattled lapwings and several different races of white wagtail. It looked very promising.

Next morning was fine and warm, for Dolalghat lies at only 1,800 feet, and we started soon after 7 a.m. I was in the usual euphoric mood in which I begin a trek, bewitched by the scenery, happy beyond words and agog with the thought of what was to come.

We stopped for lunch under a peepul tree, an enormous, spreading umbrella with beautiful, almost heart-shaped leaves that ended in a sharp, elongated point, a tree stuffed with mynahs, white-eyes, leaf warblers of many unknown species, sparrows and who knew what else.

The two-hour stop was soon over and we were on the move again, just in time to see three red-billed blue magpies waver across the landscape.

That afternoon we camped in an old rice paddy with the sun beating down on us. I sat with my back against a stone wall typing my circular letter home, for with five porters I could afford the luxury of a typewriter. I was watched from a hedge by an iron-grey bush chat, bulbuls were singing all around, the view was extensive and supper well advanced. Everything was going well and I was grateful to be there.

Next day brought the kind of country I envisaged when in wartime Mr. Churchill spoke of eventually attaining the broad sunlit uplands. We were about 7,000 feet up, the short, over-grazed grass full of tiny gentians and birds, including several strange pipits, flitting across the path from time to time.

We swung over this exhilarating terrain at a spanking pace till we reached a rather scanty forest full of fire-breasted flower peckers, yellow-cheeked tits, minivets, warblers and other birds and fortunately I could now identify many of them.

One beautiful day succeeded another and I walked for hours on end, seeing lovely birds and nearly always with the white peaks of the Rowalling group in view, Ganesh Himal, Jugal Himal and many more.

On one of these happy, bird-filled days I was eating my rumble-tumble (scrambled eggs to me, but that's what the Sherpas called them) when suddenly the trees were filled by a chattering mass of slim birds with grey heads, green bodies and long blue tails. They were my first slaty-headed parakeets and I could now add them to the rose-ringed and blossom-headed members of the tribe that I had seen before.

After lunch we descended to a bridge that I looked at with horror, for it was a most dreadful affair of big chains suspended from posts. Between these chains hung trembling loops of wire supporting two or three planks lying side by side. It was my fate to walk across these planks, trying hard not to look at the rushing, boulder-strewn water below. Pasang was very kind and urged me forward slowly while the porters on the opposite side drew me on by the strength of their combined gaze. I have never been more thankful for anything than for reaching the other side in safety. Pasang wisely omitted to tell me that there were other equally awful bridges to negotiate before reaching Khumbu.

We went on through lovely country, camping in rice paddies, fields and woods. Pasang was adept at choosing isolated camping sites where there was nothing but the peace and silence of the remote countryside, the moon in its differing phases and myriads of stars.

After a few days we reached a point where the track from Lamo-sangu joined our path from Dolalghat. Towards the end of the afternoon I began to feel ill. I crawled up the last hill and collapsed in my tent. I was so exhausted that we had to spend a second night there. I staggered on the following morning but after half a mile had to camp again and stay another two nights. This seemed ridiculous and I set off once more, only to collapse yet again, being forced to stay in an unattractive camp site just outside Yarsa for three nights.

Pasang was very worried and so was I, for to embark on a trek to Everest and to have to lie down for almost a week in the early stages did not augur well. And then, just when I was beginning to wonder if I should abandon the trek entirely, I took a little training walk with Pasang. We went to a stream where I saw a pair of forktails and a fan-tailed flycatcher and I began to feel better and ate my supper with some semblance of relish. Pasang was as relieved as I for while everyone welcomes an occasional day off, almost a week of doing nothing was too much of a good thing and the porters had nothing to occupy their minds or bodies.

Next morning I felt fine so we started slowly up a long slope which took us to 9,000 feet where there was a convenient tea-house. These tea-houses are a feature of Nepalese treks. You can buy small glasses of a thick brew of tea, boiled buffalo milk and sugar, for 25 to 30 *paisa* or, if you insist, you can have 'black tea' without milk and with or without sugar. All Sherpas and porters love to stop at tea-houses at least once a day, particularly if they also sell *chang* (Nepalese rice beer).

A little farther on the thick forest became more open, and flying from tree to tree we saw a flock of white-throated laughing thrushes. Laughing thrushes, which look like very big thrushes but are really babblers, are a delightful and varied family with phenomenally loud voices. They make no sound when you see them and usually fly off whenever possible but if they are not aware of your presence they will suddenly give vent to enormous gusts of sound, sometimes like bursts of hearty laughter, sometimes shrieks like over-excited girls going down the big dipper, a wild, hair-raising cacophony. Pasang decided to make lunch on this hillside and I happily stalked the laughing thrushes till it was ready.

I was greatly restored by lunch for Pasang was an excellent cook. We walked on till we came to the Sikri Khola, a shallow stream studded with little islands and on one of these, easily reached by a few strategic leaps from stone to stone, Pasang pitched my tent. It was ideal to camp in mid-river with white-capped river chats, grey wagtails and whistling thrushes darting by as I ate.

Next morning we left for Those but to reach it we had to cross the river by the same kind of bridge that had caused me such agonising anxiety some days before. This second one was worse than the first. It had great gaps in the wire through which timorous memsahibs could so easily fall. I was convinced that I would but I *had* to see Everest.

Full of pride that I had surmounted this grave obstacle I swung through Those with Pasang. In the paved main street was a post office. I looked in and saw a great pile of letters strewn all over the floor with a few men sitting silently and immovably in front of the mound. I had once been told that it took three weeks for a letter to go from Namche Bazar to Kathmandu and now I could quite believe it. But as porters can do the journey in six or seven days, if pushed, why post anything?

Camping in Those was not easy. Pasang was very fussy and couldn't see anywhere suitable. He finally strode into the river, which was about a foot deep, and crossed it to a beautifully isolated island site, knowing my preference for such places. We all followed. It was a warm night for we were at only 5,000 feet and after supper, happier than ever, I sat on a groundsheet, my legs covered with my down sleeping bag, my back against a low stone wall, typing my diary for the day's events by the light of a brilliant full moon. There were birds all around (I heard my first Indian nightjar) and when I opened the tent door next morning a duck flew past and down the river. It wasn't light enough to identify the species.

From Those we wound our way up the river valley towards the Bhandar pass. It was wide and open with a softly purling stream that was calmer than any I had seen before. I have heard rumours that the valley will one day contain a road to Namche Bazar. It would be sacrilege to spoil this serene and lovely place, but sacrilege seems to be the bread and butter of the road builder.

After a leisured lunch at the foot of the Bhandar pass we began the climb to 9,000 feet. We had been at 9,000 some days before but had gone right down to Those. Kathmandu is roughly 4,500 feet and the Base Camp about 17,500 feet but there is no continuous climb of 13,000 feet as one might think, rather a constant switchback.

We camped halfway to Bhandar under the first fully-flowered rhododendron of the trek. That night it was very cold and before we left in the morning Mingma, the oldest of the women porters, (Mingma being a name applicable to both sexes), warmed the handle of my walking stick above the fire.

When we reached the top of the pass we looked down on the village of Bhandar which has two particularly lovely *chortens* (Buddist shrines) and is the beginning of real Sherpa country. We lunched there and then lost all the height we had gained by plunging down through bird-filled forest to the Likhu Khola, a fast flowing stream at 5,000 feet.

We stayed next to a field where a family was planting potatoes. They all hoed with small hand hoes and the children dropped the potatoes into the holes made by their elders. What struck me most forcibly was the skill of the women who all wore long necklaces, sometimes two or three of them, and hoed like maniacs, their neck-laces swinging perilously close to the flailing hoe but never once getting caught by it.

Well beyond our camp was a bridge even more horrible than the previous two. Pasang stepped lightly over it, followed by Kyak Tsering and Gyalzen, leaving the girls to cross last. As they shuffled forwards, wearing ankle-length full skirts and baseball boots and carrying sixty-pound loads, the boys on the other side seized the iron chains and shook them. The bridge swayed more sickeningly than before but the girls laughed as much as the boys and with admirable balance completed the crossing without any sign of discomfort or disarray. Would I had been able to achieve such estimable equanimity.

Our destination that day was Sete, a little village on the way to the Lamjura pass, our highest point yet at almost 12,000 feet. Sete had no camping facilities but Pasang, by dint of diplomacy and much hard work, at last obtained permission for us to camp in a potato field before it was sown next day. This big field seemed to be composed entirely of dust. So dusty was it that Pasang and Gyalzen cut rhodo-dendron branches and laid them in a semi-circle in front of my tent so that if Sir wished to get out in the night, as she invariably did after a dinner beginning with soup and ending with a large mug of coffee, she would not plunge her bare feet into thick dust and afterwards find her sleeping bag full of it. It is in such little touches as these that the lovability and good sense of Sherpas are manifested.

One of the nicest on that winter Everest trek was Kyak Tsering, a large man with a wide smile and protruding teeth. He was thin, rather gangling and very tall for a Sherpa. He had the kindest heart in all Nepal and when anything needed doing, particularly if it were some-thing unpleasant, Kyak Tsering was always the first to volunteer. He was the one who shifted the biggest load, carried the extra wood, chopped down branches, always smiling, his head tied up in a tea towel with the ends rather rakishly arranged. He was a most charm-ing character but on an expedition a few months later he was killed by an avalanche, leaving a wife and four young children. Sherpas on professional expeditions are always well insured and their depend-ants are possibly better off financially when their husbands are killed; but what woman wants a good income and no husband or father for her children?

Next morning we left early and had lunch at the top of the climb before crossing the pass. There were a great many birds about, all of them new to me because we were now in a high life zone containing pearl-spotted laughing thrushes, barwings and different tits. The top of the pass was almost entirely covered with rhododendrons but in the mid-winter cold the dark green leaves were all rolled back on themselves and looked like Venus pencils. Just as we were about to cross the highest part a thick mist descended. The path, a mixture of snow and ice, was very slippery and wound across a steep face. With Pasang in front and Gyalzen behind I inched along, not really helped by a string of cattle on the way down to Those which forced me off the path as they passed. The mist thickened and through it I heard multiple twitterings but could not see a single bird. We reached the highest point, marked by a small Buddhist shrine with many soiled and tattered little prayer flags, and then began the descent to Junbesi through thick hemlocks and deodars, grating our way down the stony track and meeting many more cattle coming up, although here there was ample room for us all.

At last Pasang made camp in a small clearing, lit a fire and moved to put up my tent, only to discover that Kyak Tsering, who was carrying it and the sleeping bags, had thought we were going to camp at Junbesi, some four miles further down. Pasang leapt down the mountainside to break the unpleasant news to Kyak Tsering that he would have to carry his big load back up the mountain. They were both very, very tired that night.

Next morning, delighted that I had crossed the Lamjura without a trace of altitude sickness, we trotted down to Junbesi, a large open village of big, prosperous-looking houses and a celebrated monastery that I did not hear about till after we had left. Below us a beautiful old *chorten* gleamed whitely in the sunshine and near it was a different gleam, the bright silver of corrugated iron that roofed one of the first Hillary schools, now packed with healthy little Sherpas.

Beyond Junbesi were hillsides where cattle grazed and we trudged on happily but then I had another attack of tiredness so Pasang, with the boundless ingenuity which he could always summon in emergency, managed to find a camp site on a tiny patch of hillside. The ground was white with rime next morning and Pasang and Gyalzen piled dead stalks and twigs on the fire and in the resultant quick blaze shook the frost off my tent before packing it, skilfully removing frost and preserving the tent in several rapid shakes.

We went quickly down to the valley and after much urging I sampled *chang* at the Ringmo tea-house. I detested it and went on towards Takhsindu while the others enjoyed themselves. It was an exhausting ascent to Takhsindu, hatefully steep though not very long but when we reached the pass the view was superb, fold upon fold of shining snow peaks and, in the foreground below, a beautiful monastery.

We were allowed to take our lunch in the courtyard where I took a memorable picture of Kyak Tsering diligently beating up my rumble-tumble while Gyalzen and Pasang made *chapattis,* thin rounds of unleavened bread, cooked quickly in a fatless frying pan and finished off by a brief sojourn in the wood ash below. In the right hands, which Pasang posessed, *chapattis* are delicious but in the wrong ones they are leaden slabs of indigestible fodder.

The forest below Takhsindu was thick with birds, many of them entirely new to me, and we went down and down for what seemed miles, finally stopping for the night at a little settlement called Manidigma. This was full of laughing thrushes of various kinds, warblers, woodpeckers and many other species that I couldn't find in *The Birds of Sikkim.* While I was searching through the book, Mingma, fully aware of my love of flowers, and particularly dahl, cut down a small tree of it and planted this at my tent doorway so that I should smell the wonderful perfume throughout the night. It was an enchanting gesture and I could only thank her warmly, while inwardly condemning her unwitting vandalism. Mingma was a darling and it was not until years later that I learnt she was Kyak Tsering's sister.

Next morning our lunchtime goal was the Dudh Kosi, the famous river that drains the western side of Everest. I gazed at the milky-green water from the melting ice above, rushing over huge glaciated boulders, visualised the inaccessible slopes from which it sprang, and felt that at last we were really getting somewhere.

But an hour or so later I began to feel ill and realised that I was in for another of my tiresome collapses which might mean a couple of nights at the Dudh Kosi. However, what better place to collapse with white-capped river chats and plumbeous redstarts flittering about, dippers making an occasional appearance, grey wagtails and whistling thrushes flying past, and a wallcreeper, that lovely French-grey bird, flicking its raspberry-pink wings in and out as it climbed over the rocks?

The biggest thrill was provided by the monkeys, a large troop of macaques that climbed and sprang about among the boulders on the opposite side of the river. The only way for them to cross it was by the good modern bridge, but it was obvious that they did not want to use it with people watching them. They hung about, getting nearer and nearer but unable to nerve themselves to cross. Pasang, sure that they would come eventually, insisted on concealing himself, with my camera and 300mm telephoto lens, in a bush which commanded a view of the bridge and waited patiently for the monkeys to conquer their fears. As I seldom saw a Nepalese catch sight of a monkey without throwing something at it or making loud noises I was well able to understand the animals' reluctance to expose themselves to such treatment. After an hour or so a few brave specimens bolted across at high speed and swung up into the bushes on our side. Pasang got his picture, rather out of focus but still quite good, of a monkey going hell for leather straight towards us over the bridge.

After two nights I recovered completely and we went on through several dirty settlements to Kharikhola, an interminable village with a long descent to a stream and another equally long ascent to a clearing where we camped. We had been nineteen days on the way, slow progress which made Pasang feel ashamed. I didn't mind at all and was enjoying everything bar my boring collapses.

I woke next morning to freezing cold and ground covered in thick snow. I said to Pasang that I supposed we had better stay in our tents and wait for the weather to improve. He said that on the contrary, the porters had no tent—surely a bad mistake on the organiser's part, they were all wet and cold and we must go on and up *immediately* or we might not be able to get over the Puiyan pass.

I did as I was told. The snow grew thicker and I could see very little through the blizzard as we climbed slowly upwards. We had been going for some time when we met a friend of Pasang's from Namche, who was a rather high official. He was dressed in the usual Nepalese cotton trousers, a thin sweater, a jaunty cap and nothing more and was trotting gaily along under an umbrella. Pasang introduced me to this smart vision who at once removed his gloves, shook hands and conversed in impeccable English. This was as delightful as it was unexpected but there was no time to waste in pleasantries and we had to hurry on to the guest house on top of the pass.

Pasang took me to the upper floor where Gyalzen and the porters, having commandeered much of the available room, had my lunch already laid out and a splendid fire going. It was very cold and the wind whistled through the cracks between the stones but the fire was good and I began to thaw out. The blizzard continued and through the eight inches of snow trudged porters going to Namche's Saturday market. There were others on the way back, their unsold wares still in their baskets, a bad omen that presaged thicker snow ahead. The thing that impressed me most deeply was that these men were trekking in little sleeveless tunics of thin material with a blanket wound round their shoulders, a little cap on their heads and bare legs and feet.

After lunch the snow stopped and Pasang said that we must go on. We began the long and precipitous descent to Puiyan, which I found very difficult to negotiate in thick snow. Suddenly I could move no more and lay down at the side of the path feeling dreadful.

Pasang looked down at me with great concern. Was Sir going to expire in the snow? Sir didn't know but felt that it was probable, for even her strong will was powerless to move her exhausted body.

The party for my first trek, Pasang in centre with my camera.

ingma with the dhal tree which she cut for me.

Itinerant Nepalese flute seller.

Top: *View from the pass above Takhsindu monastery.*

Bottom: *Pomori with Lindgren behind.*

Kyak Tsering, the indefatigable porter, was called to the rescue and bidden to carry Sir until she felt better. He did so, heaving his inert load for a few hundred yards until Gyalzen took over. Kyak Tsering had a second spell of weight lifting but then I recovered sufficiently to stagger to the bottom of the hill under my own steam and from there it was not far to Puiyan village. Pasang decreed that we must stay in a house where the porters could at last get warm and dry, a stipulation with which I fully agreed for they had no change of clothing and were completely soaked and very cold.

We reached a house in which the owner allowed us to stay but Pasang decided that the usual practice must be observed and porters and Sir must be separated. My tent was erected in an open-fronted cowshed, the sleeping pad put down and my two sleeping bags arranged on it. I went to bed at once, thankfully clutching the hot-water bottle which Gyalzen had filled for me. It was 3 o'clock and I drank quantities of tea which warmed and stimulated my over-tired limbs.

The snow began again and Pasang and Gyalzen shuttled up and down from the upper floor to the yard below, digging channels to redirect any melting snow that might flood my 'bedroom' while I lay at ease and watched them. I asked where the poor cows would be going while a foreign woman usurped their shed?

'This isn't a cowshed', said Pasang indignantly; 'this is a guest house!'

I remembered our conversation at Tharepati and reflected that some stupid people never learn the difference between the one and the other. It was only later on I discovered that all Nepalese guest houses are three-walled affairs. I don't know why. Maybe the hosts don't want their guests to be so comfortable that they are disinclined to move on.

The snow thickened as I lay typing in my bed, a sight that amazed the many children who came to look at me while light still existed. Small wonder, really, for they could never have seen a typewriter before nor an elderly foreign lady lying in bed using one.

Next morning was brilliantly sunny, the sky absolutely clear and the trees, caked with balls of snow, were full of hungry birds searching for food. We continued the downward path to Serte, where there was no snow at all, lunched by the stream and then began the climb to Chaurikharka. This was rather far for one in my somewhat debilitated condition and we stopped at Muse, just short of it. There were caves where the porters could sleep in case of another blizzard, for as they were now completely dried out they naturally did not want to get wet again so soon. The snow had gone, there was a full moon and the stars were frosty bright. Pasang and I sat by the fire looking at them and, as we watched, saw a satellite speeding over us: there was something incongruous in our very primitive condition at the entrance to a cave, with a candle for illumination, while overhead buzzed one of the supreme examples of technology.

We reached the beautiful village of Chaurikharka next day and there saw our first long prayer walls, all inscribed with the Buddhist prayer of *Om mani padme hum.* These carved stone walls, erected by devout Buddhists who wish to attain merit in the after-life, must always be passed on the left. Where they exist the path is double so that people can observe the rule from whichever direction they come. Although no Buddhist, I always follow my porters obediently to the left of every Mani wall or stone.

All Nepalese villages are interesting but there was something particularly appealing about Chaurikharka. Whether it was its setting, its lovely *chortens* with the Buddha's eyes watching from all four sides or the fact that here we really did seem to be getting closer to our objective, I don't know; it was in some way special.

We stopped for lunch at Ghat, on the banks of the Dudh Kosi, where the stream seemed to have more than its fair share of white-capped river chats, wagtails and dippers. Pasang and the porters made lunch while I sat by the river's edge photographing these Asiatic dippers, more gingery-brown than the European species and without the white breast, as they pursued each other up and down the river in courtship flight.

The next afternoon, at Jorsale, a second blizzard struck. A blanket of fine snow wrapped us round closely but far from warmly and it looked as though we would have to use a guest house once more. Luckily there was one in the village. It looked both dark and dirty but who cared? Pasang and Gyalzen erected my tent inside and I again retired into my sleeping bag, by far the best place for waiting out a blizzard.

As Jorsale was not far from Namche Bazar, where Pasang's wife and family were waiting for him, Pasang, with my full permission, plunged into the blizzard to walk to the end of the valley and then up the 2,000 feet climb to Namche. It was something I would not have relished in the dark but he was both speedy and sure-footed and I knew that he would make it with ease. It was agreed that if the morning were fine the porters and I would follow him up.

In the middle of the night it became necessary to leave my tent. This was a problem, for the guest house was at the side of the main path to Namche and there was no cover. It was still snowing hard and with extreme reluctance I wriggled out of my cosy down bag, drew on my cold and heavy nailed boots, my sweater and my anorak and stepped into the street, hoping that no one would come by as I attended to the call of nature. The snow beat down on my bare back as I crouched and it was only when I had returned to the comforting warmth of my sleeping bag that I remembered my umbrella which would have provided some measure of shelter. I wonder if Colonel Roberts envisaged such an emergency when he recommended me to take one?

The morning was bright and sunny and we set off in high spirits. Less than halfway up the very steep and stony path we met a boy with a huge Thermos flask of tea and a large bag of freshly boiled potatoes, plus a little ground chili in which to dip them. He had been sent by Pasang with refreshments to speed us on our way. We sat down gratefully on the nearest porters' chairs, laughing and chatting as we feasted on the delicious potatoes which in this part of Nepal had a flavour far exceeding anything that I had tasted elsewhere.

As we neared Namche, a large village built in terraces on the steep slopes, we saw a small flying figure coming to greet us. This was Pasang's eldest daughter, sent to escort us to her father's house. She grasped my hand in hers and led us quickly to a house halfway up the slope, through the dark lower room, up the dark stairs and so into the light. Here we met Pasang's wife, Namdo, very tall for a Sherpa, beautiful and welcoming, his two younger daughters and his mother, short and active but, said her son, 'Very, *very* old, more than sixty!'

After lunch the snow began again. Pasang decided that it would be wrong to erect my tent in the little patch of ground outside the house; I must stay inside with them.

Their house was the usual Sherpa home but bigger than many others that I saw later. The ground floor, into which the front door opened, was for cattle, hens or any other livestock and dry leaves, twigs, branches, hay and general debris strewed the floor. This was all right in the daytime but when it was dark it was fraught with difficulty for in the corner at the back of this room was the only entrance to the house proper, a staircase with an indefinite number of steps. I never saw how many there were.

At the top of the stairs we took a sharp turn left along a passage with a rail to stop one falling down below and emerged into a long room, lined on the right wall with shelves holding large brass containers of water and various stores. Opposite this stood a stove, a square stone structure with various holes in it. This stove, which was used both for warmth and cooking, was fed by rhododendron logs in the main and rhododendron is an exceptionally close and heavy wood as I found when I tried to lift it. There was no chimney to remove the smoke and create a good draught. No Sherpa houses have this facility considered so essential in the West and in consequence the room was often very smoky when the fire failed to draw properly.

It then became necessary for Pasang, Namdo or any other member of the family to kneel before it, take a deep breath and blow the flickering embers into life, which must have tarred the lungs of the blowers to no small extent. Maybe this is a contributory factor towards the chronic bronchitis, T.B. and other chest diseases that exist so widely in Nepal.

The room was warm, especially if you were near the fire, and soon we were all sitting there in a double row and I, being both elderly and foreign, was given the seat of honour, next to the stove in the front row. Beds and benches were ranged along the wall and on them sat other guests, for Pasang's was evidently a very popular household. Pasang and Namdo were a charming and handsome couple, and visitors were legion, all regaled with either *chang* or tea.

Pasang and every other Sherpa I ever met was very fond of *chang* and stopped to drink it whenever it was available. I found it disgusting but this was not a fair criticism, really, as I heartily dislike the taste of beer, sherry or wine of any kind. I politely refused *chang* whenever it was offered but Pasang insisted that I tried Namdo's which was, he boasted, the best in Namche, in fact in all Khumbu. I drank one small glass of it and agreed that, whilst still not to my taste, it was indeed far better than any other. After that, honour being satisfied, I was allowed to stick to tea.

I was interested to see how Namdo, who was as efficient as her husband, made Tibetan tea. First of all she made a large pot of tea and boiled it for a short while. This done, a tall, thin churn was brought out, the tea poured into it and several spoonfuls of yak butter and a little salt added. A plunger was then thrust up and down at good speed for some time and when Namdo considered that the mixture was thoroughly blended she poured the tea back into the pot, re-heated it and only then judged it to be fit to serve. She poured it into small bowls which fitted neatly and securely into a metal saucer on a stem and one drank it by holding this stem and tilting the bowl gently towards the mouth. As time went on and I continued to stay in Pasang's house, imprisoned by successive blizzards, I became accustomed to this strange concoction and even grew to like it. It had a certain 'body' and was warm and pleasing.

That first night my things were put into a second room that also served as a little chapel and here I lay in solitary state while all the rest of the family slept in the main room.

Next morning Pasang woke me with tea and said it was a lovely day but although the blizzard had stopped the snow still lay thick around and he thought it would be unwise to start. 'Perhaps tomorrow', he said, but agreed to take me out for a short walk to survey the route that, all being well, we would follow next day.

First came the question of the lavatory, now a matter of pressing urgency. There was a public lavatory in Namche, he said, and he would escort me. In the middle of the street stood a little house on stilts. The staircase to it was a short, thick tree trunk which leant against the floor of the house and the steps were merely notches cut in the trunk. These were not easy to negotiate in nailed boots and one could only climb it when the door was open to show that no one else was inside. I scrambled up the 'stairs' and went in, finding to my surprise that there were dirty drawings on the walls, a piece of Western 'culture' that visitors might have refrained from passing on. The stench was indescribable and I prayed fervently that my stay in Namche might not be unduly protracted.

This grisly ritual concluded, Pasang and I climbed the hill behind Namche and came out on the path that led to Thyang Boche, so near and yet so far away. Snow lay thickly everywhere and single yaks and *dzomos** were picking their way along the hillside vainly trying to find something to eat. We slithered along the narrow and rather treacherous path. The inner side was full of snow and ice that had slid down from above but the outer side was fairly clear. I was rather scared of this for the drop to the valley of Dudh Kosi below was precipitous.

Pasang said we *must* go on to the corner for from there we should see Everest clearly and also moderately close at hand.

We pressed on and we *did* see it, a breath-depriving moment, for there it stood solidly in all its glory, flanked by Nuptse and Lhotse, a rather pudding-shaped mass of enormous size, blue-white and splendid with a long plume of snow streaming from the summit. At last!

We lunched in Pasang's house and in the afternoon I went round the village to look at the yaks penned in various yards, trying to talk to the children who followed me round. Trekkers were not so many in 1970 and elderly lady trekkers on their own in midwinter were something to look at. And for my part I looked with far greater wonder at white-fronted redstarts and white-browed rose-finches, both of them new to me and exceedingly beautiful.

And then the snow began yet again. It continued all night and all the next day. Luckily Pasang had some English paperback thrillers which grateful trekkers had presented to him. I was very glad of them for my own stock of reading matter was running low.

There was always something going on in Pasang's house for from eight in the morning until nine at night visitors came in: Namdo's sister, also tall and handsome, her husband, various cousins, uncles, aunts and friends and everyone who came sat round the fire and drank *chang* or tea.

* Female product of a Yak and a Cow.

Namdo never stopped working for an instant, brewing *chang,* churning tea, washing up and throwing the water out of the window, tending the children, making noodles, cooking omelettes but never, it seemed, eating, drinking or sitting down herself. It was a busy, fascinating scene of which I never tired.

Occasionally I had to don my boots, wrap up warmly, stagger down those black and secret stairs and through the icy, slippery streets to the lavatory past houses hung with orange icicles, the colour produced by the snow that melted on the smoke-grimed, impregnated wooden roofs. It was a good hundred yards to that noisome building and I was surprised at the powers of endurance I developed which enabled me to pay my malodorous visit not more than twice a day at the outside.

Next day was fine and brilliant, the sky serenely blue, the snow all on the ground with little in the air, and we set off. Pasang Doma singing lustily and rather raucously as she bore her vast burden up the steep slope. Snow had narrowed the path even further and we scuffled along less than half of it, struggling to keep our footing. The scenery was more open than at Namche itself where the view was almost all mountain with very little sky. The incomparably lovely Ama Dablam lay directly ahead and everything combined to create a picture of superlative beauty.

When we had gone several miles we came to the village of Trashinga where Gyalzen, having slipped ahead with the porters, had lunch almost ready and Sir's Dunlopillo pad laid out, not on the snow-covered ground but safely placed on top of a wide and low stone wall. We sat there happily, warmed by the bright sun and hot food.

While the porters were clearing away the lunch and repacking I heard an unfamiliar avian noise. And then I saw what made it: beautiful, rather dumpy little birds about the size of small farmyard hens. The males had grey backs and breasts of lemony green streaked with crimson, with crimson markings on their heads and bright crimson under tail coverts; the females were brown with orange heads. All were pecking diligently at the snow in an endeavour to get through to something edible. Hasty consultation of *The Birds of Sikkim* showed them to be blood pheasants and there were about thirty of them. When we had crossed the Dudh Kosi (that here looked most abominably cold and unwelcoming) I again heard them in the undergrowth. They were a trifle portly but at the same time elegant and their colour combination was most unusual and completely distinctive.

Just above the Dudh Kosi was a teahouse and here, built over a small stream that ran down to join the main river, was a series of little huts, each containing a prayer wheel. The force of the water turned the wheel automatically so that perpetual intercession was made for the benefit of the faithful, entailing no effort by the people concerned. If I were a deity I think I would be more inclined to pay attention to one genuine personal prayer by a believing supplicant rather than the longest intercession produced by mechanical means.

The final part of the climb to Thyang Boche was through the forest, which seemed to be composed almost entirely of conifers. The little trees in the valley to our right were draped with a kind of lime-green growth that looked like the Spanish moss of the United States but powdered with snow, and when we came out on to the open hillside there was more snow with which to do battle. There were other Sherpas and lamas on the path and occasional men driving their yaks down to less inhospitable pastures. Still we climbed. I was beginning to think that we had had more than enough of it when Pasang turned abruptly to the left through a painted gateway and we were at last in the fabled loveliness of Thyang Boche.

Before us stretched an apparently limitless courtyard fifteen inches deep in snow in which some motionless yaks stood quietly enduring the cold. To the left was the monastery itself and beside it and to the right were the subsidiary buildings and lamas' quarters, with a backing of green-black conifers. This closed and silent area was hemmed in by enormous peaks, Ama Dablam, Taweche, Thamserku, Kangtega, and everything was muffled and blurred in the all-prevading soft mohair of snow.

It was a magnificent but chilling sight and we made our way to the guest house, this time with four walls, in the corner of the grounds where Gyalzen rapidly made a fire. Black-faced laughing thrushes, with the peculiar black-and-white facial markings that give them a slightly demented look, are normally wild but here they were demonstrably hungry which made them tame enough to cluster round us in the hope of food. There was no sound at all except the occasional desperate baying of a perpetually chained guard dog.

Pasang said custom demanded that we go to see the Head Lama if he were at home. He would go to find out. The Head Lama was at home and would receive us at 5 o'clock. Pasang went to buy from one of the lamas the white scarves which, together with at least twenty rupees each towards the upkeep of the monastery, it was polite and customary to proffer to the Head Lama.

I was slightly nervous for I had no knowledge of Buddhism and its procedures and although I wanted to meet the Head Lama I had no idea of the correct way to behave on such an occasion. I need not have worried for Pasang presented Sir by her correct title, we proffered our gifts and were invited to sit down.

The room in which we were received was beautifully decorated with holy paintings and we sat on a comfortable sofa and drank the Head Lama's excellent coffee. The atmosphere was extremely cold and every so often an attendant lama brought in a brazier full of embers at which we warmed our hands but this, though welcome, was not enough to combat the freezing air at an altitude of little less than 13,000 feet. I did my best to appear alert and interested but the Head Lama had no English. On the other hand Pasang seemed to please and interest him and they talked on and on and on. I understood not one word and after some forty-five minutes I said to Pasang that I thought we should be going. He said, 'No, the Head Lama has just offered us tea.'

The attendant appeared once more, removed the coffee cups and brought in an enormous Thermos flask of most delicious Tibetan tea which was given to us in very fine cups with metal lids to keep the contents warm when we were not actually drinking, a necessary provision at that altitude. We drank our cup of tea and the two further cups that are apparently considered to be correct then, mentally numbed by the long period of unintelligible conversation, physically numbed by the cold and almost awash, we made our respectful farewells and went down through the snow to the guest house and supper.

I was awakened in the night by a strong wind which roared through the courtyard, shaking the guest house as it passed. It did not last long but it was violent.

Next morning Pasang called from the other end of the long room, where he was sleeping in a little alcove, that it was very cold indeed, wasn't it, and had I heard the earthquake in the night?

I said no, I had heard nothing but wind.

'There was no wind,' said Pasang, 'only the earthquake.'

Collapses, blizzards, earthquakes! What next?

During the morning it began to snow again and I realised that we should not be able to go up to the Base Camp for the route would now be impassible. If it cleared in the afternoon, said Pasang, we would go up towards Pangboche so that I could see what it was like and then tomorrow we would go down. It was a sad decision but I knew it was the right one.

The sky cleared temporarily after lunch and we took the route to Pangboche where the alleged yeti scalp is kept in the monastery or *gompa*. The route was wonderful, all snow, ice, dark green, tightly curled rhododendrons and large conifers, with great trails of the Asian form of Spanish moss hanging from some of the trees. We slipped and slid on ice and snow until we came to the bridge over the Imja Khola, which had great chunks of ice in it, and then regretfully turned back. I wondered if I would ever get there again and if so, when.

Towards dusk in thick cloud as I was sitting reading in my tent and vainly trying to get warm, Pasang came rushing in crying, 'The peaks! The peaks!'

I rushed out, taking my camera with me, and there saw Everest and its companions in the one patch of clear sky, their tops turned a rich apricot in the rays of the setting sun, gleaming with bewitching beauty in the last of the light. It was a fitting farewell to those great heights.

In the morning, cheered by the sight of white-winged grosbeaks, we went sadly down, not directly to Namche but turning right to Kunde, the village above it where Hillary had built his first hospital, now staffed by a new Zealand doctor, Dr. Selwyn Lang, and his wife to whom the British ambassador in Kathmandu had given me a letter.

I went to the hospital to deliver it. Mrs. Lang thanked me and then said tentatively, 'I wonder if you'd like a shower?'

After all that cold and discomfort it seemed almost too good to be true and I arranged that next morning, immediately after breakfast, I would go to the hospital complete with soap and towel.

Pasang and the porters spent the night in a rather rich Sherpa's house while I lay in my tent outside. When I woke up I felt cold, and when Gyalzen brought my tea and opened the tent door I saw that there were several inches of fresh snow.

I went to the hospital and had my shower, the feeling of hot water trickling down the back of my neck after nearly four weeks trekking being so sensuous and comforting that I could hardly believe my luck.

Mrs. Lang invited me to take tea in the kitchen, normal English tea out of a normal cup. She told me that the hospital cook had a small curio shop in the corner of his kitchen. He had some really nice things and I bought fourteen pounds' worth of treasures, which in 1970 was exceptional but then, I excused myself, I had bought nothing in Kathmandu. When I came to pay for my purchases I found that Pasang didn't have my purse. This had been placed in my rucksack which had already gone down to Namche with the porters. Pasang was almost beside himself with fear that he had made a mistake and my money had been lost and ran down to Namche at once. Mrs. Lang and the cook thankfully believed my story.

As I looked out of the window it was obvious that yet another blizzard had started and it would be prudent to go down to Namche as quickly as I could. I followed Gyalzen, finding it almost impossible to see through the whirling snow. A tall man came by wearing high Sherpa boots and otherwise inadequate clothing and walked just before us all the way. When we got to one peculiarly nasty and difficult stretch there he was standing right in the middle of the path.

Surely not a hold-up during a blizzard?

And yet he did want us to stop. He pulled a little roll of cloth from the front of his tunic, unwrapped it and showed me some Indian silver rupees of the early years of the century. He badly wanted to sell them. I would not have been interested anywhere, still less in the middle of a howling blizzard in this obscured and difficult terrain.

By the time we reached Namche the snow had stopped. We made our way to Pasang's house where we found him happily drinking *chang* and clutching the lost purse. He promised to send the money up to the hospital next day and we all breathed sighs of profound relief.

Clean and refreshed I spent one more night in his hospitable house and next day left for Lukla, the small New Zealand-built airstrip in the mountains from which it was very difficult to get a plane. Those who wish to leave on Monday must get there on Sunday and preferably Saturday.

Pasang and I got a plane out on our second day. It was just before seven-thirty in the morning, the sky was clear as a good conscience and with the unreal brightness that precedes bad weather. Pasang and I climbed into our seats, fastened our belts, waved to Gyalzen and Kyak Tsering and were gone, looking back at all those fabulous peaks so unbelievably close at hand, with Everest towering well above them all, white and wonderful. The sight was something to treasure for ever.

Annapurna

The spring of 1971 saw me back in Nepal, all set for another trek, this time to central Nepal and the Annapurna Sanctuary. I was to start trekking from Pokhara where I would pick up my Sherpa and porters after flying from Kathmandu.

Everything but the exact date of starting was carefully arranged with Mountain Travel but as I was going first to Egypt and on to India I did not want to take all my climbing equipment with me. Before I left home I packed a large parcel containing all my trekking gear, addressed it to myself c/o Mountain Travel and arranged for it to be sent by airmail some weeks before I was due in Nepal.

This seemed sensible at the time but a protracted postal strike in England intervened and I was completely out of touch. Colonel Roberts' letter telling me when I was to start my trek did not arrive and no one in India seemed able to furnish a telephone number for him in Nepal.

I confided my troubles to Dr. Sálim Ali, the eminent Indian ornithologist, when I had lunch with him and his niece Shama, and between them they concocted a splendid plan. Shama had a brother who was a keen radio ham. He often spoke to an equally keen ham in Kathmandu called Father Moran who knew Colonel Roberts. If Saad Ali could raise Father Moran by radio and ask him to contact Colonel Roberts as to when Miss Forster's trek was supposed to leave, Father Moran could then radio back on the following day and leave a message. This kind of thing was strictly forbidden, so they said, but in such an emergency it was decided to risk it.

That night Saad duly called up Kathmandu and very luckily found Father Moran who promised to do his best on behalf of the distraught English lady who was biting her fingernails in Bombay.

I dined with the family on the following night when it was hoped Father Moran would call back with news. In the middle of dinner Saad, who lived in the flat below Sálim Ali, came panting up the stairs to announce that Father Moran had telephoned Colonel Roberts and discovered that Miss Forster was due to start her trek on

10th March. It was then the 3rd so Miss Forster, bowed down with gratitude for this ingenious ploy carried out on her behalf, departed for her hotel in a far easier frame of mind.

Next morning I booked a flight to Calcutta and on to Kathmandu and telegraphed my hosts in Calcutta asking them to meet me at the airport that night. There was no one to meet me and when I telephoned I heard that my telegram had not arrived and they were giving a party, so I took a taxi to their house and joined in.

I stayed two nights in Calcutta and cabled Mountain Travel giving date and time of arrival in Kathmandu.

Again there was no one at the airport. I took a taxi to the Shanker Hotel, where I had stayed before, and asked if Mountain Travel had booked a room for me. They had.

I telephoned Mountain Travel. Had my parcel of equipment arrived? It had not and neither had my telegram. It seemed that this would not be an easy trek.

The absence of the parcel was a shattering blow. I hadn't the money to buy a down jacket and hood, climbing boots, thick socks and sweaters (as a knitting designer I couldn't bear the thought of buying such things!) Even if I had had the money many of those items were not then available in Kathmandu. It was unthinkable to miss the trek, but how could I go to 12,000 feet without boots and in thin summer clothes?

Salvation came in the person of Elizabeth Blower, a friend of the Harrops, whom I had met on my very first trek. Mrs. Blower, who deserves a comfortable seat in heaven for her unparalleled kindness to a total stranger, decimated her wardrobe and lent me two pairs of trousers, a double anorak, three thick sweaters, warm underwear, socks, gloves, a fur hood that tied under the chin and was always referred to by my Sherpa as 'Mummy's Yeti hat' and her son's boots which fitted. This was the most fantastic luck as I have notoriously difficult feet and find it almost impossible to buy boots or shoes. And here was a pair of the right size that were soft and comfortable as suede gloves. It seemed like the answer to prayer.

Now well equipped, and carrying Mrs. Blower's rucksack too, I left for Pokhara on 12th March, only two days behind my original schedule. I heard later that my parcel arrived on the 13th.

There was the usual delay at the airport and while waiting I talked to a handsome young American couple who were travelling on the cheap with one porter. They were doing it through Rover Treks, a concern new to me, which hired out all equipment from tents and sleeping bags to saucepans and also engaged Sherpas and/or porters. All the clients had to do was to pay the Sherpa and provide his food and also pay any extra porters that they might engage en route.

These two, Mal and Joan Sterrett, had brought with them from America a quantity of dehydrated food, something that I thought might be a good thing for me on future treks as I am not one for unlimited rice. They were walking in the same direction as I was at first but they were going all the way to Jomsom, back to Chitre, over the Deorali pass to Chomrong and returing to Pokhara through Ghandrung and Landrung, while I, considerably older and not so tough, was going only to Chitre and over the Deorali, but then right up to the Annapurna Sanctuary and back to Pokhara by the same route that they were taking.

After much waiting we were eventually sent to Pokhara in what we were told was an aircraft of the King's Flight that usually took only luggage. Instead of the glorious views that I remembered from my first trip we were packed lengthwise on two interminable benches with our backs to the windows and our faces to the luggage which was roped more or less securely to a central fixture which quivered disconcertingly. This time we saw nothing at all of what is undoubtedly one of the loveliest flights in the world.

We reached Pokhara safely and disembarked on the airfield which was then a large grassy expanse, with the airport office situated under a big tree, and people, buffalo and goats wandering everywhere until a few seconds before a plane landed or took off.

My Sherpa for the trip, Pen Uri, found me, introduced himself and took me and my luggage to the Mountain Travel office nearby. Here I saw my porters, an endless string of tiny little things, all male and all, except one, under 18 and inexperienced. They were utterly indistinguishable at first, even their names being remarkably similar but I gradually got to know and like them although none won my heart as completely as the Sherpas on my first and second treks had done.

The porters packed everything into baskets and at last we started, a tedious plod upwards through the bazaar. The bazaar town was thronged with people, including two wedding processions with several men holding what I thought were large curved swords decorated with ribbons. These proved to be trumpets, and with these and an assortment of drums the party strode down the hill, making a joyful noise. Little flat cakes of bright yellow and violently shocking pink were drying on the roofs of many houses where numerous flies were having first pick. I wondered if these delicacies were part of the wedding breakfast.

I had already noticed that every woman in Nepal was festooned with some kind of jewellery and the ladies of Pokhara district seemed to be even more addicted to it than the Sherpas. Here it was of a different type, composed of many strings of very small glittering beads set into a fancy gold crossbar called a *tilari*. Other bigger necklaces were made of what looked like large lumps of pale coral interspersed with gold. These ladies all wore gold earrings, some as much as three inches in diameter, rings on their fingers and nose rings, drops or studs at the side of one nostril. They wore glass and other bracelets galore and a few odd brooches for good measure.

I felt curiously undressed and dull amongst this ubiquitous finery and decided that I too would have jewellery on my trek. I went to the nearest bead and bangle stall. Every town and market, however small, has someone sitting among piles of glass bangles, strings of beads and red tassels attached to black cotton to plait into the hair. The woman in charge looked at my hand, squeezed it painfully tight to see how small she could make it before attempting to press bracelets over the knuckles and shook her head ruefully as she considered its enormous size. This was a sad snub for one considered at home to have a fairly small hand of size $6\frac{1}{2}$.

She picked up three bangles and indicated that I should try them on for size. I was unable to get them even half way on. She seized my right hand in her left, compressed it with agonising force and began to jam the bangles over it. Every time she came to some protruding joint or awkward bone she pummelled or temporarily dislocated it, so it seemed, at which I gave a shrill scream. A crowd quickly collected and by the time she had forced six bangles over my aching knuckles both I and my hand felt bruised and jellified. Strangely enough the bangles didn't break. Now decorated in suitable Nepalese fashion, I stopped screaming, the crowd departed and I went on. I thought bangles were enough and didn't stop to consider a long, hampering necklace or a nose ring.

As we continued our upward trudge through this apparently endless street I heard a loud cry followed by a shocked howl which turned to a miserable wail. A woman wearing an opulent necklace of turquoise and coral, symbol of status and wealth combined, had had it broken by the clutching hands of her small son. The mother was almost beside herself with fury. She screamed with rage and attacked her offspring unmercifully, hitting him on the head, back, legs or anywhere she could reach in the intervals of scrabbling amongst the filth in the gutter in an effort to retrieve her priceless treasures. The child screamed at the top of his considerable voice as his mother pursued him, bashing and scrabbling alternately, until the child, infuriated and revengeful, bashed back. It was a disturbing scene but we could not interfere.

We met several trains of donkeys, all with rather horsey faces and long ears but they were definitely not mules. Some were in moderately good condition but many had bare patches on their backs and others showed open sores. The leading animals had woollen plumes in a little holder on their foreheads or embroidered frontispieces over their brows and many had bells reminiscent of those worn by Swiss cows. Apparently these donkeys make the long trek to Jomsom and back continually and some of them did not look happy.

Our camp site for the first night was just outside the town and afforded magnificent views of Annapurna and Machha Puchhare. Annapurna is a many-peaked, widely spreading giant, but for me and for many others too, the cream of the whole Himalayan range is the fish-tail mountain, Machha Puchhare. This, from some angles an exquisite single peak is, when you have come round it to the Chandrakot, a twin-peaked eminence of unsurpassable loveliness. I sat down, tired out, to have a cup of tea, leaning against a stone wall and watching the sunset throw a veil of deepening apricot over this superb mountain. I took its photograph once or twice that day, as I was to do on every other day that I saw it, for it was never the same from any two points. And then a full moon came up and made it lovelier still.

All this augured well and I hoped that my many troubles were now over. They were not. My Sherpa was small and rather simian in appearance, very different from the somewhat austere and immensely capable Pasang. Pasang called me Sir on the first trip and Miss Forster on the second but Pen Uri didn't call me anything at first. Once I thought I heard him call me Mother, which seemed unlikely, but later on I was astonished to hear him refer to me as Mummy, a form of address which he employed consistently ever after. I learnt afterwards that this is a term of affection for older women but at first I wasn't pleased by a team of men who all called me Mummy, an unsuitable appellation for a spinster in her early sixties.

Next day I woke to a glorious morning and was ready to start at 7 o'clock, as trained by Pasang, But Pen Uri wasn't nearly ready so, having been told which path to take, I went on alone and soon fell in with Mal and Joan. We walked together along a broad, crowded path, thick with Nepalis, trekkers and strings of burdened donkeys.

The houses changed in character from region to region and I noticed that those covered with reddish clay that I had seen in the Kathmandu Valley were here replaced by others with designs of what looked like stylised daisies painted at very irregular intervals on various outer walls. Everyone seemed to be very busy and here and there at the roadside sat a man with a Singer sewing machine, (I never saw any other type) ready and willing to undertake any odd stitching that might be required.

Mal, Joan and I walked on, their Sherpa in attendance but mine nowhere to be seen. He and the porters turned up at 9.30 having had 'a lot to do'. Our communication was not as easy as it had been with Pasang for Pen Uri's English was passable, not fluent, and my Nepalese didn't exist.

At the end of this long, straggling village we came to what seemed to be the bed of a wide river with rice paddies in which a lot of wagtails and a few waders were feeding. After a few miles we left the river bed to climb up a steep winding path and round the nearest houses I saw cinnamon sparrows, lovely, almost orange sparrows that made our own house sparrows look dingy in the extreme. I don't really care for house sparrows and much prefer tree sparrows but in Nepal nearly all the sparrows that nest in houses above 6,000 feet *are* tree sparrows.

Mal and Joan pressed on more quickly while I clambered up the very steep slope, sweating profusely, to a beautiful village called Naudanda. This lay on a narrow ridge and just outside the village we pitched camp in a sunken field with a stupendous view both fore and aft. On our right lay Annapurna 1, 2 and 3, Annapurna being a confusing, multi-peaked mountain; Machha Puchhare, now showing both its peaks, and also Gangapurna. I had brought a typewriter with me on which to write a glowingly descriptive circular letter to friends at home but this sight was too good to lose and I gazed at it, spellbound, until darkness fell. I could still gaze at it after that under the full moon and the letter writing had to wait.

That night I didn't feel well and by the morning I had developed a streaming cold and high temperature and was unable to move. This depressing state of affairs continued for three days, my temperature rose to 103 and I had no appetite, a splitting headache, an incessant cough and a raging sense of frustration that did nothing to reduce my temperature.

All the time that I lay in my tent, tormented by the heat, or outside on my Dunlopillo under Pen Uri's serviceable black umbrella, a large party of children and some adults from the nearby village sat staring at me with a fixed scrutiny. One little boy sat there for ten hours one day. I remember seeing his unblinking gaze fixed on me as I closed my eyes in an attempt to start my night's sleep and when I opened the tent door next morning there he was, still looking. Perhaps he thought I was going to die and he would be the first to see the body carted off.

My antibiotics did no good and I then saw that they were out of date so I wrote a note to the hospital at Pokhara asking for some more, and sent it down by a porter, together with twenty rupees.

That afternoon, when my head was so hot and throbbing that I was almost demented, my camp site was invaded by a mass of small boys. They were carrying a football and all of them were shouting. We were apparently camping in the field in which they always played football on Sundays. A wordy tug-of-war took place between the vociferous children and Pen Uri. The children, yelling in concert while they bounced the football noisily up and down, insisted that they *must* play and Pen Uri, assisted by his Sherpa henchman, Pinto, insisted that they must *not*. They repeated that they always played *here, on this very spot* but as we had been there for three days and no one had mentioned it before, we were disinclined to believe them. After all, none of the inhabitants of the village who had been not once but many times to look at the poor lady lying there had told Pen Uri that my bedroom was the village football field.

Peace reigned at last but an hour later another lot arrived, apparently the opposing team, quieter at first but even noisier when they got into their stride. Pen Uri defeated them too, or so I thought, but afterwards both teams returned, some thirty to forty screaming, terrifyingly energetic children. I was reduced almost to tears. The heat was prodigious, the noise ear-splitting and the besieging hordes all stood within a yard or so of my bed, most of them coughing and a number of them spitting. Pen Uri, small but splendid and quite invincible, finally dispersed them by threatening to go to see their school teacher next day. Surprisingly enough this did the trick. They left.

The porter returned with twenty Penbritin tablets and a diagnosis of flu. I do not recommend flu on a trip, which wastes precious trekking time by forcing one to be in bed, but I always seem to get something somewhere and if I had to be ill and recumbent this was a most beautiful place for it. The birding was superb, mostly raptors: king vultures, Egyptian vultures, lammergeiers, serpent eagles and once a black stork all sailed over just above my head.

Next day, my temperature had gone down and I tottered to my feet and moved off for a mile or so. The glorious weather broke and rain was falling. My waterproof outfit was a man's long, black, plastic mack with a very big detachable hood bought for me by a porter in Kathmandu market, and a small collapsible Chinese umbrella.

I was concerned to see that the porters had only pieces of plastic sheeting to wear or very large plastic bags. They tried unsuccessfully to cut these open with a tin opener and Mummy gained much face by getting two men to hold an end each and then ripping the tin opener down the fold like an assistant in an old-fashioned draper's shop. Mummy was getting better.

The rain went on steadily so we soon made camp and in case it should get worse Pen Uri scraped out an inch-deep trench all round to take any surplus water, cutting a further little channel to drain it away. Fortunately it did not rain much more.

Pen Uri had an assistant who was kind and sweet but who had been very lightly endowed with brains and could not remember anything for more than a minute. I didn't like buffalo milk or powdered milk in my tea and had lemon or lime when it was available but when Pinto brought my tea tray it always held a mugful of either powdered or condensed milk let down with water, a kettle of hot water, a teapot of tea which leaked rapidly, a tin of Nescafé and a tin of drinking chocolate. I always smiled kindly, said 'lemon' and made squeezing gestures with my hand and he then ran off and returned with lemon. The next day I was given exactly the same trayful as before, without lemon.

We had trouble about meal times, too, as Pen Uri liked to have lunch at 9.30 and I liked it at 1 o'clock. I very often lost in this unequal struggle because he said, and I had no means of checking it, that we must lunch at his selected spot as there would be no available water for some hours. Next day I jibbed at taking lunch so soon after breakfast and said firmly that we'd have it at the bottom of the hill down which we were to travel. I am not quick going downhill at the best of times and this descent was exceptionally long, steep and strewn with rolling stones and by the time we reached the bottom it was 1 o'clock.

We lunched by the Modi Khola, a delectable and bird-rich stream as all Himalayan rivers seem to be. There was a serpent eagle over-head as there was on so many days of this trek, displaying with a wonderful, swooping flight, quivering its wings and screaming shrilly. Serpent eagles are fine beginners' birds and no one can mistake them for anything else for they have a broad, black-edged white strip along the end of the primaries, all round the trailing edge of the wing and across the base of the tail, an unmistakable inch-wide white ribbon that is always visible in flight. Add to this its long, square-ended wings with up-turned fingers, a spotted breast, bright yellow bill and feet and it is evident that anyone of average intelligence can identify it.

After lunch I paddled in the stream which was deliciously soothing, and later fell asleep, sure indication that the morning's walk had been long and hard. It was tea-time when I woke and returned to camp.

It was not there. I called repeatedly but there was no answer. What was I to do, alone on a Himalayan hillside with no warm clothing, no tent, no food and no porters? I began to feel a quite unreasonable panic surging up when suddenly, two fields off, I saw a waving figure running towards me.

It was Pen Uri, far more panic-stricken that I had been. They had searched everywhere, they thought that Mummy had gone into the mountains. It had not occurred to them to look by the stream close at hand where Mummy was snoozing peacefully, regaining some of her flu-sapped strength.

The new site, about a mile away, was by the river near to a bombax tree. This wonderful tree, also called silk cotton, is tall with right-angled branches and large, pinkish-red, round-petalled, waxy flowers that are rich in nectar. The bombax is beloved by birds of all kinds and they were everywhere, beautiful blue-black, hair-crested drongos with lovely, curling tail tips, two kinds of oriole, many different species of bulbul and in the river nearby were forktails, redstarts, dippers and whistling thrushes. There was also a great Himalayan kingfisher, a huge black, white and grey-speckled bird swooping up and down over the water and plunging headlong for its food.

Pinto brought my dinner to the river bank where I sat blissfully watching and eating by turn. That is one lovely thing about camping in Nepal, porters and Sherpas never seem to mind how far they have to bring your meals, in fact they seem to prefer you to be at a respectable distance. They never complain about bringing a meal 200 yards, but 10 yards away is far too near the kitchen for their liking. The same reserve applies to one's tent which they always erect some way away from theirs when they have one. This is not very chummy when it is cold and there is only one fire, which I insist on sharing at meal times, but in the main, Sir, Memsahib or Mummy is put at a remove.

Next day was hot and sunny, I had completely recovered and we moved on through beautiful, fairly flat country and lunched further up the same river, where a whole family party of great Himalayan kingfishers were hurtling up and down.

This was apparently sanitation day and everything the porters possessed, and all my smalls too, were washed and hung out to dry while lunch was prepared. With all this washing going on I decided that I might as well wash my hair which was badly in need of it after several days of flu. Pen Uri took charge of the operation and first laid my Dunlopillo sleeping pad out on the stones by the river, a fair imitation of the contour couch of luxurious American hairdressing establishments. A small tin bowl of hot water was brought and after many verbal and mimed requests a second bowl of cold water made its appearance. The most difficult bit was yet to come. I needed a mug with which to pour the water over my head and asked Pinto to bring one. Now Pinto, not too quick in any language and knowing absolutely nothing of English, knew that when Mummy asked for a mug she wanted tea or coffee in it. He brought Nescafé. No. He brought tea. No good. He then brought the drinking chocolate but memsahib waved them all away. What could be the matter? It was some time before I managed to convey effectively that what I wanted was an *empty* mug. *Why* did Mummy want a mug with nothing in it?

When at last it came I had to start work, peeling off my blouse in front of what was by now an assembled multitude for anyone passing by had, of course, stopped to watch what was going on. I managed the shampoo, fervently blessing the man or woman who invented those little plastic sachets. When the shampooing was completed I had to rinse my hair and the scant pint of water I had was not enough. Getting some more out of Pinto was a tedious and lengthy task. He finally brought the kettle-teapot full of hot water and poured it over my head as I lay in a semi-recumbent position on the stones. I set the hair as best I could, watched by an ever-growing and absolutely entranced audience, and it dried quickly in the bright sun. Examining the result in my glass later I thought that I looked exceptionally repulsive but Pen Uri insisted that it was 'much more better' than it had been. Whatever must it have looked like before?

When we moved off after lunch my entourage presented a wonderful picture for every porter's basket was draped from top to bottom with damp laundry. On the way we met a string of ponies returning from Jomsom, stumbling carefully down the now precipitous path. I wondered how often they fell and broke their legs, for I saw one which had been mended in the wrong direction. Many of these animals looked very sweet and some were quite perky and cheerful while others were bowed and depressed. One was accompanied by a foal of not more than a fortnight and a stone was thrown at her whenever she stopped to let the foal suckle. Many wore wire muzzles, presumably to stop them wasting time by grazing. I asked Pen Uri if they were ever groomed or brushed and he said no. Stupid of me to ask, really.

For the whole of the next day we walked through thick rhododendron forest. I could not get used to the beauty of rhododendrons. On my first trek I saw only red ones of two different species but here the majority were in varying shades of pink. When I looked up the trees were shaped like cumulus clouds, the deeply dark green fans of leaves thickly starred with many different pinks: blush, deep rose and a strident shocking pink of a brilliance that I have never seen equalled. Where the blooms were thickest some had fallen, covering our path with petals. It seemed unutterably regal to be walking on a flower-strewn path, a luxury as unreal as the transformation scene in the pantomimes of my youth. The fragrant pink carpet, soft as the flooring of an expensive cinema, was infinitely more sensuous and beautiful. And when we reached about 8,000 feet there was a tall tree full of pale flowers whose petals looked like thick white kid. I stared and pondered and then came to my senses. These were magnolias, their creamy stars contrasting to perfection with the glowing pinks.

Before I started my trek Bob Fleming, Jnr., told me that I ought to see at least 130 different species of bird during the four weeks. I had already seen 84 in the first ten days, three of which had been passed in a flu daze with my identification faculties hardly working. Birding in a foreign country is always full of surprises but today's biggest was at Gorepani, a 10,000 feet pass where I saw a large thrush near the top of a tree. Its breast had some markings and I hoped that it would turn out to be a mountain thrush with dark brown crescents on its creamy chest, but as I drew nearer even wishful thinking could not make crescents out of its obvious large spots and the bird seemed rather grey. It saw me and flew off, making the fairground rattle that I knew so well at home. I was looking for Asian species and never expected to see a perfectly good missel thrush 10,000 feet up in the Himalayas.

Gorepani was a lovely pass and at the very top was a perfect camping site into which we settled with alacrity even though it was only lunch time. Dhaulagiri, Fang, Annapurna and many more made a spectacular background with a foreground of multi-coloured rhododendrons. The sky was an intensely deep blue and against it every mountain looked whiter than white and glittering into the bargain. I sat down for a prolonged gazing session from which I only roused myself to eat a large lunch.

Afterwards I began to explore this charmed district which contained almost everything a keen birdwatcher could desire. There were grey-headed thrushes, large rusty birds with smoky-grey heads, orange-gorgetted flycatchers, which were dark blue and brown, their orange gorget represented by a tiny crescent at the throat which showed only when the bird turned its head in my direction and threw it back slightly, rose-finches, warblers of many mystifying kinds and several fourteen-rupee birds.

And there were white-collared blackbirds. These, bigger than European and American blackbirds, were sooty black, with a white collar, thicker and whiter in the male, and a splendid song and they sat most obligingly on the tops of trees.

It was here that I saw a chaffinch-sized creature of the most marvellous blue that was very slightly greenish but by no means turquoise. Its throat and breast were pure white, its flanks a reddish orange and its shape, streamlined and elegant, was as lovely as its colouring. The gorgeous creature proved to be an orange-flanked brush robin, known in Europe as the red-flanked bluetail. Pecking about on bright green grass sprinkled with the fallen flowers of pink rhododendrons it was sensational.

The sky soon clouded and slight rain fell so I sheltered under a tree with several other trekkers, including two young Americans carrying enormous packs. George, who was 24, described himself as 'a retired business executive'; Gene, thin, handsome and very tall, was a tennis professional. We got on enormously well and as they were sleeping at a house in the village below I invited them to come to have coffee at my camp after supper.

As we sipped our coffee later, they asked if they could come back very early in the morning to take pictures of the sun rising over those stupendous mountains. I agreed.

I had only just washed and dressed when they arrived, cameras and inter-changeable lenses at the ready, and we sat and waited eagerly for the sun to strike the tops.

After we had all taken photographs in quantity and had had breakfast Gene said why didn't we visit the Poonhill? Why didn't we?

The Poonhill was apparently an excellent viewpoint, although it was hard to imagine one better than our present station, and visitors were exhorted to visit it by a sign on the path below which urged us, to 'VISIT THE POONHILL, only an hour up and down' ending a flowery description in execrable English with 'the glaring beauty of the sunrise from the Poonhill is unforgettable.'

At 8 o'clock we set off. There was no marked path and we wandered in an upward direction for nearly a thousand feet. I began to flag, but Gene was a kindly creature and looking down from his 6 feet 3 inches at the struggling old lady behind gave her what birds crossing the Atlantic by boat are termed to have: assisted passage. A few doughty pushes in the rear and I was up, to be rewarded by the most wonderful view in the world and undoubtedly the highest of high spots. It reminded me of the view from the cockpit when flying from Calcutta to Kathmandu, a vast ring of blue-white, icy peaks thrusting into a gentian-blue sky, the brooding mass of Dhaulagiri, the coronet of Annapurna, the aptly named Fang and the graceful twin fishtail of Machha Puchhare.

Even without 'the glaring beauty of the sunrise', it was unutterably lovely. We felt humbled by this supreme manifestation of nature's power and beauty but above all grateful that we were there in perfect weather and also in isolation. Although we were acutely conscious of our insignificance we were at the same time riotously gay and excited and stayed there for at least an hour taking innumerable pictures of icefalls, glaciers, the peaks and each other. We came down at speed, flushed and deeply moved by the experience.

We were also very hungry and I dispatched Pen Uri's scrambled eggs and *chapattis* with delight, first having sampled an American concoction which George and Gene insisted that I should try. I thought a salted cracker spread with peanut butter and topped with a small square of Nepalese cheese and a spoonful of peach jam sounded nauseating but good manners forbade me to refuse. It was in fact absolutely delicious.

After lunch we struck camp with the greatest reluctance and started down towards Chitre, arriving an hour later. I bade a reluctant goodbye to George and Gene, who were going to Jomsom, and protested to Pen Uri that I didn't want to stop at Chitre which was far too soon to make camp. Pen Uri said firmly that there was nowhere else to stop on the way to the Deorali pass and for that night it was Chitre. I did not know then that most Sherpas like to stop in a recognised camp site whenever possible because there they meet all their friends. All Sherpas seem to be friends with all other Sherpas and they are inveterate gossips, too, who will talk not only till the cows come home but almost till it is time for them to be driven out again.

I settled into camp with an ill grace for there are few things I dislike more than well-used camp sites which have become dirty and are very noisy. It is also difficult to find an unused tree or bush for one's morning retirement and this is an important consideration.

Suddenly there was a great noise and into camp swept a vast conglomeration of people, a rich American family, father and mother of my own vintage, grown-up children, grandchildren and a retinue of Sherpas and porters. They were all very nice, very gay and enjoying it immensely and the hubbub they created was extraordinary. They too were going over the Deorali pass next day and wanted me to go with them but I well knew that if about a hundred of us, or so it seemed, charged through the countryside together there wouldn't be a bird left in the district.

We started at about the same time next morning but I found so many shy birds that would not come out unless I waited patiently that the family and I soon became separated: I only hope they didn't think me too curmudgeonly. On the forest path I found a dead bird, a green and yellow tiny that looked as if it might be a Tibetan siskin. I put it in a small plastic bag and carried it with me in the hope that I might find someone who would take it back to Kathmandu and deliver it to the Flemings for identification.

This part of the trek was lovely, a little used path up a wonderfully sloping hillside studded with huge deodars and giving fine views of Dhaulagiri. It was far less frequented than anywhere else that I had been, so wild and strange that I would not have been surprised to find a tiger in one of the gullies, although I should have been terrified if I had. The air was often filled with strange noises and my mind turned to the rare pheasants but search as I might I could not find any.

This slope was colder than anywhere we had been so far and I needed my two sleeping bags and hot-water bottle. When I emerged at 6.15 to take pictures of the sunrise on Dhaulagiri the ground was white with rime but the view of a pink-flushed Dhaulagiri, with feathery deodars in the foreground, was exquisite.

We reached the top of the pass by 10.30 to find it almost obscured by masses of *Primula denticulata.* I have this in my garden but I had never before seen it growing wild and in quantity. Among it was a mass of filthy Western litter, so unpleasant and degrading in content that there was no alternative but to collect and burn it. While I was engaged in this necessary but unsavoury task who should appear but Mal and Joan Sterrett whom I had last seen outside Pokhara.

It was very pleasant to meet again and we joined forces to lurch down a very steep and slippery path. As we descended, quantities of the lovely mauve primroses that I had seen on my first trek appeared. I was also surprised, in my ignorance, to see a lot of bamboo mixed with the deodars, some of it with snow still lying around the roots. Till then I had always thought that bamboo grew only in damp, jungly areas but here it was doing very well in totally different circumstances.

We came down to smoother conditions and a cattle settlement and Pen Uri elected to make camp in the middle of what seemed to me to be a solid mass of trampled cowdung.

We three fussy Westerners decided to stay a little higher up. Under the tree where my tent was eventually pitched I found a pile of scarlet feathers with white tips. These belonged to the *Satyr Tragopan,* one of the special pheasants I particularly wished to see.

Mal, Joan and I talked almost without stopping for, while trekking solo is fine, one gets lonely on occasion and congenial people who speak one's own language are more than welcome.

Next morning was one of the most beautiful days imaginable in a country which seems to have so many. There were deep pink rhododendrons in profusion with a fair number of magnolias to enhance their beauty, an undercarpet of sweetly scented daphne with *Primula denticulata* and the lovely mauve primrose everywhere. As we walked up and up and then down and down the usual Nepalese switchback we saw from every high point complete hillsides glowing pink and it was evident that in a week or so, when all the rhododendrons would be in full flower, the whole countryside would be deeply flushed with the glory of spring.

We came to a forest of very old trees with moss-encrusted trunks. In the depths of this moss nestled orchids, most of them single blooms on very short stalks. They were singularly beautiful, snowy white with five spreading petals and a large white central trumpet, the throat speckled with yellow, red or magenta. These fallen stars, trapped by the mossy trunks, added further richness to an already elaborate display of natural beauty.

At this point trouble overtook us. The porters had vanished. Pen Uri called until he grew hoarse, but all in vain. It appeared that where we had to turn left to the village of Kymru the porters had gone elsewhere. The Sterretts' rather unsatisfactory porter, to whom Pen Uri was giving excellent lessons on how to look after his clients, was told to go along the other track to look for the missing men. He came back within five minutes, saying that they were not there and was brutally sent off again to have a closer look. He soon returned, apparently determined not be be separated from his employers.

We followed the downward path through lovely forest for almost an hour but there was still no sign of the porters and Mal and Joan decided that we were lost. Pen Uri disagreed. At last, immensely weary and longing for food, which was all with the porters, we saw Kymru far, far below us. The whole distance between us was filled by a terraced mountainside of interminable length, with no distinct path. Sometimes the next terrace was only a foot below but sometimes it was four feet down and I had an arthritic knee which heartily disliked bending. I decided to take my mind off my miseries by counting the number of terraces but after 250 I gave up and stumbled doggedly on.

When we reached the bottom we found a swift and quite wide river between us and the village and no visible crossing place. Pen Uri, undaunted and perfectly fresh, insisted on taking me over the river pickaback. This was embarrassing for he was far smaller than I, but he insisted so, clinging to him and with my feet dragging in the water, I forded the river on my splendid steed.

We walked into the village and there found the porters who had come by what was evidently the right path and had arrived some hours earlier. Pen Uri tore the supplies from their baskets and within fifteen minutes presented me with *chapattis,* scrambled eggs and coffee. It was 3.30 and my only food, since waking at 6, had been tea, biscuits and a small plate of porridge.

Next morning we began the real business of getting to the Annapurna Sanctuary. Colonel Roberts' route sheet said that the trek was for experienced climbers only and I had to admit that some of it was a bit teasing. There were many places where the path was a shuffle along a little indentation in a horizontal stone slab lying at a steep angle. Both Pen Uri and Pinto were very good at extending a helping hand at these perilous times when a false step would have sent me slithering down far too far.

The path follows the Modi Khola valley but the river itself was so far below that we could see nothing of it. But there were many other things to see, including a peregrine falcon, the southern blackbird, so very like ours, and grey-winged blackbirds with their echoing bell-like song which, besides being extremely melodious, is very loud indeed. There were forktails whenever we reached a small stream, black eagles and serpent eagles and this day I saw my first hoary barwing and a black-browed flycatcher warbler.

This first day on the last stretch of the sanctuary trek was chiefly memorable for the first sight of *Coelogyne cristata,* the lovely yellow-throated white orchid which pours in quantity down the trunks of trees or exposed rock faces. I had seen it many times on my first trek but there are some things about which one can never become blasé and *Coelogyne cristata* is one of them.

That night we came to Chomrong, a long village that straggled down a hillside. The only place that Pen Uri could find to camp was a ploughed field with dumps of manure dotted thickly over it in readiness for spreading next day. The porters were bidden to put earth on the nearest lumps to save Mummy's nose and despite the drawback we all slept very well.

Next morning Mal and Joan left for Kathmandu via Ghandrung and Landrung, taking with them the small bird in the plastic bag to deliver to Bob Fleming. We said goodbye with real regret and vowed that we would go to stay with each other in England and Washington, D.C., a vow that we have all kept twice.

I went on to the Hinko Cave which I badly wanted to reach because in that area Bob Fleming had said I would surely see Hodgson's grandalas, the bird that I wanted to see above all others in Nepal. The Flemings had shown me a skin of an unbelievable ultramarine blue, shining and glistening with an almost unearthly quality, and set off by black wings and tail. Another thing they said about the Hinko Cave was that it could be slept in quite warmly and comfortably.

The path was strange, winding through heavy bamboo forest, the edges thick with *Primula denticulata.* The track was pretty nearly awash and I was so occupied with keeping upright and avoiding the deepest puddles that I was not able to look for many birds. But when we did at last come out into the open there were lovely things to be seen, including an unexpected woodcock which flew up from the river bed at about 9,500 feet.

As we neared Hinko we came on a lot of rather spiky bushes and, flying above them, was a large flock of birds, mostly brownish with a long, light bar on the wings. These were indeed the grandalas but they were mostly females. There must have been about two hundred of the longed-for creatures but the light was against me and not a scrap of blue did I see. It was exceedingly disappointing, even worse than the eight scarlet finches I saw outside Kathmandu, all of them females and therefore completely green.

But disasters were about to begin again. On the previous day the porters had used some particularly noxious, dirty water in which to cook their rice and the effect had turned even their strong Nepalese stomachs: some felt slightly ill, some felt very ill and besides that they all decided that they had had enough. They had no warm clothing and not enough food for going to 12,500 feet and it was a waste of time to argue that Pen Uri had told them at the start of the trek to bring both. They were cold, hungry, and they felt ill, and, said Pen Uri, squatting realistically and making all too graphic gestures with his hand towards the rear, 'They have much shooting!'

So down they went, leaving Pen Uri and Pinto with five men's loads and no porters. We packed into the Hinko Cave and had a long discussion as to what to do. I did not want to go back but how could we go on without porters? We could, of course, leave our things in the cave and take up provisions for only a couple of days but this did not seem to be a wise move.

We were soon joined by a couple of wild-looking men who were hunting goats and pheasants but finding none, I am happy to say. They looked to be most terrible thugs but Pen Uri quickly enrolled them as porters although they demanded an inflated rate of pay as the loads would be so heavy.

Later still came a lanky young man from New Zealand called Geoff who was hiking on his own with a huge pack that contained very little food but provided spiritual nourishment in the form of a flute. I was glad to have another English-speaking companion and listened entranced to stories of his extended tour round the world which he intended should last for many more months. He ended with a little flute recital which was really lovely in those isolated mountains.

The weather worsened as evening approached and Pen Uri decided to pitch my tent inside the Hinko Cave. This wasn't really a cave at all, merely a huge overhanging rock which afforded shelter. The wind was in the wrong direction for comfort and whistled with ferocious zeal. I spent an uncomfortable night, the discomfort heightened by the presence of other small inhabitants of the cave which found their way into my sleeping bag and left traces of their presence which remained with me for some days.

Contrary to all expectations the Annapurna route was proving rather a disappointment. The approaches, Gorepani, the Poonhill and the country between the Deorali pass and Kymru, had been magical but now, when we were nearing both Machha Puchhare and Annapurna, the magic was diminishing. The Modi Khola gorge was too tight for me to see anything and what little view there was, was obscured by bamboos. For much of the time it was a watery trudge with no birds and mammals to speak of although there was one moment at Hinko when Pen Uri saw a small red-and-cream animal. It must have been a red panda, which I knew occurred in that area, but I wasn't quick enough to spot it. What with missing the panda, seeing no blue at all on the grandalas, the steadily deteriorating weather and the desertion of all the porters, life was not rosy. Geoff was a great help: cheerful, intelligent and interested in absolutely everything, he was just the right companion on a sticky wicket.

We left Hinko and picked our way with difficulty over large snow patches on a steep slope and continued on and up towards the sanctuary. These snow slopes were extremely treacherous and Pen Uri and Pinto or Geoff went one behind and one in front to help Mummy when she sank above her knees and seemed unable to pull them out.

Where there wasn't snow were large clumps of some unknown variety of poppy. They weren't the familiar blue poppy, *Meconopsis baileyi,* which I know well because its discoverer's wife lives near to me in Norfolk, where it grows profusely in her garden. This poppy had long, narrow leaves, deeply notched throughout and of the most wonderful glowing green which had a golden light suffusing them from within. The plants withered remains showed that each had one large flower stem with several branches and this stem grew to about three feet in height.

There was also a very stunted tree which had bunches of little pink flowers growing in tight heads and smelling as sweet as daphne.

We stumbled on, through worsening weather, our boots soaked through and our socks and trouser bottoms wet enough to wring out.

As soon as we could find enough level ground, we decided to camp and Pen Uri thawed us out slightly with hot tea, though the trouble with hot tea at altitude is that it is not so hot. Pen Uri unpacked my sleeping bag as soon as he had put up my tent, and filled my hot-water bottle but this, too, felt only luke-warm.

Geoff joined me in my tent and we lay gloomily gazing out of the door at the inhospitable rock face on the other side of the gorge, a grim, unforgiving, deeply-stepped mass, the flat terraces thick with new snow, the vertical areas black and menacing. We shivered and had little appetite as we watched the snow fall from the leaden sky slowly but with an obstinate thoroughness.

I couldn't help wondering then why I continue to make these arduous and difficult expeditions at an age when most of my contemporaries stay cosily at home. Why do I have few clothes, cheap food, an unpainted house, shabby curtains and a rusty car in order to save up enough money for such extended trips? It seemed then to be masochism of the craziest kind.

But even as I shivered and complained I knew that a fine day would bring back my spirits and I would be in my boots, even if they were still wet, wrapping round me every scrap of the splendid Mrs. Blower's clothing and pressing ever upwards to the sanctuary. Geoff, younger and more resilient, lay by my side and we passed the time playing noughts and crosses on a very thin piece of typing paper and thinking aloud about the meals that we enjoyed most, none of them including either rice or tea.

Later in the afternoon the sky cleared and Geoff went to explore the upper valley, returning for a horrible supper of rice and cocktail sausages which, even when curried, were disgusting, preceded by a very thin chicken noodle soup. As I was on a four-week trek I had to have seven packets of powdered soup, using a quarter of a packet each day. But why were all seven packets chicken noodle which I didn't much like anyway? Such small privations assume a disproportionate aspect when there is little of more vital moment to consider.

Geoff was full of enthusiasm for his excursion. He had been most of the way to the sanctuary, he thought, the going was not so bad as it had been lower down and he had found fresh tracks of some animal with pads and claws some thirteen inches apart. The tracks, not the claws, he explained quickly. *Could* it have been a snow leopard?

My spirits rose. Perhaps tomorrow would be fine and I could see grandalas looking blue and a snow leopard too, which would compensate for every one of the difficulties and disasters.

Next morning was gloriously fine with a brilliant blue sky and sun touching the snow to an even greater dazzle. We left Pinto and the two tough porters to guard the camp and set off early. It was *very* cold. I put on everything I had, even the Yeti hat which was very warm indeed but did nothing to enhance my appearance. But who cared?

We trotted steadily upwards, crossing great tracts of snow which was fortunately frozen solid at that hour and presented no difficulty. Far too soon little puffs of clouds began to appear and Pen Uri said that we must make haste. I added a flock of snow pigeons to my bird list, several lammergeiers sailed over, there was a Himalayan cole tit and both red-billed and Alpine choughs.

With few rests and much protracted effort we reached the sanctuary and there, beneath a rock, sun bathing, was a Japanese who had passed us about a week earlier with his porters. I didn't feel at all well disposed towards him for his progress up the valley was marked by a trail of tins, plastic bags and other rubbish, even an old plastic mackintosh torn in strips.

Pen Uri felt friendlier that I did and went down to join the party, one of whom was a relation. One of the things one learns quickly when trekking is that every party met en route contains a relation or, at the least, a dear friend of one's Sherpa who must be talked to at length. Pen Uri spent such a long time with his friend or relative that Geoff and I climbed to a ridge overlooking the sanctuary, an almost vertical slope, up which Geoff kindly dragged me and there we sat, surveying the impressive scene.

This Base Camp area was a large open space of glacier with various peaks of Annapurna standing all around, but although it was termed the Base Camp it was not even halfway up to the summit: the view was superb, the snowy mountains crystalline and tinged with cobalt blue. All were magnificently patterned with both snow and ice and looked so enormous, towering right above us, that we felt unbearably insignificant. We could see how apparently unclimbable the recently scaled south face of Annapurna appeared to be. There were so many peaks around that we could not possibly identify them and Pen Uri was still talking to his friend and so couldn't help us. All we knew was that, close at hand, Machha Puchhare was still the loveliest by far, a superb mountain that was faultless from every angle.

We tore open our lunch packet and began to eat, marvelling at the scenery, although for sheer beauty it couldn't touch the Poonhill. As we ate, I noticed a small, unidentifiable passerine unwisely venturing into this inhospitable terrain and, within a few minutes, it was being chased by a hen harrier, a kestrel and a raven, whether for food or devilment I do not know. To my great surprise, it managed to elude all three. I had a whole new reel of film ready in my camera, but I was so hungry that I had to lunch first. And then Pen Uri appeared and said that it was snowing and we must go down.

I am allegedly the slowest eater in Britain and I had hardly begun my lunch, but Pen Uri was insistent and, in cases like this, it is unwise to argue with one's Sherpa. He did not want to be lost on the mountains with Mummy even though he had a very stong and tall young man with him to help out in any difficulty or emergency. I begged to stay just a little longer but Pen Uri was adamant.

I took a few pictures of my beloved Machha Puchhare, now being rapidly obscured by large and heavy snow clouds, waved, without cordiality, to the Japanese and began the descent. Both Pen Uri and Geoff were very good to me, as we trotted down faster than I could comfortably manage. One went in front and one behind. It was snowing hard for most of the way but it had eased by the time we reached camp. Dear Pinto had seen us coming and had tea ready and a hot-water bottle too, to warm my sleeping bag.

One very good and unforgettable thing I experienced in this camp was the hot stone seat. When the porters make a fire this is always held in place by large stones. One of these was removed at supper time and replaced by another and when the original stone had cooled slightly it was given to me to sit on, one of the most memorably luxurious seats that I have ever had.

Next morning was fine after a night of rain and we slithered down over a mixture of snow, mud and general debris. Soon after we started, Geoff said that he intended to go right on down to Kymru that day, a marathon trek. I knew it would take me three or four days at least but it was as nothing to this tall and sinewy New Zealand athlete. I was very sorry to see him go.

The weather grew steadily nastier; moderately fine mornings raised our spirits and then thick banks of cloud appeared and rain or snow obscured the view for the rest of the day. Unfortunately Pen Uri seemed unable to get our new porters going. They were a couple of older men, tougher than tough and totally undisciplined, and Pen Uri, not nearly as inflexible or well organised as Pasang, could make little impression on them. During this rather difficult time and in such bad weather both Pen Uri and Pinto were very good to me, exemplifying to the full the Sherpa ethic of looking after the client, Pinto even going to the length of removing his shoes to stand ankle deep in thick snow to keep me from sliding down a precipitous slope towards immersion in the glacial stream below.

We had a rather dreary journey downwards and the two new porters did pretty well as they wished, on one occasion going ahead when they were carrying all the food and on another staying behind with it, in both cases leaving us without any lunch. Fortunately Pen Uri, who had been helping by carrying a small load when the porters left, had 'a little something' in his rucksack.

It was on this day that Pen Uri decided he must have a good wash to remove several days' grime and I, stimulated by his exertions, managed to wash my own hair in the one inch of water that ran steadily over a rock from a minute stream. My towel, brush and comb were all with the errant porters so I combed the sopping mass, as best I could, with a sliver of bamboo broken from the nearest clump and shook it dry in the sun.

But there was one awful day when there was no sun at all and the rain was so violent and heavy that we judged it better to take shelter in the next village, Chomrong, which was still a couple of miles away. I was thoroughly drenched and miserable before we turned into a house where we were warmly welcomed. I stayed on the verandah, which was dry, the porters brought my kit and I changed as best I could, watched, needless to say, by the whole family. After this the porters, who were Chomrong men, went home, Pen Uri and Pinto disappeared and there seemed to be no one about.

I was dry but cold so I walked along the verandah and saw the glow of a fire through the window. Window is a misnomer, really, for this was a space some one and a half by two and a half feet, divided by inch-wide strips of wood with inch-wide spaces, between which were other strips of wood at the same intervals so that the amount of air and light getting in was infinitesimal.

I found a door and went in and there by the fire sat the lady of the house with a small baby by her side. The fire was in a sunken hole in the floor in which wood burned under and around two iron trivets. I was put in the place of honour next to it, on a piece of stained material. Pen Uri, Pinto and several others soon appeared and we were offered Tibetan tea which I accepted gratefully. It was a thick, sugary, milky brew laced with salt and pepper and it soothed my frozen person. Madam, who was apparently cooking something, was almost invisible through the smoky murk. It was an easy kitchen to run for she sat cross-legged before the fire with a pot of water, several pans and little boxes of this and that all within reach.

She picked up a pan containing nine ears of corn and removed the kernels by the simple expedient of rubbing one ear against the other, throwing the cores into the fire. The baby set up a piteous, hopeless wailing but the young girl sitting near it was apparently not its mother and nobody attempted to comfort the smoke-grimed, mucous-covered morsel. Grandma, presumably, thrust an ear of corn towards it but this wasn't appreciated and it continued to wail feebly for it had no toys, no dummy and nothing to support its back.

Grandma meanwhile put a large frying pan over the fire and poured the corn in, shaking it gently backwards and forwards for about twenty minutes. She poured the result into a dish and then gave me a generous plateful. Every grain had swollen to about twice the size, burst and browned, and it was absolutely delicious. This Himalayan popcorn, together with my sugar, salt and peppered tea, did me a world of good and I soon began to view life quite differently.

I went out on to the verandah with Pen Uri to discuss the night's sleeping arrangements, for the size of the family seemed to be building up and I couldn't visualise spending the night on that filthy floor with chickens and dogs running in and out and everybody coughing, particularly one girl who had a streaming cold and kept blowing her nose on the end of her sari.

I decided to sleep on the verandah where I had already staked out a claim and was sitting there, thanking God that I was in this village and not lying in a tent suffering a deluge of rain, when the baby's mother appeared and asked if I had any medicine for it.

I asked what was wrong with it and Pen Uri said that it had 'many wounds'. I wondered what could have produced wounds on a small

Opposite: *Pasang's beautiful wife, Namdo, with two daughters and a friend*

Top: *'The Fighting Men'*.

Bottom: *Rhododendrons in front of Dhaulagiri.*

baby. Did they have battered babies in Nepal? Its mother pulled up its dress to show me. The sight was horrrifying.

The poor little child had nothing on at all, bar an unspeakably foul dress of ancient chiffon velvet: no underwear, not even a nappy. Its poor little body was filthy and its legs from ankle to knee were a mass of healed and unhealed scabs. All down one thigh right from the groin was a huge raw area and scabs seemed to cover almost every part of its anatomy. No wonder it was wailing.

I told Pen Uri to tell the mother to clean it up and to put some cotton clothes over it at least to keep the dirt from the open sores but the mother merely laughed and said she had nothing, no clothes and no medicines and what could I give her?

I had no baby clothes, no medicine that could help and the nearest hospital was very, very far away at Pokhara. My mind turned to the three missionary nurses I had met in a village near Gorepani, one Dutch, one German and one English. All of them had said that if it hadn't been for their faith they would have gone home soon after they arrived, for the sights they had seen had been so dreadful. They told me many horrifying tales of their experiences and I remember their saying that most mothers lost one, two, three and sometimes even more children and that none managed to rear all those that she bore.

I began to appreciate even more the work that Bethel Fleming and her helpers were doing and to realise the need for more hospitals and clinics in the remoter areas of Nepal. Tourists see the glory of the country, the majesty of the peaks and the charm and courage of the Sherpas who guide them, but they know nothing of the struggle for existence that goes on in so many of the picturesque but insanitary houses that they see around them.

My sleeping bag lay on the straw mat placed between the door and the window and Pen Uri brought me a lantern so that I could read but a young girl snatched it from me and used it instead to illuminate a paved area below on which her brother was sluicing himself with cold water, spitting copiously meanwhile. I should not have thought anyone could have needed more water on that loathsomely drenching day.

Next morning I was waked by the sweet repetition of a cuckoo, something I love to hear at home in spring but which was unexpected in Asia at 7,000 feet. I got up early and went to find the lady of the house to say to her the only word of Nepali that I knew, 'Namaste' which is greeting.

Pen Uri settled the financial end of the matter and I went off to do a little birding, finding a forktail, a black eagle and a grey-winged blackbird, all looking their best in the suspiciously bright sunlight, with the backcloth of Machha Puchhare as compellingly beautiful as ever.

An American I had first met at the Hinko Cave was also tramping on. He had seemed rather dim then, striding fast and resolutely through the country and noticing nothing. Now, meeting him again a few days later, I mentioned Hinko and he said 'What was that?' I said it was the cave where we had met and he replied that he hadn't noticed one. This day, as before, he was 'making good time' but nothing else.

He asked what on earth I was doing, just standing about. I said that I was watching birds. He looked amazed and said 'Holy Cow!', perhaps a fitting expression in a Hindu kingdom, and made off quickly.

One meets an enormous variety of people when trekking, although this year I'd been more than lucky with Mal and Joan, George and Gene and lastly Geoff, but on the way down from Hinko we met a very strange young man with spectacles, a thick beard, a wisp of hair tied at the back with a bootlace, and wearing a scoop-necked cheese-cloth tunic. He was on his way to the Annapurna Sanctuary and asked where he could stay and where he could buy food.

I told him that there was nowhere to stay and no food to buy.

'But surely,' he said, 'there's a shop at Hinko?'

'No,' I said firmly, 'No shop anywhere and no houses either. Nothing.'

'Oh well,' he said, with a saintly sigh of resignation, 'I'll just have to eat some flower with my rice!' and pulled from his shoulder bag two large clusters of pink rhododendrons. Maybe he would find some remains among the tins that the Japanese had scattered about so liberally but it astonished me that anyone could be quite so feckless.

We plodded back along the way we had come, as far as Kymru, and then went up the hill towards Ghandrung through marvellous forests where torrents of *Coelogyne cristata* spilled down the mossy trunks of old trees whose branches were also laden with gorgeous birds of many species. It was a long and tiring walk to Ghandrung and when we got there it rained and rained and rained. It rained and blew so violently during the night that I was frightened that my tent would blow down and was forced to join Pen Uri and Pinto in the shelter of the village school in which they slept themselves, having pitched my tent in the courtyard.

At Ghandrung and also at Landrung, where we went next, my patience grew rather thin for people came to watch and stare until I felt like something in a zoo. If zoo animals really do feel as I did under this unblinking scrutiny then all zoos should be abolished at once. I began to realise that privacy is something totally foreign to the Nepalese culture.

Next morning at Landrung I saw a lovely sight, a party of women leisurely cutting corn. They were cutting one ear at a time, happily gossiping as they worked. What would have been their reaction to a combine harvester?

It was near Landrung, too, that I saw a man shearing a sheep, another beautifully unhurried process. The sheep stood patiently, clasped round the neck by a strong youth who sat on a large stone. The man stood at the rear of the sheep with a big knife and from time to time picked up a large tuft of wool from the animal and cut if off. It must be very relaxing to live life at this gentle pace.

We were lower by then, it was mid-April and migrant birds were pouring in. All the new species were interesting and some were particularly lovely but the most beautiful of all was a cutia. I had looked many times at the picture of a cutia in Sálim Ali's *Birds of Sikkim* and thought how wonderful it would be to see one and this morning, when it was luckily fine and sunny, I looked deep into the forest and there on a tree trunk in full view was a splendid cutia. It had a rich chestnut back and a black-tipped chestnut tail. Its primaries were black-tipped too and its underparts snowy with the exception of fine black stripes on its flanks. Its head was a deep, slaty blue with a black stripe over its eye. I watched it to my heart's content and even the non-ornithological Pen Uri was impressed.

On the same day we saw a serpent eagle sitting on a tree about twenty feet from us and it needed almost superhuman effort on my part to prevent our thug-like-porters from shooting it. They were tough customers in every way and that day one of them trod on a thorn which had penetrated far into his bare foot. I watched with horror while Purna, oldest of the porters who had gone back home because of the cold and who had now rejoined us, prodded with a large safety pin into the sole of the man's foot, delving ever deeper until he lifted the large thorn out. I proffered antiseptic cream but it was waved away and, to my astonishment, all was well, as my stoical employee trampled along with dust and dirt grinding into the open wound.

The weather grew steadily worse and each day the rain started earlier and the sky grew greyer and more discouraging. The final part of the trek which would land us at Suiket, was a perilous and very steep descent down which we stumbled and slipped. It took far longer than I care to remember, my back hurt, my knees hurt, I was a misery and rather wet.

We got down at last and Pen Uri pitched my tent some way from the fast-running river. I asked if it were all right there and he said oh yes, indeed it was, because they didn't get so much rain at this altitude as they did higher up. He made me a pot of tea and I settled down with it to read my book.

I had been reading for only ten minutes when the rain began again, pattering on the tent. The pattering changed to an imperious rapping and then to a continuous drumming and I lay in an agony of apprehension wondering what was happening.

Suddenly the tent door was unzipped and a worried Pen Uri stood there saying, 'Mummy, I think we ought to go down to the main house. Please come out quickly.' I looked out of the tent door and saw that he was standing in four inches of water.

I put my boots on once more, wrapped my flimsy mack around me and stepped out into the flood, splashing through the rice paddies which had become a series of small lakes and with Pinto's hand to catch and pull me over, leapt across the foot-deep river which an hour ago had been a meagre trickle.

I was ushered into the nearest house, a guest house run by a woman who had her eye to the main chance. I was provided with a rush mat and a blanket but not invited to the fire before which our two highly paid thugs sat comfortably, not attempting to help with dismantling the tents and removing the stores and baggage which Pen Uri, Pinto and Purna carried out at a distance of some two hundred yards at least, leaping backwards and forwards each time over the steadily rising stream. All three of them were completely soaked and Pinto had no change of clothing. It was a long time before I was able to persuade him to wear one of the Blower sweaters to avoid pneumonia.

The rain redoubled and I was grateful to be in a house, for I doubt if any tent could have successfully withstood such a watery assault. The house was two storeys high and had two doors in alignment and as I was put to sit between them I was not cosy. The fire was inside a kind of stone square with holes in the top and was constantly fed with a supply of resinous wood which smoked so strongly that I could neither see nor breathe properly.

The lady of the house bestowed on us the most flashing of gold-toothed smiles but nothing else although she produced gargantuan dishes of rice for her husband, brother and herself. She eventually sold Pen Uri a chicken at an extortionate price but the bird was so hard (not to be wondered at, really, as from vibrant life to its appearance on my plate was little more than an hour) that I couldn't cut, let alone chew it. I managed to eat the giblets, at home reserved for dear pussy, but here reserved for Mummy as they were softer.

Pen Uri arranged that Mummy should sleep upstairs as it would be too crowded below — how right he was — and took my damp sleeping bags and soaking Dunlopillo mattress up a precipitous and chancy ladder to a kind of attic. Here I spent the night with icy wind whistling through the logs that nearly filled the open space they called a window and with choking smoke rising from below.

Next morning we swung off to Pokhara in remarkably good fettle considering the spartan conditions under which we had passed the night. The rice paddies, now all shallow lakes, held a fine crop of green and wood sandpipers, red-wattled lapwings and spur-winged lapwings which provided the silver lining to the all too heavy cloud.

On the last leg of the trek we stopped at the Tibetan camp which had some very nice small rugs for sale, each about eighteen inches square. These, when suitably backed, made lovely cushions. The man in charge spoke excellent English and told me of another lady who had been there recently and she, too, had been looking for birds and plants.

'She was very, very old, *even older than you,*' he said, slightly incredulously I thought, 'and every morning her Sherpas would go to her tent and open it to see if she was still alive.'

We reached Pokhara somewhat the worse for wear and saw a taxi at the top of the village street which for a rupee apiece conveyed us to the Mountain Travel office, an ignominious end to a tiring day.

There had been many disasters on this trek and the worst was then to come, in the form of a letter for Pen Uri, telling him that his mother had died suddenly. It was a very sad ending. I shall never forget the glory of the scenery, the superb rhododendrons and other flowers, the wonderfully varied birds and the people I met but equally unforgettable was the disgusting, unpredictable and spirit-dowsing weather which almost defeated us. But it defeated the International Everest Expedition, too, which provided a grain of comfort.

Everest – The Base Camp

For my second attempt to reach the Everest Base Camp I decided that I wanted something simpler and cheaper than Mountain Travel could provide. I also wanted to bring food which would be more to my taste and might lessen the attacks of dysentery to which I was only too prone.

I took the advice of Mal and Joan of the Annapurna trek and went to Rover Treks. This was run by a man called Mike Cheney, chief assistant to Colonel Roberts of Mountain Travel, who wore his Mountain Travel hat when dealing with moneyed clients and his Rover Trek hat when coping with poorer trekkers. In addition to equipment and porters, he provided a great deal of necessary advice and information. From then on I was on my own, having to pay the porters and all incidental expenses myself instead of doing the whole thing with one payment in Kathmandu. This meant taking a lot of money with me, which I disliked intensely.

I took a large amount of dehydrated food, milk powder, fruit crystals and Nescafé. I looked with a trifle of anxiety on my Sherpa sirdar, Lobsang, for he was only nineteen. Mr Cheney said he was experienced, though I did not think that he could be at that age.

I need not have worried. Lobsang was excellent, resourceful, hard-working and a first rate disciplinarian. He was, in fact, far more 'on the ball' than many twice his age and nothing stumped him. He had a sweet smile, an engagingly boyish appearance and a great deal of interest in clothes, bringing no less than four pairs of trousers with him, a couple of hats and several sweaters all stowed in a commodious rucksack which was the gift of an American client,

Lobsang's English was not too bad but he had picked up many Americanisms from his previous clients and doubtless found my slightly pedantic speech a little strange. He knew nothing of such English euphemisms as 'spending a penny', but, in company with many Americans, Lobsang said he was'going to the bathroom'. As we walked along the path together Lobsang would often smile disarmingly as he slipped into the bushes saying gaily, 'Bathroom, Memsahib!'

When trekking with Mountain Travel I was taken by Land Rover to the starting point. With Rover Treks the porters and I all went by a very antiquated and scruffy bus. We took four hours to get to Lamosangu, not very far away, where the Chinese had built a large power station on the banks of the Sun Kosi.

It was very hot indeed and I discovered that I had stupidly left my cotton skirt in Kathmandu and had nothing to wear but corduroys. I found a stall in the market and bought two metres of printed cotton. I had no needles and thread except short lengths for vital repairs so I folded in the raw edges, wound the material round my waist and secured it with a length of string, rolling any spare length over the top to hide the string. It was not a garment that a designer could be proud of, but it served its purpose.

It was too late to start trekking as it was then 3 o'clock so we made camp, watched by the usual crowd that always collects. This made life rather difficult for me that afternoon as there is no sanitation in Nepal except in towns. There was no cover of any kind on my bare hillside and I had to contain myself until darkness fell at 6.30 because of the curious crowd that was all around. This is one of the trekking drawbacks that travel agents do not mention but it is very real nevertheless.

I went to bed early as it is not possible to read or write without some form of illumination. Lanterns are provided by Mountain Travel but Rover Treks clients use candles which are rather tricky in a tent. Lobsang soon evolved a good candlestick by filling an old mug with earth and wedging the candle in place with small stones.

Next morning at 7 we began our trek, going up through thin forest, the first hour yielding a Peking robin and a ruby-throat, followed closely by two dark grey cuckoo shrikes.

As we walked along I asked Lobsang if he thought I'd make the Base Camp.

'No,' he said without hesitation, 'not more than Namche Bazar.'

I observed rather coldly that I had already been far beyond Namche but I don't think he believed me.

We stopped for a rather late lunch at a place where I elected to spend the night too, for my experience has taught me that while I may 'go like a bomb' in the morning I can't keep it up all day without risk of collapse later. A little desultory birding around the camp in the afternoon was fine and I did this every day with Lobsang and one or other of the six porters, excursions which became known as my Base Camp training walks.

On this first full day we wandered away from the village where adults, children and clothes were all being washed at a communal pump and saw a great many small birds of various species and also hen harriers and a serpent eagle. On the way home the sky became full of small golden birds which, when at last we managed to find where they had settled, turned out to be Himalayan goldfinches. I had seen only one before so this was a rich bonus as there cannot have been less than two hundred.

The first night did not match the beauty of the day for I was wakened by a prodigious thunderclap. The sky was filled by lightning as golden as the finches, thunder roared and raged around us and a strong wind tore at the tent. I visualised myself naked on the bare hillside with my tent whipped away by the gale but all was over in a few hours, my quivering nerves settled down and when I woke in the morning the sky was bright blue and peace was restored.

The long morning's walk towards the top of the 8,000 foot pass showed us strings of snow mountains and was just as beautiful as the trek from Dolalghat. Most of the area was very skilfully terraced and the people of the district were obviously good farmers for the terraces were firmly supported by stone facings and everything appeared to be in good condition. Farming in Nepal is by no means easy for nearly all the crops have to be grown on terraces, some of which lie up to 10,000 feet above sea level. No tractors here, either, but ploughing with archaic ploughs drawn by oxen and much of the hoeing done by hand. I wonder what it will be like in fifty or even twenty years from now?

That night I camped to one side of the path on a little hillock which was high enough for me to see the exquisite panorama: line after line of snow peaks which the setting sun painted every warm shade from apricot to rose. My soup cooled as I watched, but this was a small price to pay for seeing those pulsating colours on the snowy mountains.

When Lakhpa, one of the porters, brought my washing water next morning he opened the tent door and there was the sun rising to tinge the distant mountains with pink and gold. I wrote home that night saying with truth, 'In the unlikely event of my achieving paradise it can't possibly be lovelier than this'.

We left camp very early and in the first bit of sunlit scrub found countless red-vented and white-cheeked bulbuls and a rusty-cheeked scimitar babbler. What splendid names these Asian birds have! A flock of little buntings, serpent eagles, the first Himalayan griffon vulture (a vast bird, big as a flying grand piano), crag martins and many, many others filled the morning and all the time those glittering peaks were piercing the gentian-blue sky.

The days were gradually acquiring rhythm: hot water at 6, tea at 6.15, porridge at 6.30, packing and departure by 7 at the latest, walk till 11.30, coffee, lunch, rest and, if unavoidable, another walk to the

selected camp site, or else a Base Camp training walk, tea, identification, if possible, of the day's birds, diary, supper, bed.

My bird list grew rapidly, as it always does in the first few days of a
trip, augmented, too, by rising higher, for different species of birds
live at different altitudes; add to this that I was walking at the time of
the migration and the tally further increased.

This day brought the first rhododendrons of the trip, all of them
scarlet. Some of the trees were untouched but others had been badly
hacked about for fuel.

The villages we passed through were picturesque, dirty and swarm-
ing with new life for this was the season of birth. Puppies were
everywhere, all the goats had kids which were skipping around with
enchanting *joie de vivre,* cows had calves and hens had chickens. And
women had babies, and babies, and babies.

We reached the top of our 8,000 feet pass, dropped down immediately and camped just over the brow of the hill on a roughish hillside.
To the right lay a tall and untouched rhododendron forest, blazing
with fiery blossoms. On our left was another, shorter forest, glowing
more fiercely in the setting sun. I lay surrounded by these floral
flames and over the brilliant backcloth floated a pearly grey hen
harrier with black-tipped wings.

A young Belgian trekker came by, almost overcome by the beauty
of it all, and I invited him to take a cup of coffee while we talked. This
is one of the best things about travelling solo with your own supplies:
you can and do talk to many other trekkers on the trail and if it is the
time of day when you have a fire you can dispense hospitality in the
form of coffee. I took a vast tin of Nescafé weighing nearly two
pounds and it was the best thing I did.

At Bursa, which had a fine new bridge over the wide, fast-flowing
river, it was so very hot that I wondered if I could paddle. On the
bank I met three young Americans, a girl and two charming young
men of twenty-two. All three were carrying enormous packs and they
decided that while I paddled they would swim. They took off everything and plunged into what they admitted was a quite icy river. We
exchanged details of our professions and the two men turned out to
be navigators of rubber boats that shoot the rapids of the Colorado
River, carrying eight passengers at a time. They gave me a pressing
invitation to do it with them and said that if there were no boat going
at the time they would set up a special trip just for the three of us. I felt
that not many young men of twenty-two would offer to take a
grandma (not literally but in point of age) on a trip through a
whitewater river and I was both grateful and flattered. They were all
greatly impressed by my energy in undertaking a trip to the Base
Camp and the girl said she would like to shake the hand of someone

so remarkable! I was far more impressed by them for, despite their vast packs, they were going extremely fast and I fully expected to meet them on the way down before I had even reached the top. Sadly enough I never saw them again.

Lobsang and the porters were now beginning to think that perhaps there was a sporting chance of my reaching Base Camp. I therefore introduced them to the delights of a sweepstake. There were seven of them so I wrote Base Camp and the names of the last six stops on seven pieces of paper and they drew lots. Each one paid 50 paisa, about 2½p in English money, and the holder of the the the paper bearing the name of the highest place I reached would have the lot.

When we reached the lovely forest where I had seen the laughing thrushes with Pasang, I found that it had been sadly thinned, though it was only three years later; men were even hacking down a rhododendron in full flower. Volatile red-headed tits were bouncing about in some of the lower trees and on a remaining tall stump sat a chestnut-bellied rock thrush singing his free and fluting song.

We went on to the open hilltop where we saw a flock of Hodgson's mountain finches. We couldn't get very close to them, seemingly inevitable with these nervous little birds. Lobsang, who had a predilection from airy camp sites, thought we could stay here but memsahib, thank goodness, had the say-so in matters of this kind and said firmly, 'Not really *right* on top of the hill, Lobsang, please; down below, in that fold of the landscape'.

And there we stayed, in a snug little basin beneath the crest, ringed by a mixture of conifers and rhododendrons, with birds all round and everything one could possibly want. Anywhere that had rhododendrons was all right by me.

When I went to my tent after lunch, it was to find that Lakhpa, bless his heart, had decorated the front opening, the central pole and some of the guy ropes with clusters of rhododendrons as he knew how much I liked them. Lakhpa really was a darling, only eighteen, ignorant of most things but immensely willing, good-natured, good-tempered and permanently hungry. If ever I had too much on my plate I called for Lakhpa and he would finish what was left almost before I handed it to him.

After lunch I tried to see the Hodgson's mountain finches more closely but failed signally for they are excessively neurotic. They flew fast and close as dunlin and panicked as terns do and I had to leave them unseen. They live at high altitude from anywhere above 9,000 feet and are locally common if you can find them. Next day, we came on another flock. I stalked them from behind the shelter of a stone wall and was then able to note the diagnostic points of this rather drab and not too lovely species. Sálim Ali's *The Birds of Sikkim* says that at even higher altitudes they have a relative, Blandford's mountain finch, which has a rosy tinge, as I had too by then, so perhaps I might be lucky if I reached the Base Camp.

At the Sikri Khola we again camped in mid stream and after I had done my training walk with Lobsang and Sanila, another porter to whom I became deeply attached for his many qualities and sweetness of character, I was sitting washing my feet in the gathering dusk when there was a great cry of 'Memsahib, MEMSAHIB! The bird!'

I saw nothing but a couple of plumbeous redstarts until Lobsang pointed at a huge buzzard which had flown past earlier in the day when I had been unable to identify it. But now a man had been walking along the path by the river, carrying one of the scrawny chickens that abound in Nepal, when the buzzard had swooped down and caught the chicken in its talons. The owner had held tight to the shocked and punctured bird, which lived to tell the tale, but only just. The buzzard, foiled, had flown off to a nearby rock where it was now sitting, supperless and furious for, as it was nearly dark, it would be unable to hunt for anything else.

I told Lobsang to buy the poor chicken for our supper but he pinched its bleeding breast and said it was too thin for the price asked, and refused to pay. The owner walked away, clutching the ailing bird.

I could not decide which buzzard it was for it had dark carpal patches, a white head and body and a dark tail with white shafts to the feathers. It may have been some variant of the long-tailed buzzard and I longed for some explanatory book to consult or, better still, for one of the Flemings to be with me to sort it out. The buzzard was full of temerity to go so near a human being, but the result was a minus for both it and the chicken, which I felt sure would not survive the night with a gaping hole in its breast and a system which must have been in deep shock.

It was a glorious spring morning when we left the Sikri Khola for Those and walked through forests thick with rhododrendrons, great pillars and umbrellas of solid scarlet. There was bulu too, a lovely plant related to the rhododendron, with sprays of little white bells that were oddly reminiscent of lilies of the valley surrounded by dark green, patent-leather leaves.

One of the great glories of Nepal is its plant life, the viburnums, the St. John's wort, the countless flowering trees and bushes, the plants that grow beneath them and the orchids that hang down from above. I felt anew, as I had on my previous treks, an enormous sense of privilege at being there. It is so breathtakingly lovely that I felt it should be reserved for an élite, not the élite of breeding or money but those who deserve a superb reward for some tremendous achievement.

When we came next day to the terrifying bridge near Those, dear, noble little Lakhpa stepped on to this fearful, flimsy horror, turned round, grasped my hand firmly and walked carefully backwards all the way, leading me slowly to safety with Lobsang hovering equally solicitously in the rear. I was so relieved when we were over that I would have kissed both of them on the spot had I not been sure that it would have embarrassed them profoundly.

Those has quite a lot of shops and several of the porters stayed behind to spend some of their wages. Lakhpa, a typical teenager, had a sartorial blowout and invested in a pair of crutch length striped cotton shorts of deplorable quality, a donkey-brown pullover brushed inside, thin, navy knee length socks with fancy clocks and a pair of brown plimsolls, the lot bought for 36 rupees, which was then about £1.50. Two other porters, Sandra Bahadur and Sukrabir, bought scarlet and royal-blue pullovers respectively and all three came roaring back to camp arrayed in the new finery. When I had first met them I found it hard to tell them apart and distinguished them only by what they were wearing. Now, just as I had got them straight, here they were with totally new outfits.

We camped again on the island but this time there was no full moon. There was, however, an old man clad in garments containing more holes that cloth, who had been catching fish all day and brought twenty to sell us for our supper. After half an hour's protracted bargaining Lobsang settled for them at 13 rupees and we had a lovely fishy fry-up, although the fish were very small and twenty did not go far among seven of us.

Next day we left at seven. It was very cold indeed and Lobsang resolutely refused to let me wade through the river to the path as the water was much colder in the early morning. Memsahib must be carried. To my great surprise every porter at once volunteered for the dubious honour.

I am almost five feet six tall and all my porters were considerably shorter and also much slighter than I. I knew that they were strong, wiry and accustomed to carrying a daily weight of sixty to seventy pounds but I was nine stone undressed and considerably more when clothed. Still, Pen Uri had done it easily in 1971 so I agreed although this was a much wider river. Lobsang permitted no argument and Sanila was finally selected to bear the burden.

I divested myself of my camera, binoculars and spectacles and gave them to Lobsang and, full of trepidation, climbed on to Sanila's back. Soon we were off with everyone shouting instructions to me to hold my feet up so that they did not trail in the almost freezing water. Sanila struggled on bravely and in the deepest part, with water well above his knees, gave a fearful lurch. I expected that at any moment I would be immersed in this petrifyingly cold stream minus my spectacles so that I would not be able to see which way to get out. All was well, Sanila recovered his balance and ploughed on with great determination to deposit his human load safely on the other side. I was deeply grateful and humbled by such devotion to duty.

The Bhandar pass was this time full of rhododendrons and other flowering trees and I took a great many photographs. And then the worst happened. I dropped my light meter on the stony ground and it broke. I am not a skilful photographer and without a light meter I could only guess at the correct exposure. After long discussion with Lobsang we decided that next morning, very, very early, one of the porters would go back to Kathmandu to see if Mr. Cheney could lend or borrow a light meter, as it would be truly terrible if I reached the Base Camp and was unable to take photographs to prove it.

The choice again fell on Sanila who set off for Kathmandu at 6 o'clock, bearing the damaged meter, a note for Mr. Cheney, food for the journey and money for the bus to and from Lamosangu and accommodation on the way. He came to see me before he left and promised to be as quick as he possibly could because he realised how many good pictures I was missing.

In Bhandar we recruited a temporary porter to accompany us in Sanila's absence. He was an old man, said Lobsang, about forty, but he would manage somehow. Padum Bahadur was a very nice 'old man' who had been in the army and wore a British battle-dress jacket which gave me a homely feeling.

As we dropped down through the forest to the Likhu Khola I heard a terrible commotion and spotted red-vented, white-cheeked and black bulbuls scolding hard and many other birds flying about in an agitated manner. I thought that there must be a great owl somewhere to cause so much agitation but after much searching through this avian bank holiday crowd I spied the cause of it all, a tiny Himalayan barred owlet not much bigger than the bulbuls. It moved when I called to Lobsang but obviously didn't go far, as the noise did not subside. Among all the excited small birds I found a tiny barred woodpecker with a yellow cap, and a white-browed blue flycatcher, a navy blue morsel with a white eyebrow and breast and two navy-blue lapels. Try as I would, I could not get near enough for a picture even with a telephoto lens for the volatile little minature was off and away before I could focus.

I did not see the owl go but calm gradually returned and we continued our several thousand feet of steep stumble; by the time I reached the end my knees were definitely disinclined for further exertion. Despite this I was not prepared to stop at something called THE FIRST SHERPA HOTEL EVERYTHING CHEEP and continued to a flat piece of ground at the river's edge where we camped.

The locals at the 'cheep' hotel told Lobsang that 'cheepest' of all were the fish to be found in the river, so many that you merely had to dip a hand in to pull one out. Encouraged by this, Lobsang and the porters spent a blissful afternoon damming the stream with boulders and herbage. They didn't even see a fish of any kind but they had a lovely time.

When we came next day to the dreadful bridge I sat down to rest and recuperate on the other side and, as I watched other people inching over, I asked Lobsang if Nepalese bridges ever broke and people fell in?

'Oh yes', he said, with a peal of merry laughter. 'Last year there were fourteen people in the water!'

I was horrified and asked if any were drowned.

'Oh no', said Lobsang. 'But very funny, very wet! *Fourteen* people in the water!'

And he laughed again at the joyous memory.

We went on, after this, to Khasindu at the foot of the Lamjura pass where a market was in progress. The place was choked with Sherpas and not a tourist to be seen. Judging from the interest I aroused, they did not appear to have seen many of them before. Maybe it was because I was looking so repulsive in my makeshift skirt tied on with string, and on my head a too-small Indian cricket cap of white cotton. It was the biggest headgear I could buy in Calcutta, where it would appear that all the inhabitants have pin heads. Unless, of course, mine is unnaturally large.

The people in Khasindu were very different from those we had seen so far: with their high cheekbones and deep set eyes they were obviously of Mongolian origin. The women all wore necklaces, some of them elaborate confections of turquoise and coral, and many having charm boxes set with turquoise. I bought glass bangles again and this time was given a lesson in how to push them over thumb and knuckles without too much pain.

We left Khasindu at noon after an early lunch and began the climb to Sete, a penitentially steep and long ascent which should be made early in the morning when it is cool. That day it was extremely hot and I plodded on and on for several hours, sweating profusely, until about fifteen minutes before the village I collapsed on the path. Lobsang, improvising at his best, found a site close at hand, discovered a water supply far down the hill, necessitating more work for the porters, and there we stayed.

I enjoyed two nights at Sete, a pleasing little settlement backed by a large forest, now sadly thinned. There was a beautiful view down towards the valley and, nestling in a hollow just off the path and surrounded by a few sheltering trees, lay a tiny monastery. When I recovered we went to see it and met the one lama, a small man with a single tooth, a straggly beard, two vociferous dogs and a rather peevish grey cat. I am a pushover for all cats of whatever size and this one looked as though a little loving would not come amiss. I was mistaken. Pussy was exceedingly sour and would have none of me. Her querulous mews were becoming increasingly penetrating so the lama made preparations for her supper. He took two tablespoons of *tsampa,* which is roasted barley flour, from a jar, moistened it with Tibetan tea and formed it into a kind of damp cake which he presented to his hungry cat. She ate it as she was obviously ravenous, but with no appearance of relish and she mewed protestingly from time to time. What she had for liquid I did not discover. I thought rather guiltily of my cat's diet of fish, rabbit, brown bread and whatever green vegetable was going, washed down with fresh milk. I could well imagine his cold, disbelieving stare if presented with this austere menu.

The lama showed us all round his little monastery with great courtesy and then Lobsang and Lakhpa, who accompanied me, went to the outsize prayer wheel, painted with every kind of Buddhist symbol and *Om Mani Padme Hum,* and pulled it round energetically by its thick leather straps. A bell clanged as each revolution was completed. We then thanked the lama, gave a donation and left.

Next morning we climbed to the pass and spent the night there. It was greyish but not misty and I was able to watch red-headed bullfinches at tolerably close range, white-collared blackbirds, woodpeckers, ocellated laughing thrushes, swarms of different, high-altitude tits, almost everything I could desire. I was glad to find that on Lamjura, as before, altitude had no effect on me, in fact, when acclimatised, 12,000 to 13,000 feet seems to be my best height.

Before starting on this 1973 trek I had been given a leaflet telling me what to do in the case of altitude sickness, the first symptoms being sickness, reduction in the output of urine, headache and loss of appetite. The output of urine, it said, was especially important and this should be measured daily. I wondered by what means this could be done in trek conditions and was thankful that my outflow was unimpeded so that I need not worry.

When we set off next morning the sun shone brilliantly on numerous starry yellow flowers of unknown species, purple primulas such as I had first seem at Melemchigaon and plenty of sweet-smelling daphne. White-browed rosefinches perched on the bushes, steppe eagles were migrating in good numbers and the sky was full of alpine choughs.

We lunched on the very top, with Nepal spread before us, a superb site where a wren was singing vigorously as he ferretted in and out among the stones. Here we met a German writer, Heinz, his American wife Betty, and her niece. The niece was a tall girl whose shoes did not fit her rather large feet. She was walking alternately in gym shoes with the toes cut out, or barefoot, a course of action which seemed crazy to me but which she found less agonising than walking in shoes that produced blisters. I could not really understand why she hadn't kitted herself out with ample supplies of comfortable footwear before starting. They were a delightful trio and they had coffee with us and then went on, going faster than I did despite the shoe trouble but they did not stop to look at birds which took up so much of my time.

We went down the steep road towards Junbesi and when we had gone half way I thought it would be a good idea to stop. Lobsang found a camp site and we settled in, a small fire was lit and I went to look for birds before tea. When I came back the camp had gone but Lobsang was lurking nearby, ready to guide me to our new home.

'Why did you move?' I asked.

Lobsang gave a broad grin. 'Too much cows' bathroom!' he said.

Looking for birds with Lobsang was not what it had been with Pasang. This was not Lobsang's fault but the result of cutting down forest, both for fuel and to make room for growing more food. There were birds, of course, but far fewer than there had been for forest birds cannot live on grain terraces or in potato fields.

As we left next morning, sharp-eyed Lakhpa noticed a large bird fly through the trees and from this lead we tracked a woodcock. We then went down to Junbesi, the fields around it looking exquisite, covered with a miraculous natural embroidery of *Primula denticulata* in all shades of mauve from palest lilac to magenta, with touches of white and deep pink. The flowers ranged in size from bullseyes to golf balls.

We camped on a tiny bluff above the stream at the lower end of the village with bulu and pink rhododendrons of many shades all round us and a field of *Primula denticulata* at the back. Who should appear by the stream in the afternoon, having a good wash of both feet and 'smalls' but Betty and her niece. They were waiting in Junbesi while Heinz, the German writer, went down the valley to Sulu to buy another pair of shoes for the niece who could no longer manage with what she had. As her feet were size seven Heinz was not too hopeful of success but nevertheless went to see what he could find.

Suddenly I had an impulse. I would give a dinner party that night and ask the three of them to join me. Betty and her niece accepted eagerly and said they knew that Heinz would, too, and they left to take their washing home while I planned the evening's menu from our scanty provisions.

They arrived at six, Heinz carrying a beautiful bunch of rhododendrons and *Primula denticulata* and niece wearing the new shoes which he had tramped so far to get. He had found that the shop contained only one pair of plimsolls but, to his surprise and joy, they were size seven. He bore them home triumphantly, sure of a great welcome; it lost some of its fervour when the niece discovered that the shoes were both for the left foot. However, with pieces snipped out here and there she was able to go on.

As it was almost dark Lobsang made us a big fire and we sat on a groundsheet on the cliff above the river. When dinner was served, each porter brought something so that all could share in the great occasion.

We began with a whole packet of asparagus soup — no hateful chicken noodle on this trip — following it with dehydrated curry and rice, a little dehydrated stewed apple and a few of my remaining biscuits, finishing with large mugs of Nescafé. We had two candles on the ground to add to the festivity, although we didn't really need them as the moon was full in the velvet sky.

My guests pronounced this simple meal a banquet as they had been living for the past eight days on *tsampa,* potatoes and rice, a diet of what I term 'no taste tastes' that must have palled very quickly.

It was one of the nicest and most romantic dinner parties ever. We parted with every expression of regret hoping that we might meet again, possibly when they were on their way down from the Base Camp and I was still struggling upwards.

We left next morning in good weather, passing over whole hillsides misted with the Parma violet of the primulas. We made camp at Sallung, a Sherpa village from which you could see Everest if you got up very early. Our camp was on a primula-strewn hillside and I was lying there sipping my after-lunch coffee when I heard a cry of 'Sanila! Sanila!' from the porters sitting far above me.

There, sure enough, bounding up the hillside towards us was Sanila, wearing a new hat and a new sweater and looking as fresh as an early spring morning. He had left Bhandar at 6 a.m. on Thursday morning and had reached Mr. Cheney's office on Saturday night. Mr. Cheney had *very* kindly sent his own old light meter, and Sanila had gone into the town and done his chores, bought his new clothes and set off back, arriving at our village, between Junbesi and Ringmo, by 2 o'clock on this following Tuesday. I have seldom been so pleased to see anybody and with an effort restrained myself from hugging him, giving him a well-deserved tip instead. Dear Sanila, he was the perfect porter.

Our next stage was to the Takhsindu pass and monastery and on the way we stopped at the Ringmo tea-house where the porters happily drank black tea laced with salt. I tasted it and recoiled in horror, preferring to go without. There was a strong wind blowing and the tea-house area was both dusty and smoky so the woman in charge brought out a straw mat and carried it up the hillside to a place where I could sit above the smoke. She then settled down for a chat which had to be in dumb show as neither of us possessed a word of the other's language. She particularly wanted to know if my teeth were false, as hers were her own, and she champed loudly on nothing to show me how good their condition was. How many English café proprietors would bother to treat a passer-by in this chummy fashion?

Refreshed by their noxious brew the porters shouldered their loads and we went on to Takhsindu. The weather was hotter and finer than on my winter trip. When we reached the pass it was clear on our side but a swirl of mist enveloped the monastery and the memorable view was completely obscured. Memsahib therefore opted for camp on the top of the ridge with a fine view to the rear, a wealth of rhododendrons and other flowers and a fair number of birds.

After tea we went for a training walk along the ridge and then both Lobsang and Lakhpa disappeared. Just as dusk was falling the two of them materialised, bearing the most magnificent garland composed of two huge clusters of rosy rhododrendrons, interspersed with single heads, bits of daphne and balls of *Primula denticulata,* a garland so large and beautiful that I almost cried with pleasure and gratitude. I put it in water for that night and wore it throughout the next two days until it was quite dead.

Next morning I went down to the monastery which now had a thriving shop to supply the many trekkers who came by. We saw the two holy rooms with seven little bowls of water that were changed daily, countless paintings of the Buddha, ghosts, demons and dragons, the holy books, each in its separate box, the drums for beating at religious ceremonies and many of the lamas' enormous traditional hats. The steep stairs we had to climb were each at least fifteen inches high and very difficult to surmount.

We saw all that we were allowed to see, deposited money in the offertory box and with a last look at the monastery in its memorable setting plunged into the rhododendron forest down towards Manidigma. The forest was in full bloom, frothing pink and white for as far as we could see. There were no scarlet trees here, but there were many magnolias, their thicker petals creamily opaque among the translucent rhododendrons. It was a heady mixture and I walked downwards in a blissful trance, keeping a wary eye open for birds. There were cuckoos, both the 'ordinary' cuckoo that we have in Europe and the Indian cuckoo with its different call, many strange woodpeckers, robins, laughing thrushes and numerous different flycatchers.

This time there were no monkeys at the Dudh Kosi Bridge and we camped just above it. I washed my hair in the glacier water, which was unspeakably cold, a serpent eagle sitting all the time in a tree nearby quite unmoved by my antics.

We ploughed on and up towards Kharikhola where I met a clergyman/schoolmaster who had just taken a party of schoolboys all the way from Darjeeling to Gorakshep, the last stop before the Base Camp at about 17,300 feet. He told me that where the Italians were busily preparing for their attempt on Everest helicopters were buzzing up and down the valley several times a day, saving the cost of porterage but making a hellish noise. He said that the Base Camp itself, which he hadn't visited, was so modern that it had coffee vending machines and porters polishing glasses. This sounded a bit much to me but I decided to form my own opinion when I got there, *if* I did.

We camped just below Kharte, very near to where I had spent that first snowy night in 1970. The sky looked rather grey and murky and I wondered if we were in for a repeat performance. While Lobsang and the porters were making camp, we were visited by a rowdy party of a few men, four or five women and a collection of children, all bearing empty baskets on their backs and shouting and screaming at the tops of their very loud voices. They crowded round me, although Lobsang did his best to restrain them, and finally roared off, their upward progress marked by diminishing screams.

Just before settling down to supper I made a little sanitary sortie thinking that if the now purplish sky foretold rain I had better venture out while I could see where I was going. I found what I thought was a secluded spot and was busily engaged when there was a burst of noise that seemed all too familiar. The vocal thunder rolled rapidly nearer as the boisterous party of the afternoon ran down the hill, spied me engaged in an irreversible process and lined up on the terrace immediately above me, pointing, giggling, shouting and generally behaving in a manner calculated to madden one. I was furious but unable to take steps of any kind to resolve the situation.

This time Puiyan was easily reached and I couldn't recognise the almost snowbound guest house were we had stayed previously. The pass was very lovely, almost entirely pink with rhododendrons, and had extensive views that I had never suspected before. Rain began at lunchtime so we went upstairs to the fire, which, as usual, smoked abominably. As we crowded round it, I heard an unexplained growling and asked what it was. Someone pointed to the ashes, wherein lay a small, smoked dog, its coat matted and its general attitude apprehensive. A dog's life in Nepal can't be much fun.

Between Puiyan and Namche we met a lot of people of many nationalities and I was always glad to stop and chat if they spoke English, for Lobsang's command of my language was not as good as Pasang's and conversation was pretty well restricted to food and weather.

I met three English people who had just been right up to the Base Camp. One of them was a doctor who said *of course* I'd get there, 'but *only* if you go slowly'.

They had heard all about the old lady, who spent so much time watching birds, from a Swede to whom I had talked earlier on. They had also met an American in Kathmandu who told them to look out for me as I was very interesting. I was unaccustomed to such fame and all because I was old and stopped to watch birds, while nearly every other trekker was young and did not.

When we got to Serte I was tired and decided to have a rest day well away from the main path as this was Thursday and all the Nepalese from a vast radius were on the track, carrying goods to Khumbu for the Namche market on Saturday. The path was almost solid with them and a strong smell of humanity filled the air. There were no available camp sites near the bridge and we found a place on a little island with various small streams running by, convenient both for washing and the kitchen.

During the night the river rose slightly and the porters' tent was flooded, though not badly. Happily they thought this was very funny and everything soon dried out in the strong sun. At nine o'clock one of our porters disappeared and after lunch Sanila went down to the village to look for him and found him dead drunk in the tea-house. Lobsang decided that Memsahib should speak severely when he came back but this was not until five the next morning. In the meantime I stretched my foot outside my sleeping bag during the night and found that this time the river had chosen to enter my tent, so giving equal treatment to all. This little contretemps surmounted, I tackled the unpleasant task of dismissing the erring man, who had been absent on a drinking spree on three previous occasions.

When we reached Namche I was in a state of high excitement for the weather was really beautiful, I was going well, the high peaks were getting nearer every hour and I thought I should make it. Lobsang thought so too, by now, and the others were becoming surer.

But there was one big snag. The three Tamang porters, Sukrabir, Sandra Bahadur and Sanila, announced their intention of going back to Kathmandu. It was the same old story. It was too cold and they had no thick clothes for the heights. This meant that we were now reduced to Lakhpa as porter with Lobsang as sirdar.

Sanila was in a quandary. He longed to come with us as he liked me very much and wanted to see me achieve my ambition and he got on very well indeed with both Lobsang and Lakhpa. I could not bear the thought of losing him and suddenly had an idea. I had brought two pairs of long johns with me and one was a man's pair, the only thing available in our local shops when I left. I thought it would be better for me to manage with the woman's pair for three weeks and to hell with being dirty and to give the man's pair to Sanila if this would induce him to stay. I threw in a pair of fur-lined gloves bought in Kathmandu market and felt that I could make do with the two woollen pairs I had. Lobsang also offered the loan of a thick sweater. Sanila wavered and then accepted, wrapping the thick long johns round him beneath his voluminous cotton trousers and pronouncing them to be quite marvellous, for as he was very short he could turn down the tops to make a double thickness round the waist so that he was really cosy. This was excellent news, for now we had to get fewer replacement porters to fill the gaps.

Lobsang was in his element in Namche with plenty of friends to talk to. He had more friends than any Sherpa or Nepali I had ever met. All were greeted with rapturous gaiety, broad smiles and explanatory cries of 'Memsahib, he is My Friend!'

We went into the main shop, whose proprietor was, of course, Lobsang's Friend, to see if we could find a pair of Sherpa boots for me. Sherpa boots, rather like Wellingtons in shape, are made of heavy black felt with thick yakskin soles that are curved up slightly with the felt sewn inside. They are decorated with embroidery and red, blue and green braid and are kept up by patterned braid ties wound tightly round the top of the calves. Alas, there were none that fitted me.

This wonderful shop sold almost everything you could think of but at astronomical prices. The proprietor's wife insisted on giving us both large tumblers of Tibetan tea which we downed politely before going to see *my* Friend, Pasang's wife, Namdo.

She was still living in the same house and Pasang's mother was there too. Pasang was away on trek but Namdo said that he was well and happy. The new baby that had been expected soon after I left had arrived safely and had been recently joined by yet another, so that Pasang and Namdo were now the parents of five healthy daughters. Namdo, beautiful and excessively busy, just as before, said that she had noticed me earlier going into the trekking permit office and had recognised me at once, one of the advantages of keeping the same down jacket from year to year. She gave me a warm welcome, and so did Pasang's mother and the sweeties I brought for the children were very welcome too.

We asked about porters and Namdo said this would be easy. One could be Mingma, whom I remembered with affection from the 1970 trek, there would be one more and finally Pasang Doma, also from 1970. Pasang Doma was at the moment out on a short trek but we ought to find her at Thyang Boche and we could then give our temporary porter to the woman who had Pasang Doma and Pasang Doma could come on with us.

While Namdo was explaining all this to Lobsang she was making English tea which she presented to us in two large tumblers and as soon as we had dispatched this she gave us two cups each of Tibetan tea. Our stomachs were awash but it was lovely to be back again in a Sherpa house sitting on the floor with tea.

Namche had altered considerably since my last visit, the wooded hillsides were now almost bare and the place filthy but it was enormously vital and exciting, the gateway to the heights. My sense of delighted anticipation grew and I was itching to be off and away.

In the morning we swung along towards Everest in perfect weather, all the peaks showing magnificently and at the side of the path were dwarf irises of lilac and dark purple, spotted and striped and surrounded by tiny spear-like leaves.

When we came to the corner viewpoint there were the three giants, Everest, Lhotse and Nuptse, clear as spring water and glittering as though a thousand polishers had been working on them throughout the night. Ama Dablam, Taweche and Tamserku lay on our right as we walked rapidly towards the Dudh Kosi. In a daze of happiness we reached the river and the water-activated prayer wheels, lunched and sped on, propelled by spiritual uplift as much as by strong leg power.

We reached Thyang Boche in the afternoon. It was even lovelier than before in its setting of mountains and glaciers, but large numbers of Western tourists had done their best to wreck its quiet, isolated beauty. All the bushes around had tins, plastic bags and sachets strewn thickly beneath them and every really steep slope had become a rubbish chute. I felt a deep shame on behalf of all the fellow tourists who had done these things for Thyang Boche is not only a beautiful place, it is also a holy place to the Nepalese and for foreign visitors to leave such repulsive tokens of their passing is inexcusable.

We settled on a camp site, arranged a second courtesy call on the Head Lama, and Lobsang found My Friends in quantity, as usual. He also found Heinz, Betty and niece, and Pasang Doma.

Heinz and his family were staying in a small house in the monastery grounds and I was distressed to hear that he was in bed, suffering from a severe attack of snow blindness. Lobsang arranged for me to visit them, which I did after supper and found Heinz in a bad way. Niece's manifold blisters having healed, the three of them had easily reached the Base Camp, leaving their belongings behind at Gorak-shep as they intended to go up and back in one day. However, a heavy blizzard made it impossible for them to return to Gorakshep. They were made very welcome by the members of the Italian expedition who treated them with the utmost cordiality and put them up for the night. The blizzard was over in the morning but thick snow was everywhere. They had left their sun glasses in Gorsakshep and this proved to be an expensive oversight for trekking down for some hours in bright sunlight had resulted in Heinz becoming totally and painfully snowblind for several days. I resolved never to leave my glasses behind from then on.

Having heard this sorry tale the two mobile members of the family, their host lama and I sat cross-legged in front of the fire, where the whole hearth was filled with small, boiled potatoes. We peeled the potatoes with our finger nails, dipped them in chili powder and threw the skins in the fire. I wouldn't have believed that I could have eaten so many potatoes but the cold, the altitude and their excellent flavour provided ample excuse.

Stuffed to repletion I at last went out into the dark night with my torch, found my tent and slipped into my two down sleeping bags. Hugging my hot-water bottle, keeping on all my underwear and with both bags drawn closely round my face so that only a bit of my nose stuck out I was as warm and snug as ever I was in Norfolk.

The ground was thick with frost when I woke but it melted even as I ate my porridge near the fire. I went to see Heinz before I left and found him much better and able to see a tiny bit. We parted regret-fully and I arranged to dine with them when I got back to Kathmandu.

Before moving off I fell into conversation with two exceptionally hairy young men, one so fully furred that his features were almost invisible. He told me that the monastery's huge Tibetan mastiff had by some mischance broken loose and the enormous, furious creature had bitten him, probably finding him indistinguishable from any other intruding animal. I proffered antiseptic cream but he seemed to think it better to sit patiently awaiting the course of events, mean-while taking extremely potent antibiotics. I advised him to set off as quickly as possible to the hospital at Kunde, which was not very far away, for expert treatment but I don't think my advice stood any chance of being followed.

I met a lot of oddities on this trek, far more than previously. The majority turned out to be really nice young things when I got to know them. Many were keen conservationists, disturbed about the state of the modern world and all of them, without exception, deeply moved by the beauty and unique quality of Nepal. Quite a number stayed for a cup of tea or coffee if I happened to be sitting or lying outside my tent and many were the instructive and illuminating conversations that ensued.

We made good time along the path I had walked with Pasang, this time free from snow, and after lunch were going well towards Pheriche when a thick mist came down suddenly. It was so thick that Lobsang decided to camp. We heard the monal, Nepal's national bird, calling all around us and one or two males, a glistening, greenish-turquoise with purple sheen, even appeared on top of a nearby stone wall. Unfortunately it was far too dark to take pictures.

The mist vanished during the night and we trotted on to Pheriche. Pheriche was new ground to me, an open valley flanked on either side by huge mountains. It lies more than 14,000 feet up and is a famous yak pasture although this was so soon after the snow had melted that to my uninformed eye it appeared to be a brown, unappetising expanse. The yaks did not appear to think so and were grazing placidly on all kinds of unpalatable-looking herbage with their backs to the prevailing wind. I took a fine picture of one in this position, the wind blowing so fiercely that the beast's tail concealed its back. The animal looked like a huge, hairy rosette with four legs beneath.

I had no idea that yaks were abundantly endowed with hair so thick and long that it sometimes stuck out like a ballerina's tutu, although they had not the grace of Fonteyn. I had also expected yaks to be black, with perhaps a touch of white but here they were, if not all colours of the rainbow, at least black, white, grey and a rich brown that was termed red. Their inner form is, I assume, rather like that of a short-legged cow but their coat is so thick that their real outline is obscured and they look rather like mobile sofas. The females, called naks, are somewhat smaller and more lightly built than the males, which really are yaks.

Yaks are widely used as beasts of burden, loaded with big sacks of very thick, striped material woven from their own hair, sacks that do not seem to be at all tightly secured, so that they sway with the animals' motion. This does not seem to disconcert either yaks or naks to any degree, for they are amazingly sure-footed and go without hesitation along paths and over narrow wobbly bridges. Nevertheless they are sometimes known to lose their balance and fall over precipices; then the good Buddhists of the region, forbidden to take life themselves, have to find someone whose religion allows them to dismember the carcase, which the good Buddhists happily eat.

Above Pheriche the altitude began to tell and I told Lobsang that I could not possibly make Lobuje which was well over 16,000 feet. We would camp where we were.

Lobsang pitched the tents and I climbed into my two sleeping bags at once for it was very cold. In the morning, when it was only just beginning to get light, there was a scrabbling at my tent door and Lakhpa and Sanila opened the zip and indicated that there were many birds outside. I was warm and cosy in my sleeping bags and much disinclined to leave them at 5.15 a.m. Lakhpa brought my tea and I was sipping it and had taken out my rollers, which I wore nightly in an attempt to preserve a slightly civilised appearance, when there was a loud whisper of 'Mem, **Mem, MEM!**' Lakhpa and Sanila appeared again at the door of the tent, saying that there were birds outside which I *must* see. I kept my underclothes on all night at that altitude and tried sleepily to struggle out of my sleeping bag. Lakhpa rushed in and unzipped it, Sanila followed and unzipped the second one, exposing my pink pyjama bottoms. I dragged my trousers away from their second function as a pillow, drew them on and Lakhpa zipped them up while Sanila shoved me into my down jacket and fastened it, picked up my binoculars, hung them round my neck and shooed me out to find several little rosefinches and high-altitude accentors right in front of the tent, pecking around in the frost and light powdering of snow that had fallen during the night. It was very cold and Lakhpa went back to the tent for my gloves. I held my glasses in my right hand while he put on my left glove and we repeated the manoeuvre with the other hand. With such superb service and loving care I could not possibly tell them that these were not new birds for me in Nepal. They were new for the trip and this greatly pleased those two angelic porters.

I was now fully rested after my day off which had been quite a social marathon, entertaining with tea and conversation, among others, a woman from Manchester University who had been to Kala Pattar, two delightful Americans and two disgruntled young Englishmen who had been to the Base Camp and complained of their treatment by the Italians. This seemed odd when Heinz had described the abundant and generous hospitality. I discovered that my two compatriots had arrived there in the evening, soaking wet and with no food or tent. It was too late to go down and they had thrown themselves on the mercy of the Italians who had, grudgingly so they said, provided a four-course dinner, accommodation in a heated tent, sleeping pills for high altitude and a large breakfast. I cannot imagine what more they could have been given and wondered if a British expedition would have been as hospitable if two feckless Italians had arrived at their camp without food or equipment. I felt ashamed.

Lobsang said that the only way to go to the Base Camp from Gorakshep was to start very early in the morning when the Khumbu glacier was frozen and could be walked on in safety. Later in the day much of the surface snow and ice melted and progress was difficult and dangerous. I resolved that when we went, *if* we went, we would set out at first light.

After the early birding the morning became brilliant and we started off up the narrowing, very rocky path which had little vegetation. We toiled up an extremely steep slope, which made me feel every year of my age, until we came to a saddle from which we had the first good view of Nuptse, its regularly humped ridge looking as mammary as some of the mosques in Istanbul.

On top of this saddle was a row of symmetrical cairns marking the graves of six Sherpas killed in a climbing accident and on another smaller ridge was a solitary cairn that marked the grave of dear Kyak Tsering. It was a cloud on an otherwise flawless day and I thought with distress of the many climbers and Sherpas who had lost their lives in the effort to conquer the peaks among which we were now trekking.

On the saddle we were joined by three young Frenchmen, teachers from a school at Pnom Penh in Cambodia. They had enough English to get by and insisted on taking my photograph as they thought it admirable that anyone *so* old should be slogging along at such a height. I wondered why more people didn't do it as I was feeling happier than I had ever been before, except, perhaps, on the Poon-hill, and not at all old. The Frenchmen were also bound for the Base Camp and said they had heard that everyone who reached there was given a glass of champagne by the Italians. The two disgruntled Englishmen had not received this benediction and I was not surprised.

The porters were well ahead of Lobsang and me when across a steeply angled slope ahead I saw Sanila coming back to us, bearing the stick I kept for emergencies for this was part of his load. He had returned because there was a very nasty portion of track in front where the path was sometimes buried under two feet of snow. At others it ran along the edge but the slope was rather perilous and it would be easy to miss one's footing. Sanila handed me my stick and backed slowly along before me while Lobsang came behind. I dared look nowhere but at my feet as we scuffled along this risky stretch for about twenty minutes.

In the middle of it I met a young American who said that he had heard of me from some friends on the way and wished he had known I was coming as he would have stayed for lunch. I invited him to come back and share mine and continued to plough along carefully. When at last I was over this treacherous snowy expanse we walked slowly to Lobuje above the edge of the Khumbu glacier. The ground was thickly laced with tiny streams, there were large and small stones everywhere and among them were lots of small bushes, probably azaleas which would be in blossom in a few weeks.

We reached Lobuje, a fairly flat area almost at the head of the valley with one or two Sherpa hotels on a ledge above. Lobsang pitched our tents well apart at remarkable speed and by 1 o'clock we were eating lunch. We should have been there much earlier but Lobuje lies at more than 16,000 feet, which was the highest I had ever been, and it 'took it out of me' as the saying is.

The young American, Willie, was very nice indeed, full of sensibility and deeply appreciative of his good fortune in being able to see the beauty that was all around us. Some of what was around us, alas, was not so good, for the Italians, and many others, too, had again left large quantities of litter which was blowing everywhere.

The glacier lay to our left as we looked down the valley to Ama Dablam, Taweche, Tamserku and many more. Willie and I talked and talked but long silences intervened in which we just gazed and marvelled as the sky grew deeper and deeper blue and the mountains shone more brilliantly white.

As soon as the sun sank behind the mountains it became desperately cold and I retired into my tent but ten minutes later I heard a strange bird call. I went to the door and there, running along the mountainside, were three snow partridges. This was all the day needed for perfection and I danced for joy and to help my circulation, returning to my tent to eat supper, a large pile of the beautiful Khumbu potatoes with their accompanying chili, plus a little of my carefully hoarded tinned butter.

Soon after this Willie came to the tent and said I *must* come out again. I pulled on my boots once more and emerged to see a full moon shining over the magnificent prospect that had entranced us all afternoon. It had been sublime in daylight but in the moonlight it had a gleaming, spectral beauty. The Himalayas possess a quality that transcends every other place that I have visited and they move me as nothing else does.

Next morning Willie, who was suffering slightly from the altitude, went down and I started off for Gorakshep, only some 600 feet above Lobuje but reached by a very up and down route. We had been going only half an hour when the altitude hit me too and I knew that it would be stupid to go on. There was nothing for it but to have yet another rest day, for it was almost unthinkable to consider the possibility of retreat less than 2,000 feet from my objective. What would the porters think if, having escorted their ageing memsahib so far, she turned back within sight of her goal? I was furious but up went the tent, down went the pad and the sleeping bags and Lobsang brewed elevenses even though it was only 8.30.

I recovered as the day wore on and held conversations with various other trekkers who were going up or down and by the end of the afternoon did a little training walk and began to think that perhaps I'd make these last 2,000 feet after all.

All seemed to be well next morning and we started for Gorakshep. I went very slowly for I was still feeling the effects of altitude but according to my leaflet this was not serious for I was still eating moderately well and the output of urine was strong and steady.

We had not gone far before we met a young German accompanied by an elderly female. I said politely how nice it was to meet a contemporary on the trek and she replied, equally politely, that she thought she was far older than I was. It turned out that we were both 64 but I was creeping along in the rear of our party, feeling 74, while she marched smartly up the track from Lobuje, reached Gorakshep, climbed Kala Pattar, which I had been warned was very steep indeed, and marched straight back to Lobuje.

With this inspiring example before me I was determined to make Gorakshep if it killed me. The path was flattish for the first two miles but then it became very much of a switchback over horribly stony and difficult ground.

While we were sitting down to rest at one point Lakhpa, whose eyes could see things invisible to me, noticed two big birds high on the hillside. Through my binoculars I could see that they were, without doubt, Tibetan snowcocks, large, rather dumpy, farmyard-hen-sized creatures with grey backs and black and white striped breasts.

My attention was diverted by another bird close at hand, a very big redstart. It flew off and I saw that it had a white head and a large white wing bar, making it, without doubt, Güldenstadt's redstart, the high altitude member of this beguiling family. The sight of two such rarities within a couple of minutes gave me a tremendous boost and I set off more strongly.

We struggled along over stones and rocks, some big as a television set, others small, sharp and square. At one point we crossed a semi-frozen river which we heard roaring down beneath the ice, but Pasang Doma, who had done this trip many, many times before, knew just where to go and we followed her closely. After what seemed an interminable trudge we came to the last ridge and there, far below us, lay Gorakshep, a sandy waste, pock-marked with large and small stones. It was odd to reflect that the Himalayas are one of the 'newest' mountain ranges that used to be beneath the sea and I remembered that Heinz had showed me a fossil shell bought from a Sherpa at Gorakshep who swore that he had found it there.

The sandy waste was filled in part by a frozen lake with damp edges. We sat down to look at this promised land and the superb mountains that surrounded it. I still felt rather poor and weak when Lakhpa, kind, sweet, considerate Lakhpa, belted back towards us from the camp site where Sanila and Pasang Doma had a fire going. He was carrying two mugs and a kettle containing a large quantity of heavily sugared tea. It was just what I needed and after imbibing it I almost trotted over the sand towards our camp.

The prospect before us was impressive beyond description. Pumori appeared to be the largest mountain in the vicinity but this was because it stood so close to us, a huge, white cone, the kind of mountain one drew as a child. Behind it was Lindgren, bearing on one face a snowy excrescence looking like a thickly maned lion and across the Khumbu glacier were Nuptse, Lhotse and many more. Everest itself was hidden.

The joy of being in this wonderful place was marred by the frequent passage of helicopters bearing supplies to the Italians at the Base Camp. This seemed to me to be a particularly unpleasant type of pollution. Pollution of a more familiar type was everywhere too, the majority being Italian, tins, boxes, plastic bags and all manner of waste, piled into a repulsive dump.

The weather was so good that I thought we should go for the Base Camp next day. The route was not merely upwards: I should have known that nothing is in Nepal. After going along the valley for a short while to a big stone, commemorating the members of international expeditions who had lost their lives on Everest, a sober introduction to the last lap of the trek, we had then to go right down on to the glacier and afterwards climb up to the Base Camp. It would be tough, I knew.

We rose very early next morning and all five of us, Lobsang, Kakhpa, Sanila, Pasang Doma and I started off, bearing tents, food and firewood so that we shouldn't need to trespass on Italian hospitality. It was a shiny, patent-leather morning with every peak sparkling and winking in the sunshine as we passed the memorial stone and began our descent to the glacier. The path was terrible, unmarked and hopelessly rough. We made fairly good time until we reached the glacier, still frozen but with dampish patches here and there, and slowly the pinnacles began to appear.

I had read many books about Everest, the glacier, the ice pinnacles and the icefall but none had sufficiently prepared me for the reality. Cliffs and pinnacles of ice were all around me, glittering in the sun and glittering still more as the surface began to melt slightly, pinnacles of every shade from cobalt to baby blue, and all the greens from deep jade to *eau-de-nil.* The colours altered as our angle of approach changed, providing a kaleidoscope of jewelled magnificence such as I could never have imagined.

We stopped from time to time and in the middle of the ascent met the French teachers from Pnom Penh, even more pleased than before to see me and full of the glory of the Base Camp. The Italians had been wonderful to them and they had stayed overnight at the camp and had actually been allowed to venture on to the first part of the icefall in borrowed crampons. It had been truly, truly *merveilleuse.*

They rushed down the glacier at a swift canter and I went laboriously upward, constantly urged by Lobsang to hurry up for the ice was melting and this was dangerous as we should be unable to cross the many tributaries that ran into the main stream. After about four hours, when we had surmounted the worst part, I collapsed on the stones. Lobsang and the porters had gone on ahead to make camp so there was no one about to see my ignominious plight. I knew that someone would find me sooner or later but it was considerably later when splendid, faithful Lakhpa appeared, again with a kettleful of strong and sugared tea and some biscuits. I ate and drank and then, considerably revived, followed him through a sea of stone to a spot where a little signpost bore both the Nepalese and Italian flags and soon after this I saw an assembly of orange tents of all sizes.

We were there! Lakhpa led me to where my tent was already pitched in the area where the high-altitude Sherpas were camped, all of them, of course, being Lobsang's Friends. Lobsang was having the time of his life and his many Friends were plying him with tea, coffee, biscuits, chocolate, sweets and apples for I heard later that the leader of the expedition owned many supermarkets in Italy so that catering was no problem.

Lobsang's friends were so generous that they even presented his aged employer with two welcome gifts: a thick bar of plain chocolate stuffed with nutty nougat and, even better, a large apple. I ate both at once, followed by a big cup of coffee. I felt fine by then and all debility had gone. *I was at the Base Camp* and this was a revivifying tonic better than Napoleon brandy.

I tidied myself and went to call on the leader of the expedition. I was told that he was busy so left a message presenting my compliments and saying that I thought he might like to see the oldest woman who had ever reached the Base Camp, so I thought.

This brought him out at once. He was a charming and most polite man who congratulated me on my achievement and asked if there were any way in which he could help me. I thanked him and said that we had everything we needed. In that case, he said, would I join them all for dinner at eight that night?

I accepted with pleasure and went back to my tent to rest and to glory in the fact that I had managed what in the last stages I had feared was impossible. The winner of the sweepstake was Sanila but

Lobsang hadn't really grasped the necessity of putting aside the 50 paisa subscribed by each participant and had no money at all for the prize.

I don't really know what I had expected the Base Camp to be like but certainly not a small city of orange tents, a few of them very big, a radio station, vast stocks of supplies, plenty of litter and what seemed like hundreds of people milling about in front of the leader's tent, before which was placed a very commodious reclining chair of black plastic leather which afforded a splendid view of the icefall. Whether he ever had time to sit in it to survey the scene I did not discover.

As night fell the sun turned the blue-white tops to a rich apricot, the moon, still almost full, shone down on us and I was reeling with happiness. Lobsang, not really much of a one for natural beauty, was also very happy but this was because his stomach was full of delicious food, his main interest in life.

Just before 8, a young lieutenant, the English-speaking member of the Italian expedition, came to escort me to the dining tent. I sat in state on the right of the leader, whose English was correct but rather sparse and on my right was the lieutenant who spoke it very well.

The evening was a tremendous treat for one who had been camping for six weeks. A tent with a floor, a dinner table laid with good cutlery and glass, and the meal served by waiters. We had soup, roast goat, pudding, cheese, biscuits and coffee and no dinner in the most expensive restaurant of my experience had ever seemed so luxurious as this one served at the Base Camp after forty nights en route. At the end of it champagne was brought in as it was the expedition doctor's birthday. He was toasted by the assembled company and my name was coupled with his 'in recognition of my achievement'. I dislike champagne and do not drink but I had to do so that night for decency's sake. It was a wonderful climax to my long, long trek.

At length the party was over and I was taken back to my tent by the young lieutenant who was due to start up the icefall early next morning and was to be one of the assault party for the summit if all went well. The leader insisted on sending back with me a large Aladdin stove to heat my tent. This was another unexpected treat which I could not refuse and the lieutenant lit it for me, kissed my hand most gallantly and departed. And there I was, sleeping in a heated tent at 18,000 feet. How good and kind the Italians had been.

We began to go down early next morning while the glacier was frozen. I thought it would not be nearly so bad as going up but, halfway down, I began to flag and realised that I should have taken a day's rest at the Base Camp. I sat down, struggled up, fell down again and at last, about two hours from camp, lay down to rest, feeling it unlikely that I would ever get up again. Lobsang went on to Gorakshep with the porters while I lay quietly on the path and waited for recovery to begin. This took a long, long time and at last, when I looked up, I saw two figures approaching. They were Lakhpa and Sanila and they were bringing a tray. It contained a kettle of sugared coffee, a plate of scrambled eggs and *chapattis,* and they had brought it a couple of miles, bless them. It was stone cold, of course, but I ate it, felt slightly better and then staggered back to camp with my kind and faithful couple, resolved not to move again that day.

It was extremely cold at Gorakshep before the sun came up, so cold that one's fingernails hurt. Washing was difficult for my sponge was a stone, my complexion milk was solid in the bottle and the outsize plastic container which Sanila filled with water from the lake was an almost immovable block. I did not realise how cold it was until Lobsang washed the lining of my sleeping bag. He climbed up on a high rock and stood holding up the bag which he thought would dry quickly in the strong wind. It froze into an immobile flag in a matter of minutes.

Personal washing was a problem too. One day, when my cardigan had become so disgusting that I could no longer tolerate it, I gave it to Lobsang to wash in *warm* and not hot water with careful instructions about squeezing and not wringing it. I passed the fire soon afterwards and there was my cardigan, boiling gaily in a saucepan. I rescued it, did my best to pat it into the right shape and a little later took it into the comparative warmth of my tent to dry off during the night. It froze completely.

As I lay outside my tent next day, recovering, two men came by. One was an English army captain and the other a professional photographer from Darjeeling. I offered tea and they sat down and chatted. Mohan Das, called Mo, a Nepali, told me that there was to be a big reunion in Darjeeling the following week to celebrate the first ascent of Everest twenty years before and he wanted a really good picture of the summit to sell there, the best photographic aspect being obtained from the lower slopes of Kala Pattar early in the morning.

I longed to go up Kala Pattar myself but did not push my luck as the Base Camp trip had almost knocked me out and I thought that another effort on the same scale would put paid to me for good. I resolved, however, to go a little way up to see if I could find the place that afforded a good view of Everest for it really seemed absurd to go so far and to have no picture of the world's highest mountain to prove it.

During this comparative rest day I tried to find out something about snowcocks, which were fairly numerous at Gorakshep, although I had seen them nowhere else, bar the one on the way. In the morning they would give odd cackling cries and then plane downhill

94

Opposite:

Bare footprints, Chinese shoes and climbing boots all going to and from Namche.

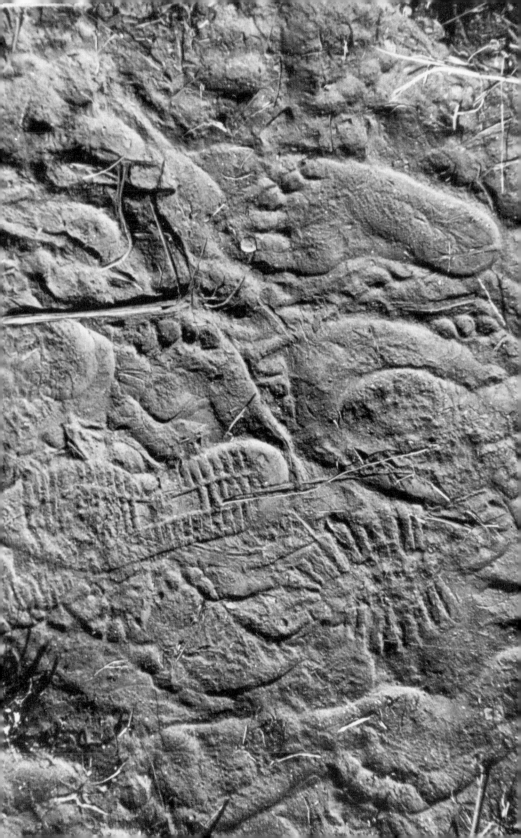

Top: *Pasang looking for birds.*

Bottom: *Chorten in Bhandar.*

Top: *Pasang and Mingma preparing 'Sir's' lunch.*

Bottom: *Inching across the Khumbu Khola.*

Top: *Ice melting on Gokyo lake at almost 17,000 ft.*

Bottom: *The Author on lower slope of Kala Pattar with Khumbu Glacier in the background*

Top: *Thyang Boche monastery.*

Bottom: *Sukrabir entertaining an admiring audience.*

Top: *Base Camp.*

Bottom: *Sanila, Lobsang, myself and Lagpa.*

Top: *Small helpers bringing in their baskets of leaves.*

Bottom: *Namche Bazar.*

Cool lunch site in a hot valley.

Porters really resting.

Peaks in the Gokyo valley.

to the frozen lake to take water from its melting edges. As they sped down they called remarkably like curlew, a call that I did not hear them make on any other occasion. The serious business of the day was feeding on roots and tubers. Their favourite food plant appeared to be something that looked rather like a very fine staghorn moss. Almost every snowcock in the area was to be seen, at one time or another, head down in a hole, digging for roots and displacing showers of dust with its large pinkish feet. When they emerged I could see that the birds were a beautiful French grey, perhaps a trifle browner, with rusty tails. Their heads had what I can only describe as buffish ear muffs and their breasts were gleaming white with thick black streaks. Their throats were marked by a grey circle with radiating spokes and they had pinkish beaks, legs and feet which had strong claws for their almost perpetual digging.

I spent a large part of the day stalking them with my telephoto lens at the ready as I believed they had not been photographed before. I sneaked quietly from stone to stone in order not to disturb them and found that in time they became almost oblivious of my presence. I was able to get about twenty pictures, many of which turned out to be surprisingly good.

Next day came the descent to Lobuje but before setting off we tried for a picture from Kala Pattar. This is a very ordinary-looking, deceivingly low little lump that one of the Americans I met had described as 'brutal'. And brutal the first bit really was, a slope of what seemed to be about one in two, with no real path, at least from the point where we started.

We climbed a few hundred feet up this agonising wall of slippery vegetation and at last came to a small plateau containing many large stones embroidered with wonderful patterns of multi-coloured lichen. They were very, very beautiful and I wondered if I could knit them with a little skilful simplification. Lakhpa, with the amazing energy of the eighteen-year-old, ran at speed towards Pumori to see what could be seen and signalled excitedly that *this* was the place.

It was indeed. Everest, clear and almost completely free from snow, stood in front of us, high above everything else, a huge, stolid pudding of a mountain. It was not nearly as beautiful as many of the others but was impressive by its sheer size, rather like Churchill sitting on a pedestal surrounded by handsome men and beautiful women but engrossing the world's attention by the strength of personality.

I took picture after picture, longed for a wide-angled lens and tried to compensate by taking photographs all round the horizon, hoping to join them up later.

Mo was there before us getting, so he hoped, incomparable pictures, aided by a battery of different lenses which his porter was carrying. At one point he told me to stand still and took a picture of me backed by the Khumbu glacier.

'This should be very good,' he said, 'I will send you a copy when I get home.'

He did, too, six copies, a super picture in which I look an intrepid explorer and not an elderly lady who has tottered painfully to the heights. He also sent me a magnificent enlargement of the summit picture which is framed and hangs in a place of honour in my office.

After the glories of Kala Pattar we went back to Gorakshep to pick up the others and began the descent. Pasang Doma had gone before us and we knew exactly where she had walked for she had been well supplied with sweets and chocolate by the Base Camp Sherpas and had left a trail of sweet wrappings behind her.

A little later we met a party of Swiss from an Alpine club, all fairly elderly and all going well. One sturdy man said to me, 'Grüss Gott! Ich habe fier und sechsig jahr und ich bin fahre im Himalayas.'

This was German basic enough even for me to understand and I replied, 'Ich auch!'

These Swiss had me beaten. I, used to walking on the flat, was doing my best in unaccustomed surroundings but they were obviously all conditioned by regular trips over their own wonderful mountains. They had come from Lobuje to Gorakshep, up Kala Pattar and down it and were now on their way back to Lobuje, some of them even intending to go down a further two hours to Pheriche.

As we went down we were passed by Mo, looking rather grey in the face and saying he felt frightful because of the altitude. He had been too high too early that morning he felt and he must descend quickly. He had left his friend Chris behind at Gorakshep, suffering in his tent, but as soon as Chris felt better he was going down to join Mo. We waved Mo goodbye and several hours later, when we reached the Sherpa Hotel at Pheriche, we found him comfortably ensconced there and feeling perfectly all right now that he was 3,000 feet lower down.

Pheriche, so drab and colourless on the way up, was now unbelievably full of flowers, tiny *Primula denticulata* and quantities of even tinier mauve primroses with flowers so small that thirty could easily go on a 10p piece, or fifteen on a quarter for Americans to judge.

And then up from Thyang Boche came a charming American girl called Julie whom I had met twice before, once in Kaziranga and once in Kathmandu. Here she was bravely trekking alone to the Base Camp, carrying her own pack. We embraced delightedly and she, remembering my penchant for birds, said that she had seen a duck that day in the river below.

I thought little of it at the time but next day I saw a strange duck in the fast-flowing glacier water, a dark-brown bird probably a pintail with pale buffish patches on its wings and a pointed tail, up-ending repeatedly in the swift stream. I could not imagine what it was doing there at 13,500 feet or where it was going and as it was several hundred feet below me and there was no path down to the river it was far too far away for a photograph to be of any use at all. This was my most frustrating example of Nepalese ornithology.

Down we went to Pangboche, hoping this time to see the yeti scalp in the monastery, but there was nobody there to open the door and we had to go on to Thyang Boche.

The difference since we had passed that way about ten days before was amazing. The rhododendron leaves, before tightly curled, were now spread and some of the bushes showed blossom totally different from any we had seen before, mostly pale pinkish-mauve flowers, only three or four to a cluster.

Thyang Boche was warmer than it had been and full of trekkers and celebrities, including Lord and Lady Hunt and other Everest climbers who had come to take a nostalgic look at Thyang Boche before the Darjeeling shindig. The hillside below was a blaze of pink rhododendrons, most of them a deep cerise, and among them strange bushes with long catkins and a red-pollened pussy willow. How I longed for a flower and tree book as well as a bird book to help sort out all the problems.

All along the side of the path, anywhere with an inch of spare space, were the purple iris and a very lovely spurge, its new leaves a brownish crimson, the older ones dark green, the flowers a burning bright yellow with a greenish tinge. The birds were legion, several species of rosefinch, heavily white-spotted nutcrackers, unknown pipits, several monal, grosbeaks, little buntings, the list was endless.

We went again to Khumjung where I wanted to see the famous Nepalese artist, Kappa Kalden, and try to buy one of his beautiful primitive paintings. Lobsang took me to his house which stood right at the top of the village. It was a typical Sherpa house, the big room filled with beautiful brass and copper cooking pots but no furniture. In another room Kappa Kalden, old and wizened, was sitting in a kind of box bed, I think cross-legged but most of his lower half was obscured by a huddle of rags, wool and old fur, making a kind of nest in which he sat painting away at a picture of little figures in a mountain landscape. He had none for sale and nothing to show, but for a hundred and twenty-five rupees, then about £5, he agreed to paint one of his special pictures, putting in *chortens,* yetis, lamas, *gompas* or whatever I wished and this would be sent to me. I paid willingly for I dearly wanted to own a Kappa Kalden picture.

Neither the painter nor his wife spoke a word of English but Lobsang acted as interpreter and after the bargain had been struck Mrs. Kalden offered us large, warming glasses of Tibetan tea. Kappa Kalden looked very old, his thin hair tied back into an attenuated pony tail, his steel-rimmed glasses tied on with string, sitting on the box bed in his bare room painting away oblivious to anything else. All the walls and the cupboard doors were decorated with his beautiful paintings of various Buddhist scenes and figures of which I knew nothing except that they were obviously of great artistic merit.

My painting was promised for a few weeks later but when I told Mr. Cheney this he said I would be lucky if I got it within a year. I was indeed lucky for it was forwarded to me within two months and now hangs beneath my picture of Everest. Also in my office is a lovely drawing of a yak done by Heinz in Indian ink on Nepalese handmade paper. All these, with a few other Nepalese treasures, transform my Norfolk office at some twenty-five feet above sea level into a high-altitude ambience.

We camped at Kunde in a field where unknown passerines alighted from time to time, flitting off before I had time to identify them, and at 6 o'clock next morning I was visited by a Tibetan trader who wanted to sell me 'a very old teapot of great rarity'. It was the same kind of teapot, exactly, as a lama at Thyang Boche, a trader at Namche and another at Lobuje had all tried to sell me.

We sped towards Namche down the path I had traversed with Gyalzen in the furious blizzard of three years before and as we reached the village I fell in with Chris and Mo, both now recovered, and just going to have a large breakfast at the Sherpa hotel, which they invited me to share as they proposed to eat up all their remaining stores. We had great chunks of fried bully beef, two eggs apiece, vast *chapattis,* butter, marmalade and innumerable cups of tea. It was more than I had eaten for weeks and so filling that I had nothing more all day.

We arranged to meet in Kathmandu and they scampered off, while I went to collect the things I had left with Namdo and to say goodbye. I bought some more sweeties for the children and carried with me a pair of Sherpa boots which Mo had bought for me by the simple expedient of sending porters to the shop with clear instructions in Nepali. This also ensured that I paid the correct price for them. Namdo said I would have to tie them round the upper calf with braid and sent a daughter to the shop to get some specimens. I chose the nicest one and asked the price.

'Present!' said Namdo sweetly.

We drank yet more tea and then bade farewell, something I hated doing because at such a distance we could never be sure that we would meet again. Namdo hung a *kata* round my neck, a token of affection which I greatly appreciated. We ran off down to the river, my *kata* fluttering in the breeze.

I was going very well then and after we reached the two bridges we went on down the gorge as far as possible so that the next day's journey to Lukla wouldn't be too long.

Lukla is a small airfield set at what looks like a very perilous angle. There were no scheduled flights on which places could be booked and it was a case of getting seats back on chartered planes which had brought in parties of tourists. We heard unpleasant tales of people being marooned in Lukla for days on end for Lukla was not an easy airfield to get into, especially in bad weather. But I had neither the time nor the strength to walk all the way back to Kathmandu.

We stayed the night at Lukla, which is rapidly becoming rather insanitary for large numbers of people have to stay the night throughout the trekking season. It was becoming increasingly difficult to find an unused bush.

The tourist pressure is accounted for by the fact that comparatively few people want to walk all the way to Khumbu and prefer to fly to Lukla and then trek to Namche, Thyang Boche and the heights beyond. In that way they can see the cream of the Himalayas in a fortnight, if they work hard. They can also expose themselves to the dangers of altitude sickness by pressing themselves to go too far too fast.

There is now, for instance, a Japanese hotel in the region of Thyang Boche where for a prodigious price guests can sleep in moderately comfortable rooms, enjoy hot baths and be assured of oxygen if they need it. There is a splendid view of Everest from every window. But who wants a view like that only from a *window?* Everest is surely something to be fought for, walked for and become exhausted for, not just another fine view laid on easily for those with money.

We stayed in Lukla in great discomfort, first in thick cloud and then in pouring rain but Lobsang was as good as Pasang had been, getting everything but the tent packed so that if the morning were fine and an early plane came in he could rush down to the airfield, find out if there were two vacant places and, if so, the tent could be struck, packed and brought to the airfield in five minutes.

There was a sound of engines, a small plane appeared and he ran down to find out what was happening. People sprang out of the ground like Cadmus' teeth, or so it seemed, but Lobsang was in there, fighting. The man in charge, however, wasn't My Friend and we didn't get seats.

An hour later the process was repeated and Lobsang almost flew down to the airfield and was then promised two seats. Memsahib dashed down with the money for them, while Lakhpa struck and packed the tent. I wrung his hands, and Sanila's too, and giving them the biggest tips I could possibly afford we left them to walk back to Kathmandu.

Lobsang and I had the same magical flight that I had had with Pasang and were in Kathmandu in time for breakfast and a heavenly bath.

I said goodbye and thank you to Lobsang with real regret for this had been an exceptionally happy trip with very few snags and disagreements and an inordinate quantity of gaiety and laughter. And, besides that, they had got me to the Base Camp.

East Nepal and Kala Pattar

I had had such a marvellous trek to the Base Camp in 1973 that it was unthinkable merely to reflect on it with satisfaction and then plan to go somewhere else. There is something about Nepal, its people and countryside that calls one back as forcefully as any sergeant major reprimanding his recruits.

1975 saw me in Kathmandu once more. This time I planned to spend the first four weeks trekking in east Nepal, which was new to me, coming round to Khumbu in a big loop for four more weeks there, culminating in the ascent of Kala Pattar.

I had to make all routine arrangements with Rover Treks in Kathmandu and then fly to Biratnagar in east Nepal, drive on to Dharan Bazar and begin the trek from there. My Sherpa and cook would fly with me and the five porters would go on the previous day by bus to Biratnagar. On the morning of the day I left I was told that the porters had not been able to get a bus and therefore my Sherpa, Pemba, would have to find other porters in Dharan.

The plane started many hours late, there was no transport to Dharan for some time and when we finally arrived there it was almost dark and too late to recruit porters or find a camping site.

Pemba took me to a hotel that was horrible beyond words and I had no alternative but to stay in it. My chief worry then, and for some time afterwards, was my money. This amounted to some £450, and I had heard that parts of Nepal were now becoming dangerous and people had had their tents slit and their money and camera equipment stolen.

Mingma, the cook, who was a Tamang, called for me at six, leaving Pemba behind to engage porters and buy supplies before joining us on the trail.

The country was parched and dull and the heat became intense. Mingma and I slogged on and on and finally chose a possible camp site. Pemba did not join us until five o'clock having had difficulty in finding porters and buying supplies. He seemed to have forgotten many necessities such as candles, baking powder, torch batteries and, worst of all, toilet paper.

I had been warned before I left that some Sherpas had been corrupted by the easy pickings of the tourist explosion. I was told, too, that many made a practice of going into the Sherpa hotels and selling off their clients' supplies. I found this hard to believe and hoped devoutly that I would be as lucky as usual.

We tramped through east Nepal for several days. It was full of houses, intensively cultivated and had very few birds, but on the other hand there were no Western trekkers leaving piles of litter. There were, however, record numbers of local people to stare. We camped on a hilltop outside Dhankuta, and as I ate my supper a sizeable party watched every mouthful go down. I asked Pemba what they were staring at and he said, 'They find you very interesting for they have never seen such a very old mummy before'.

While I ate my supper I sent a porter into Dhankuta to do some shopping and prayed that he would be able to find some toilet paper there. The Nepalese have no use for this indispensable commodity and Pemba could not understand why I made such a fuss about it. Why didn't I use leaves or grass? I tried but as the trek took place towards the end of the dry season, such leaves as remained were hard, friable or prickly and the grass full of dust. The porter came back in triumph later bearing a sheet of blotting paper, poor ammunition for an eightweek trek even when torn into many tiny pieces.

But relief was at hand, for a few days later I met an American doctor returning from a short trek. She and I stopped to discuss the delights and drawbacks of trekking, one of the greatest, in my opinion, being the lack of toilet paper. She at once drew from her pack one and a half precious rolls and pressed them into my eager hands. I blessed her memory at least once a day.

The scenery on this long sweeping trek to Khumbu was disappointing. Every tree was hacked about to a considerable degreee. The vegetation was chewed down by countless goats and even the *Mahonia nepalensis,* at home a spreading shrub but here a tree, had been cruelly pruned to provide cattle food. Those cattle must have had tough mouths for mahonia's leaves are very spiky.

On the first day I met a young Irish doctor trekking with a friend. He was working in Nepal for a couple of years and confirmed my fears about the ruthless cutting of trees and other vegetation, adding that goats were the worst problem for they ate absolutely everything. He was much concerned about the result of cutting down so much forest for the top soil leached away in the monsoon and went down rivers as silt, raising the level of their beds. In consequence the rivers overflowed and the result was worse floods in Bangladesh and elsewhere.

After a few days we left the main stream of foot traffic for smaller paths and at last came to a patch of forest with flowering trees and plenty of birds.

It was here that I had my first off day of the trip but what a good place in which to spend it. There were numerous small babblers, tits and flycatchers, Tickell's thrushes and little buntings migrating in sizeable flocks and parties of unidentifiable large pigeons.

So far the service on this trek was not as good as on previous journeys. One excuse after another was proffered for going slowly, camping in places that I did not like and forgetting necessary items. Pemba told me that porters did not like camping in the forest as they felt cold there and preferred to sleep in houses. I replied, somewhat tartly, that they could sleep where they liked but *I* was paying for the trip.

I had recovered by late afternoon and was having tea when I heard a great commotion and an unending string of porters came by, three hundred and fifty of them, bound for Kangchenjunga with a German expedition.

Amongst this vast assemblage was Pinto of my Annapurna trek. It was lovely to see him again, now much brighter, more confident, obviously happy and very smart indeed in the new gear provided by the expedition. It is part of the understood custom of big climbing expeditions to equip all Sherpas with high-quality climbing gear, sleeping bags, and so on, a gift which is worth a great deal of money.

Next morning the Kangchenjunga party were all over the place in tearingly high spirits. It was impossible to get past them as they were strung out for such a long distance and many of them were Friends of Pemba, who was incurably chatty and had to talk. And when Pemba began to talk the end was never in sight.

We approached a beautiful forest and just before it I saw a nut-cracker, a jay and a yellow-billed blue magpie, the high-altitude version of its red-billed relative, but as soon as the expedition porters caught us up I saw and heard nothing more. Every member of the party was either talking, laughing or singing, which to my untutored ear was a kind of tuneless roaring, punctuated by whoops of joy. The peace of Nepal, for which I had longed so passionately since my last visit, was irretrievably shattered by this interminable procession, their pattering feet sending up obliterating clouds of dust. I asked Pemba to make lunch out of reach of the three hundred and fifty. He did this but we were well within range of at least eighty.

This camp, he said, would be a fine place to spend the night. I felt that after a full day's rest on the previous day we ought to go further.

'Next water very far,' he said, 'about three hours.'

I said O.K., that would be fine.

Pemba was furious, but we had done less than two miles during the morning, we had a long way to go and Mummy was quite fresh.

We walked for hours on the steep edge of a rocky ridge that rose to about 9,000 feet. Six Himalayan vultures and two lammergeiers floated past beneath us and we also saw a great flock of Hodgson's mountain finches. It was a beautiful district of heavenly peace, the day was warm but not hot and everywhere we came on bushes of dhal in full flower, palest pink and exquisitely fragrant, the scent that beyond all others reminds me of Nepal.

We dropped down through thick forest to a camp site and as we passed I heard repeatedly a mournful call which I later learnt was made by the satyr tragopan, a magnificent red pheasant with white spots and a bluish face. Alas, I never saw it. There were a great many fire-tailed sunbirds flitting among the rhododendrons and we found a good camp site in a little clearing with a house nearby for the porters so that everyone was happy.

The next day we went through the sort of country I dearly love, open hillside with good views alternating with thickish forest stuffed with exciting birds. I had a Mountain Travel route sheet with me which spoke lyrically of the magnificent views of snow mountains to be seen from the ridge on which we were walking, laying particular emphasis on such giants as Makalu and Kangchenjunga.

I had brief and tantalizing glimpses of them both once or twice through the pearly mist of dawn. With only their exquisite tops rising from this diaphanous haze, they looked rather like the debutantes photographed by Dorothy Wilding in the twenties, their shoulders swathed in tulle, suggesting remote unattainability. In winter the prospect is apparently clear but in spring the copious dust from the Indian plains floats upwards in the atmosphere and masks the magical heights. This was very disappointing but had I seen it in winter I would not have seen and smelt dhal, rhododendrons and orchids.

The forests were sometimes almost bird-free and at others thick with foraging parties of maddening little creatures that flitted rapidly from bush to bush. The Flemings' *Birds of Nepal* was still unpublished and the only small bird I knew for certain that morning was the metallic, fire-tailed sunbird, largely scarlet, volatile and exquisite, which was there in quantity, very often deigning to sit on top of a large rhododendron bush.

That afternoon we camped by a big and rather muddy lake and once or twice Alpine swifts came over, zooming down to drink. This gave me a chance to see how very big they were, much, much bigger than the common swift which I had many times held in my hands: by some mysterious chance, every year or so, one swift gets sucked into the vent of my Aga cooking range at home. It is heard scrabbling in the air duct leading from the Aga to the outside world from which dark tunnel it has to be rescued and thrown up again into the free air outside.

At this camp I bought a chicken for the porters' dinner, a little courtesy that is expected from time to time. I heard a tremendous crunching noise going on later and called jokingly to Pemba that it sounded as if he and Mingma were eating the chicken's bones.

'Yes, Mummy, we are!' he called gaily. 'They're very good.'

I always knew that Sherpas were tough.

Pemba said that the porters were very tired after yesterday's long carry so we must have a half day's rest. This made one and a half rest days out of four and as I was paying them fifteen rupees a day each I was not best pleased. I knew that I should have my own stupid collapses every so often and badly wanted to press on when I was fit.

Next day took us up the Milke Dande ridge, high and lovely, full of flowers and birds such as tits, tree creepers and small babblers but again we had no view of the snowy giants. After lunch on a sunny hillside we went down to the valley listed on the route sheet as 'a steep descent of 300 feet'. This did not sound at all bad but unfortunately it should have read 3,000 feet and I was quite exhausted when at last we reached the bottom.

The country was very dull until we came to Chainpur, an enchanting little town on a hill with many paved streets, geraniums in window boxes and craftsmen selling the brassware for which the place was noted.

And who should I find there but my doctor friend Paddy and his companion doing a helpful stint with two British doctors at the local clinic. They were all staying in a charming little house and being very well looked after by a Nepalese girl who, at the moment I called, brought in tea and delicious shortbread. It was a well-timed visit.

I was very pleased to see them and to talk English once again. I stayed for an hour and a half but there was no sign of Pemba, so Paddy sent someone out to find him and tell him that Mummy was waiting. While they searched I received good medical advice and remembered to ask where I could buy a hot-water bottle, mine, sold to me as perfect in Kathmandu, having a large hole near the neck which squirted water at the first filling.

'Nowhere', they said in unison.

This was a sad blow because I did not feel that I'd survive the rigours of areas above 10,000 feet, and particularly Gorakshep, without my comforting hot-water bottle. The doctor's wife then said sweetly, why didn't I have the clinic's hot-water bottle? It was used only twice a year, if that, and my need was great. I wasted no time in polite protest and bore the trophy off with many expressions of gratitude and prayed for their health and happiness on every day that I used it.

After lunch Pemba began his daily grizzle about going too far and there not being enough time to get to a good camping site. As he was for ever stopping to drink tea or smoke, insisting that smoking could not be enjoyed on the move, I said rather shortly that if he couldn't smoke as he walked he shouldn't smoke at all. This was not popular.

Before leaving Chainpur we had to have our trekking permits checked and the inspector was a roguish individual who could not understand that a lady of my mature years was not married. This was a topic that was beginning to pall, but only with me: everyone else found it uniquely absorbing. He stamped my permit, waved me goodbye and then ran after me to the gate to say archly, 'When at last you *do* decide to marry please invite me to the wedding!'

After a very windy night when I thought my tent would blow down we descended to the Sankuwa Sabha river where everybody washed everything and also bathed. It was very hot and lovely and I longed to bathe too, but I had no suit with me and felt it would be a bad mark for Britain if Mummy slipped in to the shallow river in bra and panties in front of hordes of porters and children of all ages.

We left this beautiful river to climb to the high plateau on which Tumlingtar airport lay as I wanted to hand in a letter for Rover Treks to send home to England.

The airfield was closed and we were directed to a dirty little house nearby where we found the airport commandant lying on his bed in a darkened room feeding his baby with biscuits., He did not attempt to rise when I came in but said that he would send the letter on the next plane in five days, for 2.25 rupees.

We then set off for the Arun River and on the way Pemba found and engaged two new porters, for our little band, to whom I had become quite attached, were leaving us at the next town, Dingla.

When we reached the Arun, spanned by a large new suspension bridge, Pemba found a third porter. He was a complete musical comedy creation, short and very good looking indeed, well muscled and with enormously strong calves. He had long black hair, slightly matted, a striped scarf knotted round his head and so arranged that it looked like a rather rakish toque, a torn brick-red shirt, a striped sleeveless jacket of immensely thick wool, shorts so short as to be negligible, coral and turquoise earrings and necklace and a thick green plastic bangle. I spoke to him and he replied with a smile of angelic sweetness such as I have never seen equalled. The other two were also good looking, very young and very shy, and they appeared to be a good trio. One more was to be recruited in Dingla. I found Pemba very trying in many ways but he had several excellent points and picking capable porters was one of them. They all set to and made camp on the very high bank above the river.

The Arun was wider, fuller and faster than any river we had yet seen and fairly shallow in the centre which was dotted with a number of stony islets. Over them fluttered a river tern with large orange-yellow beak, a bird I had not seen since I was in India some years before. Two greenshanks flew up, followed by a ringed plover and a little egret; a green sandpiper was feeding and a common sandpiper flew by later. I found a black-bellied tern, four dippers and, best of all, a small flock of milky pratincoles, bumping up my bird list by a dozen species in half an hour.

Pemba made me a large mug of coffee and I was sitting drinking it when I spotted a large wading bird of a totally unfamiliar appearance, poking about among the stones in the shallows. It was a pearly, pinkish-grey with a black face, wide black necklace and long, down-curved red bill. There was only one thing that it could be, an ibisbill, something that I had hoped to see on every previous trip to Nepal.

I upset my coffee as I jumped over the clods of earth in our camping field, pushed on to the path and tried to find my way down the 100-feet bank to the river. I made it and found *three* ibisbills, pecking and picking their way about the river bed. I was so excited that I completely forgot my 66 years and felt more like a 6-year-old. At length, sated with their beauty and still shaking with excitement, I scrambled back to the camp where Pemba understandingly made me another cup of coffee.

We reached Dingla at tea time to find that our prospective camping site was now occupied by a newly built school. Pemba said the Nepalese equivalent of 'not to worry', he knew of another site well away from town. Hordes of people of all ages followed us to the chosen site and remained with us, every one of them watching me closely. They nearly drove me mad, pressing closer and closer, staring fixedly and occasionally giggling. And when I made the mistake of telling them angrily to go away this was thought to be very funny indeed and, led by a teenager in a pink dress, they pressed ever closer.

One of the porters brought me some hot water and I began to wash my feet. Surely that would make them go? Not a bit of it, they came almost to within touching distance to inspect my feet to find that they had neither webs nor claws but were feet just like theirs. They coughed and spat and spat and coughed just outside my tent. I did not fancy walking in and out over spit-soaked soil and did the unforgiveable thing: I lost my temper and with it, face. I was terribly ashamed of myself but there it was.

It was soon after Dingla that, exhausted by walking long distances

uphill in high afternoon temperatures, I needed a rest. This happened, fortunately, in a seldom-visited part of the country with no
crowds to stare and disturb. We camped by a river and again everyone washed everything and Lakhpa took the opportunity to wash my
tent both inside and out, dipping the whole lot in the river.

I was better next day so we went on up a valley with a small but
very busy river in the middle. This joined another river where a rocky
spur pushed out between them and we camped at the foot of this
spur, reaching it by a hideously difficult path along the hillside,
clinging to it by our eyebrows, Pemba leading me when necessary and
turning with an outstretched hand to catch me if my shoes, now worn
to a slippery smoothness, refused to support me. He was so difficult,
obstinate and inefficient over many things but superb at guiding a
timorous client over seemingly invisible paths and ghastly bridges.
The porters were far ahead and literally cheered us along as we
inched over the virtually impossible sections of the path. Lakhpa
came to help me over the last bit, a precarious bridge. Siring offered
to carry me over but it would have been like putting a St. Bernard on
a Labrador so, with Siring behind holding one hand and Pemba, who
had already gone across, bending forward from the bank to reach the
other, I edged along sideways, stepping very, very carefully and
praying not to be catapulted into the torrent below; and then I was
over, to loud cheers from my little band.

The three young porters were all darlings but the fourth one
decided that evening that he wanted to go home, demanded four
days' pay at once and set off immediately. He did well to receive four
days' pay for on two of them he had done nothing at all but sit. He
said he had to go home because — wait for it! he thought he would be
too cold higher up.

I wondered how Siring, Gombu and Lakhpa would manage higher
up for none had much clothing and all were walking barefoot. Surely
they would not risk that at Gorakshep? We did not know where to
look for another porter, but the resident three said they would divide
the fourth man's load among them, providing that Memsahib would
pay them the fourth man's wages. It seemed a fair bargain and I said
yes.

We saw very, very few birds in this valley with the exception of
three orange-bellied chloropses in the morning, wonderfully bright,
grass-green birds that are hard to see in trees, particularly those with
young leaves. But in the evening, near the village of Phedi, suddenly
there were several, then more, then a great many and soon the sky
was filled. The numbers thickened like those of starlings going to
roost but these birds seemed to lack any purposive direction and
merely milled about. At last they came lower and I could see that they

were dark and small, with white rumps and underparts and I came to the conclusion that they must be Nepal house martins which Sálim Ali refers to as 'particularly social', a description which fitted this gathering perfectly. There must have been at least a thousand of them, if not more, smocking the sky with their black dots. And then, not more than ten minutes later, the heavens held nothing.

Next day Pemba suggested lunch at 10.30 and I refused as I wanted to walk in the morning and rest in the afternoon. We went on for half an hour and then he said 'We *must* lunch *now*' as we were about to leave the river and there would then be no more water. This seemed reasonable and I stopped. By 1 o'clock Pemba was ready to go, saying that our camping site was '*very* far'. I knew that one and refused to budge until 2.15 as I had said many times before that I found it exhausting to walk in the full heat of the day. We finally left at 2.30 and reached camp at 4, walking all the way by the side of the river. No more water and very far indeed!

During the afternoon we met a man carrying a big goat in his basket. The goat, said Pemba, had been bitten by an animal and had nearly died and the man was taking it home. I asked what kind of animal had bitten it and Pemba said 'a levver', which I can only presume was a leopard, as it had already eaten one of the goat's legs. I asked if the owner were going to kill the animal and was told indeed no, he was going to keep it. A three-legged goat in that harsh and inhospitable territory would stand a poor chance of survival; bad enough on even ground but far worse in a boulder-filled valley.

The valley, short on birds, quivered with butterflies of every size, shape and colour in a dazzling array of fragile beauty, and there were many plants that I did not know at all. But there was one that I did recognise: watercress, which we found growing in a small stream. Pemba washed it in boiled water and we had it for supper which was a rare treat, our first fresh vegetable since Kathmandu.

Next morning at 7.30 we began the ascent to the famous Salpa pass. The route sheet seemed to indicate that this was a two-hour trek but Pemba said that it would take two days. We went first through a cool, dark oak forest, with *Coelogne cristata* growing in profusion. This forest was full of invisible birds and as we entered it a black eagle flew out just above my head. The trees ended far too soon and we came out on to open hillside which was sown with wheat. My altimeter showed 10,000 feet but Pemba said we were not even a third of the way up. This was manifest nonsense when Everest itself was only 29,028 but it would be, he said, two or three hours more till we reached water and could lunch. It was ten-thirty then and I had banked on a meal at noon but one cannot lunch without water when accompanied by a band of devoted rice eaters.

We sat down more and more frequently as I was tiring perceptibly after flogging upwards for six hours. While I rested I saw an orchid, a most wonderful bloom with pale green outer petals and a great lemon trumpet spotted inside with pinkish red. It hung down the tree trunk in sweeping trails, on which the old flowers had turned to a deep rust. It was very, very beautiful, exotic, and expensive looking.

Pemba said that water was only five minutes away and went ahead to make lunch while I tottered slowly on. At 1.30 I called despairingly, an answer came from some distance and at last Siring and Pemba came to meet me. I was quite unable to go any further, as a small helping of porridge at 6.30 had not been sufficient to sustain me for seven hours' exertion. Siring went back for a cup of coffee which made all the difference and I reached camp and lunch at 2 o'clock, saying firmly as I sat down that this was where we would spend the night.

When I had recovered and rested I began to examine the camp area. It was on a very steep hillside deep in a forest of old oaks, some with orchids hanging from them. Tragically, many of the biggest trees had had fires lit inside them which had burnt out the hearts. How the hollow shells managed to survive I could not understand but survive they did though with diminished vitality.

Later in the afternoon when I was having tea a bird appeared quite near my tent, very tame and quite unimpressed by our presence. It had a dark olive-brown back, with a pale head and its entire creamy underparts were thickly marked with dark-brown crescents. It had a paler bar along the length of its wing and a rather long, narrow tail. It was the long-tailed mountain thrush. It hung around the camp until night fell and watching it gave me enormous pleasure.

I went to bed very early for Pemba said that next day would be hard, a further five-hour climb to the top of the pass and three hours down to the camp site below.

We started early and swung along through the marvellous oak forest. Once we were alarmed by a fall of rock which sent Pemba scuttling along the path at top speed. I tried to explain that if all the trees on the steep slopes were cut down rockfalls and landslides were bound to occur but I was unable to present this simple fact in sufficiently basic English for him to understand. He merely repeated that this was 'a bad place'.

The common cuckoo was calling frequently and a somewhat dejected four-note call, rather like that of a hoopoe, proved to be the Himalayan cuckoo. Rhododendrons, magnolias and conifers now replaced the oaks and soon we reached a place where a party of Sherpas had hacked down trees and bushes and built some squalid shacks. Pemba wished to lunch there, but I prevailed on him to move further up the mountain where it was quieter and there were more trees, the branches burdened with many kinds of tit, including the Himalayan cole, rufous-breasted and brown-crested, charming as all members of the family are.

There were yellow-bellied fantail flycatchers giving their inexhaustable performance of aerial ballet but the cream of the collection was a new woodpecker. I heard it pecking but it was some time before I saw it, its black back so closely barred that it looked almost white, its underparts a lovely peachy-orange and with a black stripe down the back of its neck. It was absurdly tame and if only it had been bright and sunny instead of overcast, I could have had a splendid picture of it. It was a rufous-bellied woodpecker and its mate was close at hand, cutting a line across the trunk of a tree and quite oblivious of my presence.

After lunch Pemba said he thought we ought to go to the next water place as the top was still very far away and then we should have to go down for another three hours. I agreed to go on but I was now beginning to get wise to Pemba's strange method of computing time.

We reached the water place soon after, but it was full of very noisy Sherpas and I judged it better to go on. Very soon after this Pemba changed his mind and said that if we could make the pass there was a good camping place with water not far down on the other side. I was prodded on, discouraged from looking for birds, and told that we really must hurry to get over the pass as it was very cold and the porters had only cotton clothes and one thick rug among the three of them. I was sorry about this for I was very fond of all the porters but I really was not responsible for the fact that they hadn't brought any clothes with them. I was astonished, though, to see the ease with which they managed without shoes on ground that was difficult even when wearing boots. Their feet were horny and the skin deeply cracked all over but every dirty foot was perfectly shaped with never a sign of fallen arches or the deforming bunions of civilisation. I shouldn't think that any athlete's foot spores could ever penetrate those rock-like extremities.

We climbed ever higher and reached the pointed-petalled primroses, pools of orchid-pink, their glowing colour lighting the dark ground beneath the trees. There were also bushes of a much darker dhal, smelling even more potently than the former species and spurring me to further efforts.

We panted on and on and at 3.20 we were there, on top of the Salpa pass and unable to see a thing. It was very dark, very cold and very disappointing. It was the twenty-first day of our trek and in all that time I had seen very little of the magnificent scenery that was undoubtedly there but totally hidden from my eager eyes.

We scampered quickly down through an uncut forest of scarlet rhododendrons, very few of them in bloom at this height but promising glory later on.

The three hours to water turned out to be three-quarters of an hour. The site was beautiful but also very, very cold on this dark, dank northern face with fog closing in. I needed my two sleeping bags and hot-water bottle and wondered what the sparsely clad porters were doing. I found that Pemba and Mingma had invited them to share their two-man tent so that propinquity, if nothing else, must have helped to keep the five of them a tiny bit cosier.

Next morning Pemba reported that they were short of food and I was beginning to think that he was a poor planner. It was not very efficient to be short of rice, porridge, candles and, disaster for him, cigarettes when we should not be near a shop for some time. I was thankful for my small larder of dehydrated food which weighed so little and was so good.

The sun did not strike our rather dark valley till much later so we packed early and ran off down the steep and stony path as fast as we could to the more comfortable climate below. At the top many of the trees looked something like redwoods, dark and rather furry in appearance, but lower down there were many little streams, smaller, lighter trees, lakes of purple primroses and bird song everywhere, although the only specimens I could see were all yellow-bellied fantails, astonishingly mobile little creatures, their flight a kind of aerial knitting.

At about 10 a.m. we came to a clearing where a horde of incredibly dirty children, each with a semi-solidified cake of mucus beneath its nose, were chasing a herd of cows about with loud cries. This was Pemba's proposed lunch place but I thought it both too dirty and too early and went on to the next village where he replenished supplies and angrily insisted on making lunch by the path.

We were bound for a big village called Gudel but nobody seemed to have any idea of how far away it was. I persuaded Pemba to ask several men we met but although they were going to or had come from there they did not seem to know. Pemba said rather grandly that they were ignorant porters who knew nothing about miles or kilometers and as they didn't have watches how could they know how long it took? As they were men who spent their lives carrying loads from one destination to another a little knowledge of their route could surely have been expected. But then I thought back to Lobsang two years earlier who forgot everything almost as soon as it had occurred, and although he had been to Everest some half dozen times had no idea at all of how far it was from one point to another. Pemba, on the other hand, had a very good idea but cannily said, 'very far' when he didn't want to go on.

At 5.30 there was still no sign of Gudel so we turned into a rest house. A few moments later we all turned out again as both Pemba and Mingma thought it was too dirty to stay in. We were on a high path with a kind of cliff dropping down to the river and Pemba cleverly found a path to a wide ledge some way down with a tiny plateau below.

We made camp and had had supper when there was a great shouting from the path above and responsive bellows from my friendly Sherpa. Down the cliff path in the pitch darkness came a man, two women with baskets, a dog and a baby who had decided to join us as they did not wish to stay in the rest house for, said Pemba, 'burglars always came there'. He had not mentioned this when we had considered staying, and it seemed more likely that 'burglars', if they existed, would have attacked my little tribe, who clearly possessed things that were worth taking.

Pemba made the newcomers welcome, allowed them to cook on our fire and began a long talk. The baby wasn't well and howled dismally while the puppy whimpered for most of the night and the rest of them coughed or talked for the remainder. They left very early, still coughing, spitting and chattering.

Jungle nightjars purred during the last hours of darkness and common and Himalayan cuckoos were very near at hand. We were at about 9,000 feet and black-headed sibias, those beautiful but irritating ventriloquial birds that sound like everything else and cause endless trouble to foreign bird-watchers, were there in quantity. After breakfast we strode along the path which went gently downwards to Gudel, and there on a bush in the second-growth forest just below us was a red-headed bullfinch in full view, sitting in what looked like a bottlebrush tree and feeding on the bush just as eagerly as its European congener feeds on the apple trees in our orchards. Ten minutes later we came to another tree in which there were two males and a female. These sleek and portly birds, the male so vibrantly orange, the female much greener, with the black-and-white wings and white rump of the family, are seldom seen and this was tremendous luck.

We were passed by two Japanese who enthused over the beauty of the scenery and asked if I had seen the flowering trees by which, I suppose, they meant the continuous miles of rhododendrons. They did not appear to have noticed the primroses beneath but they, like all the Japanese I met, were running along so fast that possibly they could see only large things at eye level.

From Gudel, a very big village which had had every bush and tree within a considerable distance ruthlessly removed, we descended to the river. The path went down a frighteningly steep hillside of rice terraces. The angle was so acute and the ground so slippery that it was difficult to keep one's footing, and only too easy to fall and slither unpleasantly far. It took almost two hours to get down this revolting slope and at the end of it my knees were protesting.

A good lunch by the river, a rest and two huge mugs of coffee revived me. When Pemba came up, pointed to a green patch apparently hanging high in the sky and said, 'Does Mummy feel like going there today?' Mummy, knowing she would be late in getting to Khumbu, said yes, even though she really felt somewhat unwilling.

Before we could ascend the one-in-two hill opposite we had to cross a bridge, the worst I had yet seen. It hung some thirty feet above a raging torrent which, as usual, had great boulders inset. The handrail was missing on one side and for some unknown reason there were three steps down in the middle of the bridge. It was supported in some small measure by protruding logs underneath it but these were in moderately good order on only one side.

Pemba, at his very best on these occasions, led me over safely but my teeth chattered so noisily that I had to have a sweet to bite on to still their activity when at last we were over. It was an awful bridge.

We climbed for a couple of hours up a totally cultivated hillside with houses sprinkled all over it like confetti. The few trees were denuded of foliage and branches; the haze thickened and rain threatened. We looked back and up to see the reputed fine view of the Salpa pass which we had just crossed so laboriously but it was, as usual, shrouded in mist.

That afternoon I began to strike form and went on well, plodding up with great determination and leaving Pemba far behind, smoking and negotiating the purchase of a chicken. Mingma and I reached the top about 4.30 and the sky, which had been foretelling rain since lunch, now became both murky and menacing. Surprisingly enough it did not let fly until night-time when it rained heavily but fortunately our tents withstood it.

The morning was bright and beautiful and we toiled up yet another smaller pass over slopes trimmed with the small blue gentian, here a brighter and more intense blue than before. Down below us, isolated in a field and surrounded by beautiful uncut trees, stood a tiny monastery, secure in its isolation. Further up we came to a farm where Pemba thought we might be able to buy eggs as our supplies were running low. While the porters were buying rice Pemba spun some splendid tale of need and managed to buy ninety eggs which he said would last us for the rest of our trip. How he proposed to carry such delicate cargo in the rough and tumble of porters' baskets I could not imagine.

On top of the pass stood a lovely old *chorten*. When we reached it we found two lamas, a boy and an elderly man, who was supervising the building of a new *chorten* in memory of his young son who had died very recently. The boy was digging at random on the hillside for stone and when he unearthed pieces of sufficient size he took them to the lamas as further building material. All this was very praiseworthy but I could not understand why the new *chorten* was being built not much more than a yard or so below the old one, ruining the view of both.

We lunched a little way from the *chorten* in half-cut rhododendron forest which was full of birds and afterwards, while the porters were striking camp, I went birding, to be recalled by urgent shouts of 'Mummy , *Mummy,* come back quickly, many birds. Look up! *UP!'*

Mummy ran back uphill as fast as she could, which wasn't much of a pace, and looking up very high indeed saw that the sky was full of cranes, probably common cranes, wheeling and whirling in all directions. They mounted higher and higher and I think they were confused by the mist and could not get their right direction. I could hear their wild bugling, though not clearly as they were very high, and then they went off in the direction from which they had come. About an hour later they appeared again in echelon formation but still too high for me to be sure of their species. Possibly they were going towards Tibet to nest? Pemba said that they came to Khumbu every year and when they appeared the Sherpas knew that it was time to plant their potatoes.

At one point on the path through a beautiful forest of pink rhododendrons we met a man whom Pemba at once engaged in conversation. He had bananas to sell, tiny but sweet, so I bought thirty of them as a welcome relief from our rather restricted diet. We put them in a porter's basket and tramped on to the top of the pass. Pemba and I were well behind by this time. It had begun to rain hard and I found I had to cling to Pemba's hand to remain upright on the slippery downward path.

We staggered down and it grew darker though the rain had lessened. Two hours later we were overjoyed to see Siring coming to meet us, his striped jacket showing unexpectedly through the mist and the trees. He relieved Pemba of his rucksack and together the three of us continued the downward stumble through the pink forest, now liberally sprinkled with the waxy stars of magnolias.

Mingma had found a splendid camp site in an extensive cow pasture and produced an excellent supper very quickly. We topped it up with the little bananas. I retired early to my sleeping bags, tired out with the day's efforts and hoping that the rain would not return. It was a vain hope for both rain and wind attacked us without mercy for most of the night.

The morning had the false brilliance that usually precedes more rain and we continued downwards at the same giddy angle as on the day before, the ground even more slippery after the torrential rain. In a pasture full of *dzoms* Pemba met a friend and of course stayed to talk. I went on very slowly until I came to a fearfully difficult and glassy piece of path which I was disinclined to negotiate alone. I called for Pemba. No answer. I called again, and again there was no reply. I called a third time when Pemba at last replied 'Coming!' He didn't.

Tired of waiting, I went on alone, slipped, fell and struck my back hard against a stone. My back, never very strong, had been recently treated by a physiotherapist who had told me to take care. It took me more than three hours to crawl down, suffering a stabbing pain at every step. I lay quite flat at lunchtime, then felt better and decided to take advantage of the brilliant sunshine to wash my hair.

I washed it and set it in rollers and then, long before it was dry, the sun went in and the clouds rolled up. It was time to go and there was no alternative but to tie a scarf round my head, like a casual customer in a supermarket, and pretend I didn't mind.

We went down three hundred feet more to a bridge described in the brochure as 'a long wire bridge locally made' but which Pemba said was fine and a Hillary product. I had noticed two thin wires wound round and round two trees higher up and later on two wires stuck through a stick. I had asked what they were and had been told 'the bridge' and shown the steel plate pinned into the hillside.

The bridge itself turned out to be even worse than the horror of the previous day's crossing. I felt sick at the very thought of stepping on to it but realised that if I were to get to Khumbu there was no other way.

Pemba went into battle in his own inimitable way, taking over his rucksack and my stick, camera and binoculars and then came back for me, saying it would be better if Lakhpa led me over and he held me by the other hand. He then decided that the bridge was too frail to bear three of us at once.

I sat down for a few minutes to nerve myself for the ordeal and then we started, my three dear young porters all watching from the opposite side, willing me to succeed. Thankfully there was a kind of post standing in the middle where the two steps were situated. I grabbed it and somehow managed to complete the crossing. My teeth chattered so violently afterwards that Mingma undid the food supplies and handed me one of the precious bananas. With this padding my teeth were prevented from shaking out of my head but it was some minutes before I recovered sufficiently to go on.

We began to climb a precipitous path on which at times it was almost necessary to go on hands and knees. It led through a very interesting forest indeed where I managed to see a pair of maroon orioles, which at a distance looked like blackbirds with red tails, and some mysterious and unidentifiable doves.

There were few people on this track which was just as well because I had lost my head scarf and had to climb in shapeless corduroys and dirty blouse with my still wet hair in rollers. I was a sickening sight and I should not have been suprised if the porters had deserted.

At 10,000 feet we came to a flattish clearing where there was a guest house. My tent was, of course, pitched elsewhere but we had tea in the guest house and I spent the the next few days itching from the other little visitors that were staying there, relatives of the Hinko cave inhabitants.

There was birdsong here of a most glorious flutiness, reminding me rather of the yellow-crowned bulbuls of Malaysia, a loud, wild song of great richness. It was the grey-winged blackbird, a magnificent singer that inhabits country between about 9,000 and 12,000 feet.

Next morning there was still more climbing, again through rhododendrons, magnolias and purple primroses, a combination which cannot possibly be bettered. Here at about 11,000 feet, I found again the lovely whorls of green-gold poppy leaves that I had seen on the Annapurna trek and I found a Kalij pheasant too, something I had not seen before in Nepal.

After lunch we came down over smooth, well-grazed uplands and cultivated land and Pemba began to get excited as we neared Khumbu for there were more chances of meeting friends as he approached the home stretch.

At one point he stayed behind talking for almost an hour. I went on with Mingma and when Pemba caught us up the news he brought was horrible. Sir Edmund Hillary was in Nepal to build a second hospital, at Paphlu. His wife and daughter had been flying from Kathmandu to join him on the previous day when the plane had been unable to take off and had burst into flames, killing all the occupants. Pemba had been on expeditions with Sir Edmund and was very greatly upset. All Sherpas and many other Nepalese too were deeply distressed that such a fearful disaster should have happened while their benefactor and his family were in Nepal on yet another helpful mission. It cast gloom over all of us that night.

We camped in the dry bed of a river, and next day pressed on to Kharte, leaving the total silence of the east Nepal trails for the comparative hubbub of the Everest trek.

The first English speaker we met was an eighteen-year-old New Zealander, tramping upwards very quickly and wearing only exig-

117

uous white shorts, his snowy body liberally spattered with mosquito bites which were clustered in a cerise belt round his waist. He was off to Namche at the double and kindly congratulated me on having got so far adding, with some awe, that he thought I must be the oldest person ever to have done the trek.

We went through the forest in which trees were trembling with small birds. Every species that I could possibly wish for came out to welcome me back to Khumbu and Pemba was hard put to it to make me move upwards at all.

We reached the guest house at Puiyan for the third time and the weather was against us once more: snow with Pasang in 1970, rain with Lobsang in 1973, and now with Pemba violent wind which almost blew me off my feet. But it was fine and sunny so I could not really complain.

The downward path we took next day had been considerably improved since I was last there but the forest had been very much thinned and there were not so many birds as I remembered. The path was full of Rais going to Namche for the Saturday market, small men with big baskets running, running, running, mostly barefooted, to sell a few kilos of rice in Namche. After this they would run back to the lowlands, returning again a few days later.

Everyone was busily trotting, my porters included, but I kept stopping to look for birds and on one occasion, in some tall and rather weedy grass growing between trees, I saw a tiny orange bird with a black bib and black on its head, in size and behaviour very reminiscent of the bearded tit, the jewel of Cley marsh at home. It could not be a bearded tit in high-altitude Asian forest and I looked again very carefully. It was a Nepalese parrotbill, orange-brown and with a long tail, the first parrotbill I had ever seen in Nepal.

We scuttled down to Surkya in record time and had lunch by the stream, myself on one of my favourite sites, an island in the middle, and then set off on the path to Chaurikharkha. The path to Lukla branches off this so I decided to send Mingma on a detour to Lukla to book tickets for our return in three weeks, so avoiding undue delay when we reached the airport.

I left the porters to clean up and tramped methodically on, looking for birds and seeing very few. An hour or so passed and there was no sign of Pemba or any of the three porters. I wanted to take pictures of Chaurikharkha but Pemba had my camera. Mingma appeared, having gone to Lukla and back to Chaurikharkha in record time, but he too had seen nothing of the porters. What could have happened? Mingma and I sat down by the path and after some time Gomba appeared, looking distraught. They all thought Mummy had got lost. He and the others had been running up and down the track, asking everyone they met had they seen a very old Mummy. I was getting a bit bored with this dreary description but was powerless to explain in understandable terms just what the average English person visualises on hearing the words 'a very old Mummy'.

We trekked steadily on, allowing me one rest day at Phakding, for I was pretty tired by then. It was here that I saw a replica of a little animal that I had seen on my very first trek with Pasang and again in the river bed camp a few days before with Pemba. It was a long, weasel-shaped creature with a creamy body and a black face, legs and feet and a black bushy tail. It ran up and down trees with equal facility and I felt sure that it was some kind of marten. I learned later that it was a yellow-throated marten, an animal with a penchant for stealing birds' eggs.

Next day Pemba wanted to go up to Kunde to see his wife, from whom he had been parted for some weeks, and I said of course and sent him off at lunch time. The rest of us were to spend that night in the Dudh Kosi Gorge and then climb next morning to Namche where Pemba would meet us at the trekking permit office and take us to the camping ground. I gave him a large wad of rupees and instructed him to buy all the stores that we would need for our three weeks at altitude. And as Pasang now owned a large shop I told him to buy everything there.

When we reached the trekking permit office next day there was no sign of Pemba. I sat down and waited while Mingma went down to Pasang's house to see if some mistake had been made and he was waiting there but no one in Namche had seen him.

I was both anxious and angry for we did not know where to camp, our food supplies were running low, our three porters were going back to the Arun next morning and Pemba had been supposed to meet us with three new ones. I fumed gently for some time and tried to compose myself over tea but to little purpose. What was Pemba doing and, more importantly, where was he doing it? I didn't want to buy a lot of food if he had already bought it but on the other hand Mingma needed feeding, I had no more porridge, sugar was getting low and so on.

Mingma found a camp site and at about 5 o'clock Siring came with me to see Namdo who welcomed us with her usual sweetness, showed the babies, now grown into small girls, gave us tea, offered us an omelette and said that nobody had seen Pemba at all. I bought enough rice for that night from Namdo and some sugar and chili and clambered up the hill in the dark to our rather draughty camp site, anxious, puzzled and not in the best of tempers.

The three porters were to leave early next morning so I paid them off, adding a good lump of baksheesh for each as they had been wonderfully kind and sweet, had carried so cheerfully, and encouraged me so lovingly at those dreadful bridges. They were all very pleased and Lakhpa rubbed my hand against his cheek as he said goodbye.

At 7 o'clock Pemba appeared, said that he had been ill through eating too much 'pork meat' which he had bought without permission and for which I had had to pay an exorbitant price after he had eaten it. He had bought all the specified provisions from a friend and not from Pasang and Namdo, and said that I had not given him enough money. I had provided the sum for which he had asked and he did not explain why he had not bought the supplies from Pasang as I had directed. Nor had he engaged any new porters. I was very angry.

I repacked my luggage to take only the minimum necessary for the high altitude trip and arranged to leave everything else in Namdo's care. After supper I called to Pemba for advice on some point and discovered that he had left again for Kunde, taking two of the porters with him for the trip, leaving me in camp with Mingma and Siring. He said he would return at 6 next morning, bringing with him the two porters and also three new ones.

He came, with a scruffy looking bunch of four, at 7.30 and we set off for Khumjung at last. I called again on Kappa Kalden as I wanted another of his lovely pictures. His nice wife had died since my last visit and his daughter said that he was getting too old to paint now. As he was out on the mountains for the whole day with his cows it was evident that he was not too old in every respect.

We then left Khumjung in earnest and turned left into the Gokyo Valley. It lay virtually parallel with Khumbu and was, I saw, wilder and far less frequented, a pleasant change, for Khumbu was growing daily more stuffed with tourists.

It was very cold and windy, and on the bare hillside only a very short way from the path was a snowcock, standing quite still and looking at me with a slightly distasteful expression. Pemba had my camera and I called to him to bring it but he was engaged in talking to a friend and did not hear until I screamed at him, at which point the snowcock not surprisingly took fright. Pemba came running up with the camera but the snowcock had had enough and did not return.

We met some relations of Pemba's on that first day, including an old aunt who when she saw me burst into peals of ribald laughter. On asking why this was, Pemba informed me that she found it very funny that Mummy had 'broken shoes'. I had purposely refrained from laughing equally loudly at auntie's broken teeth which stuck out like neglected tombstones in an old churchyard.

The path lay round the shoulder of the hill and was thick with tiny bushes that looked like azaleas and which Pemba said were pink and fragrant later in the year. There was a little *chorten* at the top of the hill, and a covey of snow partridges, showing large white patches on their secondaries, flew across the valley and settled on the hillside. Quite near them a flock of large, bright orange-brown goats was grazing contentedly, beasts that I later learned were Himalayan *tahr*. Pemba said that they had been getting very scarce but were now protected and increasing.

We went along the spur and there, pecking on the ground under the bushes were white-browed rosefinches, lovely little brown and pink birds with a thick pink eyebrow that was white at the base.

Even more exciting than the rosefinches were the blood pheasants which emerged from the undergrowth and the white winged grosbeaks that were chattering in the bushes. I took out my telephoto lens and did my best but the clouds, which had been growing steadily darker, now joined into one leaden pall and then snow began to fall.

I said to Pemba what a pity it was that we could not stay in this wonderful place and he, delighted at the thought of not walking any more, said that we could and whistled the porters back from the valley into which they had too precipitately descended.

Fuel was short but they found some bits of wood and a quantity of yak dung which gave off a strong heat and an even stronger smoke. The porters, as usual, monopolised the fire but until the snow grew too thick I moved among the bushes to see all the birds I could though as the weather worsened they sensibly took shelter.

This valley was obviously very good for wildlife for we had already seen a large umbrella of red-billed choughs wheeling about in the sky, a dashing flock of snow pigeons hurtling along at high speed and two monal floating down the centre above the stream. From this side, too, we could get a good view across to Tashinga. The whole prospect was exquisitely beautiful but the weather was very unpleasant.

I now had an opportunity to observe the new porters, all of them extremely grimy but this is an inescapable facet of Sherpa life, for crouching perpetually in front of wood fires in windowless houses inpregnates their inhabitants with smoke and soot. And washing in frosty weather is inclined to make one's skin split, creating extremely painful small slits at finger tips and around nails.

Getting porters had been very difficult, said Pemba, because there were so many expeditions in the field already that the best had been taken long ago. Ours included a girl called Lakhpa, such names as Lakhpa, Mingma and Pemba being used for either sex, an elderly woman called Dodoma, a rather shambling man with slitty eyes and a perpetual grin whose name I never really mastered, and a boy called

Pinto. Pinto was unintelligent but whether this was his natural state or induced by his quite severe deafness I did not know. He was not very big and only about sixteen but he was strong and carried enormous loads with ease.

At one stage of the trek I met two British doctors who were working in Nepal and were taking a fortnight off from their hospitals. The taller of them, young and strong, about six feet in height, was sitting with us when the porters rested and said he would like to try on Pinto's load. He put the headband round his forehead and attempted to stand up but the effort entailed was enormous and sweat beaded his forehead. He said that he knew he would not have been able to walk with this load and yet little Pinto went uphill at high altitude without the slightest difficulty. I suppose the early years of a Sherpa's life are so hard that if they survive those they can survive anything.

It was the elderly woman at whom I looked with most concern. She was bent and tired and coughed almost without ceasing, shuffling along the trail often with her tongue hanging out. I was almost certain that she had TB, and felt that she should have been at home resting instead of flogging along a steep trail carrying heavy loads to great heights. She was, said Pemba, the mother of the girl he had told me about, the one who had been attacked by a yeti. I listened once more to the extraordinary tale of the young girl who was tending yaks in this very valley, he would show me the place higher up, when she heard a high whistle. She thought it was a signal from her brother but when she looked up she saw a yeti. This creature, which was about four feet high, came to the yaks, threw them over by a twist at the shoulder, and killed four. It ate only the eyes and then came to the girl, tore off most of her hair with its teeth, threw her into the river below and then, leaving her to drown, returned up the hill and ate all four yaks. How a four foot high animal managed to kill four such stalwart creatures by just throwing them over at the shoulder or how he managed to eat all four in a short time was not explained.

I asked why the girl had not run away when she saw the yeti and Pemba said very seriously that the influence of the yeti was so strong that when you saw one it was not easy to move.

When the creature had gone, walking with difficulty, I should imagine, after its meal, the terrified girl managed to pick herself out of the river, and struggle home to her village. She had been very ill afterwards and was in the Kunde hospital for some time but now was perfectly well and engaged in carrying loads to the base camp.

I was vastly intrigued by this story and more than interested to know that as we journeyed upwards we would pass the very spot where the encounter took place.

I woke to a brilliant morning but there were ominous clouds on the horizon. As I dressed I felt something sticky in the pocket of my anorak and brought out a small banana which I must have sat on at one time for it was a brown cylinder far past the edible stage. I put it on the floor of my tent for collection together with other rubbish such as spent cottonwool. Later on Pemba told me that when striking my tent Mingma had found this small heap and had said to him, 'Mummy didn't go to the bushes last night in the snow, she used the tent instead.' I told him that what he had found was a squashed banana removed from my coat pocket but he clearly didn't believe me and said that dirty things like that must be buried or the gods would be offended and send bad weather. Considerably affronted by his suggestion I repeated yet again that what he had found was a *squashed banana.* Although one is driven to adopt various shifts by the exigencies of trekking, to use one's tent as a loo and leave the results *in situ* for porters to clear up is not my idea of how one should behave. What kind of trekkers can they have had before that such a possibility should have occurred to them?

We left the spur with great regret for it was a beautiful place and dropped down into the wooded valley, so far uncut, and with wisps of pendulous lichen hanging from the trees in lime-green swathes. We had lunch in a thick part of this wood in an attempt to shelter from the biting wind that was whipping down the valley. We were joined by a medical student from New Zealand who had been with Hillary when the news of his wife's and daughter's deaths had been brought to him and said what a hideous and sickening moment this had been. We talked for a couple of hours before he left, something I valued greatly for I did miss the joys of conversation.

And then it began to snow. Pemba had a summer house at the next village, in which he stayed when he brought his yaks up to pasture, and we were very glad to stay there.

In Pemba's house they lived in the lower, windowless storey, which had a fireplace in it, the upper one, only five feet high, being used for storing hay. It was decided that the porters, Mingma and Pemba, would sleep on the floor of the house, happily oblivious of the dust, dried dung and whatever else lay on it, and that Mummy's tent should be erected outside. It was very cold and Mingma thoughtfully brought me a hot-water bottle as I lay in my sleeping bag, which was much warmer than sitting by the fire and also quieter and lighter so that I could read.

Happily, only some two inches of snow fell and next morning was one of glittering glory. It was exceptionally cold and I lessened the porter's loads considerably by wearing every piece of clothing I possessed. The trees were spangled with frost and snow and I felt like something in a decorated Christmas shop window, except that my appearance would not have seduced any customer into buying.

There were plenty of hungry birds about, including a flock of unknown finches, probably Blandford's mountain finches, and one very odd creature, an obvious finch but with a great deal of white in its plumage. I stalked it for some time but never got near enough for a really good look. But what did merit attention was a trio of very young yaks in the farmyard where we stayed, all so young and fubsy that I crooned over them in a sentimental way.

The air was sharp but exhilarating as we walked a flat upland path high above the river, with huge mountains piled on either side, a valley so beautiful that it had a dreamlike quality. A golden eagle flew past, circled round and then perched on a spur, there were occasional lammergeiers and quantities of red-billed choughs and snow pigeons, apart from odd and unknown birds that flew across the path. From time to time Sherpas went by with strings of yaks, placid, handsome, wonderfully hairy and perfectly attuned to their environment.

We stayed the night at a house owned by Dodoma, the coughing porter, because Pemba said that the porters *must* have a house to sleep in when it was so cold. I asked why they did not use the porters' tent? It was no good, said Pemba. Why did they bring it if it was no good? I asked reasonably Pemba was furious and said very angrily that he did not like that kind of talk.

At this time Pemba and I were not getting on at all well. There is some temporary friction on every trip but on the whole they go well, although none of my others had had quite the *joie de vivre* of the Everest journey with Lobsang and his attendant sprites; this time, however, the friction was becoming unbearable.

Pemba's constant whining over his hard lot, poor clothing, financial responsibilities and every other kind of drawback was very tedious. He had a job as an expedition Sherpa, two or three houses in different localities, several *dzoms* and cows, his wife had a job and he himself hired out pressure cookers and down jackets as a side line so that he was better off than many of the other men, particularly as he had only one child to support. Constant oblique pleas for help such as 'Mummy's boots are much better than mine' and 'Mummy's jacket is too big for her but it would fit me very well' and 'Mummy has many nice things because Mummy is very rich', dried my benevolence at the source.

Dodoma's house was built of uncemented stone so that strong draughts arrived from all sides, varying according to the wind's direction. The house had a minute window and a door of three wide planks that did not fit at all well. In addition to this there was a hole just inside it which led down into the yaks' quarters below. It was very difficult indeed to get through this door without being precipitated into the yakkery and it needed skilful negotiating, particularly in darkness. Dodoma owned one yak and six naks, and disappeared for long periods when she was taking them to or from pasture.

There were no fussy attributes like tables or chairs in her house and having complained to Pemba about being left out in the cold, literally, I came in to have my dinner, sitting among the others in the dust and ashes while one or all of the porters coaxed the reluctant juniper wood into flame. This glowed rather than burnt and gave out very little real heat.

The night was clear and frosty and after supper Dodoma elected to wash her hair. She boiled a large pan of water and then, coughing violently, took the pan outside and, bending over from the waist, washed her long black hair and then came in and sat down in front of the fire and waited for it to dry. She must have been exceptionally tough to withstand washing her hair out of doors in sub-zero temperature and then coming back into a draughty room with a wet head which would dry, perhaps, as she slept. It was also rather wasted effort for dust settled thickly on everything in sight.

I also had my adventures that night for Pemba had screwed up my hot-water bottle without the washer and water had soaked into my sleeping bag. I had to find the washer, get the bottle refilled and then wait again for it to dry out the wet patch before I could go to bed where, even with a sleeping pill, the combination of high altitude and intense cold produced wakefulness.

I was roused at 4.45 by a noisy cackling and peering through the door of my tent saw Tibetan snowcocks in profusion. There were at least three or four pairs in the field where my tent was pitched near the vast, safely tethered yak, and by the time it was fully light there were more than twenty calling, cackling and flighting about. I sat by my tent door eating my breakfast porridge and watched with fascination while they enjoyed their early morning exercise.

We had decided, if possible, to go up to Gokyo and back in one day but Pemba wisely insisted on taking all our gear in case Mummy did not make it and we had to stay either at Gokyo or en route. It would probably take Mummy six or seven hours to get there, he said. This made me feel rather inadequate for I had understood that the scheduled time for the trip was about two and a half hours.

We started off at 6.20, going first by the side of the river, rushing in every shade of blue and green over the usual large boulders. Lichen in many varieties clung to the rocks, one of the most beautiful growing in large flat plates composed of many small stars of soft mustard yellow; these, lying next to a reddish-orange, stippled-looking companion, provided a lovely picture.

We met the New Zealand doctor on his way back, quite transfixed by the beauty of the valley. He said it would not matter at all if I missed Kala Pattar so long as I did this walk which was lovely beyond anything he could possibly describe. He was absolutely right. The valley was hemmed in by spectacular mountains on either side of the central rushing river. The path at that point lay about a hundred feet up. There were very few settlements, but in summer it was apparently full of people who brought their yaks and *dzoms* to pasture. They also make a considerable amount of hay in Gokyo, though how they make it in a monsoon I cannot imagine.

On the first day of this Gokyo excursion we had met Pemba's wife going down with a back-breaking basketful of hay which did not appear to inconvenience her in the slightest. She was a pretty, rosy-cheeked young woman, wearing a magnificent coral and turquoise necklace which also contained some of the rare and expensive brown and white long beads, a necklace which had, so Pemba proudly informed me, cost him six thousand rupees. Mrs Pemba was very shy of the old foreign lady and could not bring herself to speak.

On this highest day in the Gokyo valley we climbed slowly and carefully over a track, in many places obscured by snow. Pemba preferred to walk faster over an area of hard frozen snow at the lake's edge. This was much easier than my own plodding progress but I hesitated to follow him at first for fear of being immersed in water just above freezing point at that altitude, 14,500 feet.

We sat down to rest near a huge buttress many hundreds of feet high. A pale grey bird flew towards it and began to climb up. I looked more closely and saw that it was a wallcreeper, flicking its raspberry wings with the black and white spots in and out to assist its upward passage. It is one of my very favourite birds and as if one were not enough it was soon joined by a second.

There were plenty of blue-fronted redstarts giving their gentle ticking note but not much else until we came to a small lake, a corner of which was just beginning to thaw out. Swimming about in this icy puddle were tufted duck, widgeon, common pochard and Brahminy duck. I had not expected to see any duck at 14,500 feet, and wondered if they were going to nest somewhere in the area or were perhaps resting on their way to Tibet. It seemed very odd to see the species that I count for the Wildfowl Trust every winter month when I am in England swimming in the shadow of those towering peaks.

My excitement was such that I could hardly hold my telephoto lens steady as I photographed the frozen lake backed by snow cliffs and dripping icicles, the 'ordinary' ducks inhabiting the thawed area and white-capped river chats, Hodgson's pied wagtails and alpine choughs adding an unusual touch to the edges. There was also a

Opposite: *Machha Puchhare from above Pokhara.*

Buying bracelets in Khasindu market.

Tule making makai.

Tibetan snowcocks feeding at Gorakshep.

strange, pink-flushed pipit, I think the rose-breasted, and a green sandpiper to add variety.

When we sat down to rest at another lake a little further on, we heard a wren singing loudly, this tiny creature being a high-altitude species in Nepal. And there on a rock stood yet another wallcreeper.

The next and much bigger lake was at Gokyo itself and there Pemba and the porters had to find a house where they could cook and eat. Mummy preferred to have a log of wood brought out on which she could sit and watch what came to the thawing lake. It already contained two widgeon and two Brahminy duck, glowing an even deeper orange against the green-grey ice and the slightly milky water, with the most gorgeous backdrop in the world behind them. There was a tiny spit of land near the lake's edge and on to it flew a citrine wagtail, its lemon-gold head brighter than any I had ever seen and this exceedingly bright yellow, allied to the orange of the Brahminys, lent an autumn tinge to the spring scene. A flock of Hodgson's mountain finches flew by and one settled moderately near me but it was against the sun so that no picture was possible.

We reached Gokyo just before eleven, which was less than five hours from the start, so that I didn't feel I'd done too badly. It was one of the most glorious days that I had ever spent, the ring of unsullied mountains pressing close around me, others extending to vast distances, and no human beings or their litter anywhere near. I sat on my piece of wood, bundled up in protective clothing, thankful for the unutterable joy of being where I was and in perfect weather.

I had lunch and coffee and still sat on, silent, rapt and grateful that my little band took so long in preparing, eating and clearing up lunch. It was not till 1 o'clock that Pemba came to tell me that we must go down. The descent was not nearly as easy as coming up had been for the strong sun had melted the frozen surface and where before we had marched at the lake's edge on hard packed snow we now sank in as often as not. But we found robin accentors, lovely little birds with breasts that were red above and white below, and yet another wallcreeper. And in one place a most beautiful redstart sat unperturbed while I took its photograph. It was probably a Hodgson's, and possibly a Daurian, but the picture didn't show enough of the salient points for absolute certainty, and I didn't 'obtain' the specimen for verification.

I had no gun, anyway, in spite of Pemba's assertion to a doubtful character early in the trek that he was not to come near Mummy in her tent for 'Mummy carries a gun and when Mummy shoots she shoots to kill!' Had Mummy had a gun and used it, it is quite certain that the person killed would not have been the one at whom she took aim, her sense of direction being notoriously inaccurate.

We reached home at about 4 o'clock to find the house ringed by Dodoma's naks, waiting to be admitted to their basement bedroom while the yak itself stood ready to be roped to the wall. I hoped the rope was strong and that nothing would occur to rouse the great beast to frenzy during the night.

That night was the coldest we had had and I could hardly bear it until I was safely inside my two sleeping bags with my comforting hot-water bottle, (blessings on the doctors of Chainpur) with both hoods pulled tightly round my head so that only my nostrils were on the outside and no breath of freezing air could get in.

I was again wakened by about a dozen snowcocks, running about and calling in what seemed to be a quite demented manner. What a piece of oneupmanship when I returned home to be able to boast of being wakened by snowcocks! I was very sorry to leave them but looked forward to seeing their relatives at Gorakshep.

We went down the valley on the opposite side, crossing several small streams before rising to the path above. All were reasonably well bridged, thank heaven. We made excellent progress and camped at a small settlement called Konar, not very far from Phortse.

I paid for the length of the strenuous excursion to Gokyo by feeling rather poorly on the following day and decided that I would take a rest day. Our little field had a dozen yaks nearby which I could watch while I lay quietly recovering my strength. Pemba spent the day in sleeping and, as usual, washing all his possessions, in between chewing small strips of the dried yak meat which his wife had tucked into his rucksack. He gave me a little bit to taste and, when the soot and dust that covered it had been removed, I found that it was not nearly as repulsive as I had feared. He told me that as Buddhists are forbidden to take life of any kind butchery is done by Tibetans or low-caste men. He did not explain why Tibetans, who are also Buddhists, are able to kill.

In November, he said, every household that can afford it has a yak killed for them. This is dismembered, hug up all over the house and left to dry out in the all-pervading resinous smoke. Sherpas' houses posses a unique scent, but I cannot begin to imagine how potent and tangy they must smell when they contain a whole raw yak hanging up to dry.

I was perfectly all right by next day which was a long one. There had been more snow in the night and everywhere sparkled under a fresh white net. We left our delightful little yak pasture and went down through woods to the picturesque and rather widely spread village of Phortse. Here we turned left along a narrow, tricky path towards Pangboche, walking high above the valley of the Dudh Kosi and seeing the Thyang Boche monastery at an equal height to ourselves half-buried in the pines and rhododendrons, its roof shining in the sun.

The path was steep and narrow, in one place so exceedingly narrow that Pemba had to lead me across by hand. Just as we began to edge along this very treacherous bit he said, 'A man fell off here last year.' 'Oh dear', I said. 'Was he killed?' 'Of course', said my kindly guide and then went rapidly ahead, leaving me to follow as best I could.

I came upon him half an hour later gazing into space. I asked why and he replied in a superior voice that he could not understand why I wasn't looking at the many birds that lay ahead.

I looked and saw no birds at all but I did see fifteen splendid Himalayan *tahr* grazing fairly close at hand. Some were feeding and some lying on the very steep incline that dropped down to the river, basking in the hot sun that was thawing them out wonderfully well after the rigours of the previous night.

I got out the telephoto lens and took what I hoped would be lovely pictures of the *tahr* and then went on, to be stopped very soon by a close up view of a monal, strutting slowly across the path, an iridescent male in full spring plumage whose shiny, brilliant feathers glinted in the sun.

We reached our lunch place just in time to see a flock of about a dozen snow partridges, which Pemba had cleverly spotted after hearing their call, emerge from a slit in the rock face.

My lunch resting place was a ledge some six feet above the path with a magnificent view across the valley to Thyang Boche. It had become so hot that I could hardly breathe. I took the opportunity to wash my hair while waiting for a meal, the only time I ever seemed able to engage in this complex operation. I can go without many things when necessary but cannot endure filthy, matted hair. Mine was soon washed and set but long before it was dry the sun went in, the superb view was blotted out and it became very cold. Pemba said that we must go at once as we had to get to Pangboche which was four hours away and Mummy was so slow that it might well take longer.

Pemba went ahead the whole time, waiting for me at difficult places with a resigned and rather martyred look. The journey took two and a half hours of tortuous tramping, alternatively up, down and along, through thick mist. At one time I heard a high whistle and looked for some large bird. The whistle came from a Himalayan *tahr*, grazing very close to the path and oblivious of my presence which was masked by the encircling gloom.

We made camp in an old rice paddy at Pangboche and had some warming tea. After we had finished I told Pemba that I wanted to see the *gompa* or monastery which I had missed on my two previous trips. Pemba, anxious to sit and gossip, said *'Today?'* knowing full well that as we were due off at 7 the next morning it was today or never.

'Today', I said firmly. 'I want to see the *gompa* and also the yeti scalp.'

We went through a maze of little streets to the *gompa*. The one lama sat by a window chanting prayers and beating a rather complicated rhythm on a big drum, the resonance echoing round the village. He stopped chanting and drumming and came down to open the door. We went through one or two dirty ante-rooms before reaching the main room, its walls and ceiling elaborately painted with the usual gods, demons, dragons and stylised clouds, and where little butter lamps burned under tiered silk lampshades depending from the ceiling. Everything was worn, dirty and in bad repair but yet exuded a tremendous atmosphere of faith and an indefinable something more. Pemba, the obstinate, tiresome Pemba, took off his coral-coloured plastic hat, prostrated himself several times on the floor and gave ten rupees to the lama. The lama then unlocked the box containing the yeti scalp and hand and showed them to us in awed silence, but I was not impressed with their genuine appearance, perhaps because I knew that they had been scientifically tested and pronounced fakes.

The lama then took us to a room below and showed us holy books, each in its separate red box; Pemba donated ten more rupees, prostrated himself once more and gave yet another ten rupees for the lighting of a butter lamp. I also gave ten rupees, and we left in a holy frame of mind which for my part was quite unexpected. It was an oddly impressive little *gompa* and I was very glad to have seen it at last, apart from the yeti relics. I was also very interested to have seen a totally different and unexpected side of my many-faceted Sherpa.

Next morning was bright and clear with all the damp mists of yesterday dissipated. The peaks seemed to grow ever whiter and brighter as the sun shone on them with full power, the fluted icing of Tamserku looking more like accordion pleating than ever.

As we passed the *gompa* on the way out of the village I saw the miserable mastiff puppy that we had seen tied outside a house on the previous afternoon still tethered there and shivering in the heavy frost. Pemba and I disagreed violently over the treatment of dogs which he said had to be permanently tethered because otherwise they bit people. Pemba's own dog, which I saw in Kunde, is a beauty and he is very fond of it but he still keeps it tied night and day for ten months of the year. Only for the two months of the year when they go up to the yak pastures is it set free to keep snow leopards at bay.

Snow leopards, according to Pemba, are a constant menace as yaks are their favourite prey — I wonder what else they live on in the severe terrain which they inhabit? — and in the monsoon men take turns to stay up all night to guard the yaks against 'the big white animals' that come down to take them. Pemba knew of a den in the Gokyo valley, and later brought me a kitten's skin to see, a grisly token which almost made me cry.

We lunched at the confluence of two rivers where one path goes to Gorakshep and the other to Dingboche. Few people went there, said Pemba, and I was determined to visit it as I had heard many glowing accounts of its unique beauty and also that of the valley above. Pemba and I and the porters went on this track and sent Mingma to Pheriche to buy food which Pemba said was running short. I had understood that he had bought all that was needed for our three weeks in the heights on his mammoth shopping spree in Namche. Apparently this was not so.

When we reached Dingboche the seldom-visited village was stuffed to bursting point with large parties of tourists and a few lone campers. I did not like this Nepalese Butlin's and wanted to go further up the valley but Pemba was adamant and would not move.

I met a couple of Germans of my own age on the path and we talked until the yaks came home for their English was as fluent as mine. We also compared the costs of shopping with our respective Sherpas and found a great discrepancy.

A little later Mingma returned from Pheriche saying that the shop there had no food, no rice, nothing. He had bought some noodles but otherwise they were starving. Pemba's mood, which had not been sunny for some time, grew blacker and when I invited the Germans to take coffee and my last good biscuits in my tent it grew blacker still: I think he realised that we might be discussing him to his disadvantage.

He came to my tent at 5 o'clock next morning and said that we should start early for Chukhung, at the valley's head, as the weather was not going to last. We would take some hard boiled eggs and my biscuits. I said that nothing would induce me to eat hard boiled eggs with sweet biscuits, which I had finished anyway, and why couldn't Mingma come with us and cook lunch as usual? Pemba told me some complex story of his brother being at Chukhung, and said that he would cook for us, except, of course, that he might not be there. It was eventually decided that Pemba and I would leave early and Pinto would follow later with food in a rucksack, though why Pemba could not have carried this up himself I do not know as two eggs, rice and the ingredients for *chapattis* do not make a heavy load. Mingma and the other three porters were to stay behind to guard the camp.

When at last we started it was still quite early. Pemba and I tramped up the valley towards Chukhung which the Germans had told me was a comparatively easy and very beautiful walk. This valley was wider than Gokyo with the Imja Khola tumbling down the centre, bordered by a wide band of whitish stones on either side.

In the monsoon the valley is thick with flowers and I could see the withered seed pods of last year's plants everywhere and also the new green shoots springing up to take their place. The flat plates of dark-green, goat-chewed juniper were also conspicuous and widespread.

As we went further up the valley it became so beautiful that I was almost speechless. I thought that at Gorakshep and the Base Camp, and recently at Gokyo, I had seen the very best that Nepal could offer but here was a valley surrounded by the highest peaks, Nuptse, Lhotse and Lhotse Shar on the left, Ama Dablam on the right and many, many more at the head of the valley and flowing from them all limitless quantities of fluted ice, in flounce after flounce. I developed a crook in my neck from looking eternally in one direction, spellbound by the glory of it all. It was a gradual climb and when we reached Chukhung at last my map said we were at 15,000 feet. I learnt later that according to the British Army it was 16,000.

Pemba's brother appeared as we neared the top. He was staying at Chukhung as porter and guide to a young Swede who was there alone, living rather expensively on supplies sent in from the Japanese hotel near Thyang Boche. Pemba and his brother, My Friend in excelsis, retired into a house to talk and the Swede, who spoke marvellous English, and I talked and talked until my lunch appeared.

Tommy the Swede (the Swedes I met this year had very English names) had been talking for about half an hour when a cultivated and unmistakably English voice behind us said 'Good morning!'

I turned round and saw two members of the British Army Expedition which was attempting to climb Nuptse, one a Geordie and the other from the south of England. This was a delightful encounter and we made a chatty foursome as we sat munching, for their high-altitude army rations included such goodies as packets of Rolo and Peek Frean's bourbon biscuits, unobtainably luxurious fare which they more than generously shared with us.

We asked for news of the expedition and heard that it was going very well. The first three camps had been successfully established, though that had been a bit tricky, but by the time the fourth had been set up the worst should be over and then they could have a crack at the top. I could not understand what they were doing at Chukhung and they explained that they had been to visit the Base Camp of the Italian expedition on Lhotse, and were now on their way back to their own base. I asked if he knew how the Japanese ladies were doing in their assault on Everest. Was it a truly all-female assault with no male porters?

I was told that they had both men and women porters and were getting on beautifully, too beautifully in some instances as the Italian doctor had been summoned to treat two Sherpas who had been fighting over the Japanese ladies' favours.

All too soon the two climbers had to go, we wrung their hands and wished them well on the way back and also on the attempt on the summit. They seemed quietly confident and were obviously enjoying themselves enormously. David, the young lieutenant from the south, gazed at the fluted mountains with the rapt intensity that I felt myself. They said they had seen snow-leopard tracks high on Nuptse and Tommy said he had seen them too, well above his Chukhung camp. I have seen lions, tigers, leopards, caracul, serval, puma and jungle cats in the wild but I wondered, wistfully, if I should ever see a snow leopard? I did not count the kitten's skin which Pemba had shown me.

At about 2.30 the glory of the day was slightly dimmed by cloud so we started back. It was a long day and I was glad to get back to camp to rest and to find that the large party from the travel agency had departed.

That evening Pemba came to my tent and told me that he proposed to get rid of a porter. I congratulated him and agreed, forbearing to mention that I had advocated this step some days before. He intended to dismiss the rather simple Pinto but I said that I would prefer to part with Dodoma, whose cough, despite all my throat lozenges, was no better. Pemba broke the news to her and she said she would prefer to go that very minute and not to wait until next morning. I paid her and wished her well although I did not at all like the idea of a sick woman going unaccompanied along those difficult mountain paths in darkness. Pemba insisted that she would be all right.

Next morning at 9, just when we were about to make a late start to Pheriche, Tommy came down from Chukhung on his way to Gokyo. I offered tea after his long walk and we had an enlightening conversation about Sherpas and trekking costs in general. He had paid a lump sum to an agency, not a great deal more than my trek was costing me, a sum which included a Sherpa and four porters, all kinds of interesting food brought to his camp and complete equipment, from tent to goggles. There was no constant argument about food and supplies for everything was included for both him and his Sherpas and his decisions were accepted without dispute. I felt very envious.

He also told me that on the previous night, at about 8.30, two women had appeared at the door of his tent and offered their services to carry his belongings down next day. They were Dodoma and a friend of hers from Dingboche and they must have gone up the valley immediately Dodoma had left me. The only person who knew that Tommy needed porters was his Sherpa, Pemba's brother. He had obviously told Pemba who retailed the story on his return to camp. When he dismissed Dodoma she must have decided immediately to go up to Chukhung to get the job.

By the time Tommy departed Pemba said that it would be better if I had lunch then and started for Pheriche later on. As I had only just finished drinking tea I told Pemba for the twentieth time that I did not want lunch at ten o'clock. This worsened Pemba's mood which was now both black and insolent. He refused to take with us any of the large quantity of wood which the porters had spent the previous day collecting, saying that it was far too heavy for them to carry. He also complained that the Sherpas had no food at all although he had told me on the previous day that they had enough to take them to Gorakshep, three days away. I was fast getting to the point at which I did not believe anything he said.

When we reached Pheriche Pemba, in a burst of bad temper, said that he was fed up and did not want to continue the trek. I said that if he wanted to go home that was all right by me and I would complete the journey with Mingma. Pemba, becoming angrier every minute, said it was for me to choose whether he stayed or went. I insisted that he must choose, because I knew that if I sacked him in mid-journey Rover Treks would be annoyed and say the difficulties were of my own making, whereas if he decided to walk out on me he would be at fault for abandoning his client.

After some time Pemba decided to stay and we walked on. At 12.30 I said we would stop for lunch as I had a few odds and ends in my pocket that would do. The porters had had theirs while I was talking with the Swede and as I ate we were joined by a dark elderly man who turned out to be Pemba's uncle, a herder for the large numbers of yak that were grazing at Pheriche. He told fearful tales of snow leopards and said that in the last two days three yaks nearby had been killed by them in broad daylight. I could not take my eyes off that mountain from then on but no snow leopards appeared.

I decided that the next settlement was too near for us to spend the night there and so we would go on to the next one. We should need wood. Uncle, by happy chance, was able to provide some for fifteen rupees. I thought regretfully of the large amounts left behind but 'Mummy could buy more, she is rich woman'.

We started off up the testing stretch that I remembered from last time and reached our stopping place in about two hours for the porters had to have their house and this was the only one for miles.

I grew very hungry towards evening and was looking forward to my supper for during the afternoon Pemba had told me of his good fortune in being able to buy a large plastic bag of various foods from a Sherpa whose employers 'didn't want it any more'. Although the money had to come from my purse he had bought it for eighty rupees without asking my permission. This ruinously expensive bag of goodies contained rice, 'pork meat' and a jar of honey. Remembering the azaleas we had seen so frequently on the way I asked Pemba what the honey was made from.

'Perhaps from bees', he answered politely.

I looked at the label and saw that it was made in Calcutta from 'dextrose, glucose, caramel and colouring' and that no bees had been involved in the operation. With the 'pork meat' in mind I said that I would have bacon and egg and fried potato chips for supper and looked forward with eagerness to this departure from the routine curry. When it came the bacon was a mass of rancid fat and leathery rind and was quite inedible. No wonder the Sherpa's clients had not wanted it.

I wondered if I were unlucky but then remembered that several young people to whom I had talked that afternoon had all alike complained of the same thing, the rapacity, dishonesty and duplicity of the Sherpas up above. I found this news distressing for in previous trips I had found Sherpas to be an enchanting race possessing almost every good quality. All in all I had never liked any people better and that they should be corrupted by the influence of the West was greatly to be lamented and made me feel more than a little guilty. I remembered with deep gratitude the overwhelming charm, simplicity, kindliness and sweetness of character that I met on my first treks.

I reached Lobuje next day feeling horrible but remembered that I had felt equally horrible there two years ago. Litter of every kind was thick on the ground. There were two 'hotels' staffed by some very tough little ladies. They were doing a roaring trade, bent on extracting every possible rupee from passers by, and even more from those who stayed. They sold very small loads of wood for thirty rupees, which was about £1.20 then, and still my porters insisted on making two fires for cooking even though they were all eating the same food.

My tent was pitched some two hundred yards at least from the hotels, in isolation from the 'traffic' and in a fairly clean area. Pemba and the porters made their camp in the soot-grimed earth near the hotels and started their fire at the end of a tunnel between two rocks through which I had to crawl to get my lunch. I looked out on to one of the Sherpa hotels where a shivering and unhappy mastiff puppy was starting its life of permanent attachment to a stick and rope.

At dinner time I again crept through the tunnel to enjoy my evening banquet. The snow which had fallen in spasms throughout the afternoon had stopped but it was damp and very cold. I was not acclimatising well and felt rather ill. As I ate in desultory fashion I could hear the puppy howling disconsolately, on and on.

I got up to look out properly and saw that it was tethered under a big rock which formed a half cave filled with two inches of water, mud, old tins, waste paper and so on. In the middle of this horrible rubbish was a very old and worn half yak skin on which the puppy sat, cold, wet, miserable and lonely. I spoke kindly and unintelligibly to it as it sat there, its large caramel eyes buried in black puppy fluff and its ears unable to comprehend endearments, especially when couched in English.

When I returned to my supper I could not eat it and began to cry. I was furious and ashamed of myself but quite unable to control my tears. Mingma and the porters looked on in great concern. The woman who ran the hotel came to see what was the matter and I said, through Pemba, that if she had to tie a puppy up it should be near the house within reach of shelter and not outside in the snow in a pool of water. The woman laughed and Pemba laughed too and said yet again that it was necessary for dogs to be 'by rope' as otherwise they ran off.

At this moment another dog appeared, a little off-white and black half-Apso which belonged to no one and was therefore unfed. The insanitary little creature kept trying to climb on my lap. I went on crying as miserably as the puppy but more quietly and then, to my astonishment, the woman actually untied the poor little thing and fed it. She hit the white one, which also asked for food, and I gave it my partially eaten curry. It didn't care for it so the puppy engulfed that too and danced about like a demented grasshopper, so happy was it to be free and able to move about away from the malodrous pool of muck.

Next morning I felt really ill and exhausted and decided to stay in bed. Either Pemba or Mingma came every hour or so to wake me up but as it was freezing hard and snowing intermittently I decided to stay where I was. I felt better by lunch time and said I would try a mug of coffee and a *chapatti* or so, with perhaps a little of the Calcutta 'honey'. Mingma came later with some almost uneatable *chapattis* and a tiny quantity of butter. I asked for the honey and he said they had eaten it all. Bought with my money and I hadn't even seen it opened!

The little off-white dog found my tent and came in with the full intention of spending his time on my sleeping bag. I really could not countenance this as he was matted, filthy and soaking wet. I offered the bag in which the tent was packed as being better than frozen ground, but he declined to lie on it and retreated into the snow. This canine drama was re-enacted several times but at last he got the message and curled up on the tent bag, shivering with frightening intensity as he slept.

During the course of the afternoon I heard voices and one of them said 'Well, if you feel too brutal, sit down and I'll try to rustle up some tea for you'.

I called from my tent to say that I had some tea and two men appeared, a black-bearded Aussie and a pea-green American who declined the tea as he felt he might return it immediately and suspected that his lunch of peanut butter and sardine might have contributed to his nausea. I thought his diagnosis was probably correct. They had been up Kala Pattar and had lost their way and instead of descending had gone up again, reached the base camp of the French expedition and had been re-directed down.

I felt better later and decided to get up for supper which, after all, meant nothing more than pulling on trousers, boots and anorak and walking to the hotel. This would not only test my state of health but would also ensure that my dinner did not freeze between kitchen and tent.

I saw that the puppy was tied up outside again but this time by the door of the house. Victory to some small extent but for how long?

This night Pemba had decided that we should eat in a house, a soot-encrusted stone rectangle owned by either My Friend or My Uncle. We were joined by the bearded Aussie, his American companion having gone to bed. The Aussie was an actor from Sydney and I passed a fascinating couple of hours sitting in the black dust and hearing about everything from Indonesia to the fall of Saigon and the condition of Vientiane, where he had recently been. I could have listened for ever but at 8.45, terribly late for trekkers, Mingma appeared with my hot-water bottle and Pemba with a large orange Chinese paper lantern — where this came from I cannot imagine — with which they guided me to my tent, picking our way through falling snow across the stepping stones in the river, a tricky exercise in the dark and without a torch.

I considered what to do next day thinking that if the weather did not improve I might even go down again as relations between Pemba and myself were deteriorating rapidly.

The morning was fine and beautiful and at 6.30 Pemba came to my tent to ask me how I felt. Having slept well and looking at the sun in all its early morning glory, I said that I felt fine.

'Will Mummy go up or down?' said Pemba

'UP!' I said. He obviously did not want to move and an hour later came again with the same question.

I said 'UP!' once more and he then began to query the possibility, saying that the tents were too wet to move, we couldn't go for at least two hours, and so on. Remembering the beauty of recent mornings and the snow of the afternoon I said that I would go ahead with Mingma and he could follow with the porters later on. Nobody thought much of this except the possessor of a waving white tail who trotted ahead of me.

The sun was hot, the snow melted rapidly and we forged ahead over the comparatively flat terrain, seeing very few birds except a number of Tibetan snowcocks, routine this year it seemed and almost common. Pemba and the porters soon caught us up, no more non-sense about a two-hour wait, and we walked on at a decent pace until I suddenly noticed, in the welter of rough, light stones all about me, a small bird that was feeding on my left. I looked closely and saw that it was a shore lark, or horned lark as the Americans call it. It was a different species from the European one for this had a pinkish back and its little face was marked in black and white instead of black and primrose yellow. It was a charming little bird and I wanted to photograph it but my telephoto lens was in Mingma's pack. Pemba, showing the nicer side of his character, said that he would run after Mingma and bring back the lens which he did in remarkably quick time. I took some good pictures and was just about to take off the lens when he said,

'Look, Mummy, there are four.'

There were indeed four by now but only two of them were larks, the other two being finches. They weren't Hodgson's mountain finches so I presumed that they must be Brandt's mountain finches, mentioned in *The Birds of Sikkim*. They were delightful, confiding little creatures, dark brown, ash brown and creamy white in com-position and seemed almost unaware of my existence, allowing pictures to be taken at very short range.

A little further on I heard a tiny snatch of melodious song, surpris-ingly close at hand. The singer was the big, beautiful Güldenstadt's redstart. It was breath-takingly beautiful and flew from one rock to another for some time. Out came the big lens again and pictures were taken but, unlike the Brandt's finch, Güldenstadt's redstart was nervous and restless.

This was a splendid ornithological morning for before leaving Lobuje I had had an eastern Himalayan accentor attempting to enter my tent, robin accentors and various rosefinches on the way and a raven and a lammergeier higher up.

I took a long time to plod to Gorakshep but when we reached the top of the last exhausting ridge to look down on to the sandy waste, Mingma, as Lakhpa had two years before, came to meet us with a kettleful of sugary coffee. It was a lovely thought and the experience of drinking it was even lovelier.

We arrived at Gorakshep in good weather but it worsened steadily. There was no snow, but it grew dark and a very cold wind sprang up. The half-frozen little dog kept pushing his way into my tent and I was quite unable to cast it out. I did wish that it would not keep trying to get in to my sleeping bag because even with my almost indiscriminate love of nearly every kind of animal I drew the line at a wet, dirty, rather smelly and almost certainly flea-ridden dog inside my sleeping bag.

I did not feel too bad at all considering the height, which was 17,300 feet, but thought it might be better to have a day to acclimatise at Gorakshep before attempting Kala Pattar, a day which could be spent in gentle training walks and an attempt to assess the avian life of the area.

That night there were rock falls and avalanches, all of them coming from the direction of Nuptse. Normally I would just have noted their occurrence but every time I heard one I kept wondering what was happening to our two friends from Chukhung and their companions. The ominous rumbles came far too frequently for my liking, often with only half an hour between them.

I woke next morning to extreme cold and heard scratching and whining outside my tent, the dog having been banished for the night to the stone shelter with Pemba and the porters. When Mingma brought my tea the animal came in with a rush, ravenously hungry, shivering and filthy and when my porridge arrived the poor beast gulped down much of it, small wonder, really, as the portion of rice put aside for it had been taken by rats.

I was becoming very worried about this dog for it belonged to no one and was starving and unhappy. I would feed it to the best of my ability while I was in the area but what would happen to it later? I could not bear the thought of it following me all the way to Lukla and being left foodless and friendless on the airfield.

Pemba and I decided on a little training walk round the head of the valley in preparation for our ascent. It was a bright and brilliant day and the beauties of Gorakshep had never shown to better advantage. I looked at the many different rocks that lay around and wished for the hundreth time that I knew something of geology.

Pemba decided to send Pinto back to Lobuje for another load of wood, and thought it would be a good idea to send the dog back with him. I stipulated that it must be fed first and given my biscuits if they had no food for it. This shocked Pemba and he gave it some *tsampa,* the roasted barley flour of which the Sete cat had thought so poorly. The dog was so starved that it ate the *tsampa* with the utmost avidity.

As this was a rest day Pemba and I lay in the sun to drink a cup of coffee before we set off. My binoculars were always round my neck and I raised them to look across the sandy waste before the ridge; there was Pinto dragging a reluctant dog along 'by rope'. I didn't care for this but could do nothing as he was too far away to hear Pemba's whistle and too deaf to hear it even had he been nearer.

We then saw a string of seven splendid yaks loaded almost to the horn tips with wood which they were taking up to the Base Camp to keep the Japanese ladies warm. The magnificent animals were followed by five tiny women, each carrying a load of wood which Pemba said must weigh at least forty kilos. I thought of my struggle up that fearful slope with Lobsang and marvelled at their strength and tenacity. To do it at all was hard enough but to do it carrying forty kilos as well! Lastly came a man with a moderately small sack on his back. This, said Pemba, contained the yaks' lunch. I was impressed by the minute amount consumed by these large beasts of burden.

We started off to the head of the valley and were soon startled by a cry from Mingma. The dog had escaped from Pinto's care and was already panting excitedly up the ridge towards us. It was no good, he was mine whether I liked it or not until I left Khumbu.

We wandered slowly upwards, climbing to little crests that overlooked the Base Camp, from which we could watch the yaks plodding methodically among the ice pinnacles, suffering none of the inertia and exhaustion that had afflicted me.

Snowcocks and blue-fronted redstarts were quite frequent, we saw the occasional shore lark and one great rosefinch, much larger and paler pink than the others. By this time we were getting quite near the Pumori expedition's base camp and Pumori itself was so near that we felt we could almost push it, a great, shapely cone of some 23,442 feet with large glaciers and jumbled icefalls streaming down its flanks.

We soon came to a cluster of orange tents with only a few people about and one Sherpa, Pemba's friend, of course. Pemba disappeared and I began to talk to the nearest Frenchman, who had a little English, I apologised for the dog which had pushed its way into the nearest tent, obviously looking for food. I explained that it was a stray and almost starving and the Frenchman said that they would be happy to feed it as they had plentiful supplies. He called for some and at once a porter came out bringing a large piece of cheese and a big bag of nuts and while we ate the nuts the dog had a field day with the cheese.

The French climber and another who joined us said their expedition would be at the camp for at least ten days more and if the weather held they planned to start their summit attempt next day. Their base camp, so he said, stood at 5,300 metres and Kala Pattar, which had two small summits, was 5,545 metres. I was feeling fine and thought that an additional 245 metres, about 800 feet, should be well within my reach, given reasonable luck.

After a little further chat, I shook hands and wished them well warmly, for they were very nice indeed. Pemba was at last persuaded to leave the friend, who turned out to be his brother, and we departed with great relief at having found a home for the dog which was so occupied with its cheese and nuts that it never noticed my departure.

I seemed able to see everything from the elevation of the French camp's ridge: the Everest Base Camp, below us, the immensities of the icefall revealed in its entirety, the plodding yaks and their attendants and everywhere snow, ice and blue, blue sky with puffs of thistledown cloud. I came back to my tent transfigured with happiness through the contemplation of so much natural beauty and lay on my Dunlopillo, chumping potatoes and scrambled eggs and drinking large mugs of Nescafé, as though I had never been fed before.

The only thing that perturbed me was the frequency of rumbles in the region of Nuptse and my mind turned constantly to the Army Expedition.

Soon after lunch I looked again at the glacier and saw the yaks *running* down. Later on the two yak-herds, both relations of Pemba (his was a large family) sat with us round our fire drinking the *rakshi* which they had brought with them, the only thing, they said, that kept them going. These herders told us that in this season they and their yaks start from Pheriche in the late afternoon, spend the night at Lobuje, leave there very early next morning and get to the Base Camp about lunchtime. They sell the wood at a good profit, have a short rest and lunch and then go straight back down, reaching Pheriche very, very late or early on the following morning. They have a big meal and rest all day before starting out in the afternoon of the next day to make the trip again.

Pemba was enormously impressed by the amount that the yak men earned. This worked out at about 75 rupees per yak which with seven yaks came to about £21 per trip. This did not seem an inordinate amount to me as someone would have to be paid to collect the wood and the yaks would have to be well fed to enable them to go so far so fast and so often.

Pemba and I made plans for the morning assault on Kala Pattar which would entail tea at an hour when the atmosphere was absolutely polar, and a start at 5. My dairy for that day says 'I've done it! I'VE DONE IT!' rather as though the ascent of Kala Pattar were something exceptional whereas in truth it is the point to which most trekkers go rather than to the Base Camp, chiefly because of the superb and extensive view.

We left with a large nosebag of food prepared by Mingma which would be eaten for breakfast on top, we hoped, and in it I put a Mars bar which I had brought with me for the express purpose of eating on the summit.

Our path lay up the valley and then curved back near the French Camp, a far easier and less agonising route than the sheer ascent of the slippery slope that I had essayed two years ago with Lobsang. I felt no ill effects at all bar a slight shortness of breath now and then, far less than I had felt all the time between Pheriche and Lobuje which to me is by far the most taxing part of the whole trek.

Pemba pointed out that one summit of Kala Pattar was 5,545 metres while another nearer to us measured 5,750 metres. As I was going so well we decided to make for that one, much nearer to 19,000 than 18,000 feet.

The way was steep but the track well marked and we followed it with ease and I stopped frequently to photograph the very beautiful patterns of lichen on the stones which also gave me a chance to collect enough breath to go on.

By 8.45 we were there, eating our hard-boiled eggs, *chapattis* and the ceremonial Mars bar. It wasn't as good as it might have been as it had almost entirely melted several times in east Nepal and had been re-frozen in Khumbu.

It is impossible to describe adequately the beauty of the scene that was revealed, many of the tallest mountains in the world rearing before us, and, something I had not forseen, a number of small lakes locked in unexpected pockets of the mountains, turning their green and frozen faces hopefully to the brilliant sun, now burning down with such intensity that I took off my gloves and down hood and even opened my down jacket.

There stood Everest, almost snow free, grey, huge and oddly unattractive, Nuptse, Pumori, Changtse just over the Tibetan border, Ama Dablam further down the valley, the fluted complex of Chukhung, Lobuje mountain, Lindgren: a marvellous panorama that was worth all the effort entailed.

Both Pemba and I were excited beyond measure, I because I was there at all, Pemba because he had managed to get his sixty-six-year old Mummy to almost 19,000 feet without incident or mishap. All the friction and distrust had gone and we were completely at one. The sky was a cloudless and serene blue, snow and ice glittered so brilliantly that I did not dare to remove my sunglasses. It was almost more that I could credit that I, ageing trout from a Norfolk village, had arrived in this superb situation without mechanical aid of any sort, just my own two feet, the use of them made possible by the porters and Sherpas who had done the hard and the heavy work of carrying for me and ministering to my wants.

Pemba's excitement was enhanced by the fact that we were having a grandstand view of the French efforts to climb Pumori. We had seen the expedition leader's wife trudging up a steep slope just above the camp when we left and now we saw two pairs of roped climbers, like tiny ants, crawling slowly but steadily up what appeared to be a vertical wall of snow. I knew it was possible that Pemba's brother might be one of the four, a possibility that lent fuel to the crackling fire of Pemba's excitement. He was a dedicated mountaineer who would talk for hours about his expedition experiences and was enjoying the French climbers' exploits vicariously.

At last we realised, with the utmost regret, that it was time to go down which we did by a different route. The first part was easy and I was surprised at how well I felt; the last was so steep that had I had a tin tray I could have slid down without difficulty in very few minutes.

Mingma and the porters had been watching our progress from below, my Dunlopillo was already laid out and Mingma was there with two mugs of steaming coffee as we appeared, tired out, flushed and deliriously happy. I lay in a state of almost complete exhaustion for a couple of hours and then retired to bed with a hot-water bottle, for the sun had gone in and it had immediately become extremely cold. But oh! the exaltation of that climb and that view!

A Mountain Travel group arrived next day with a horde of porters and Sherpas, their equipment new, expensive and luxurious with chairs, tables and everything that could be thought of to make roughing it smooth. Most of them went up Kala Pattar very early but the porters and some of the Sherpas remained in camp.

Before we left, Pemba took me over to see the sirdar of this high-class party and who should it be but Mingma, the young and exuberant cook of my very first trek who used to shin up trees and rocks to pick orchids for me. Mingma was now a totally different person, contained and responsible, with a large gold front tooth that ensured a flashing smile.

Pemba and I went slowly downward for I was by then feeling the effects of the previous day's high altitude exertion and after we had covered the steeper portion he and the porters went ahead to make camp. Mingma returned about an hour later carrying a small kettle of coffee and after I had refreshed myself we continued to Lobuje.

I found that my pleasantly isolated camping site had gone and the whole of that flat and pleasing area was filled with the tents of another large Mountain Travel party. My tent had been put on the hillside near the hotel. All that was going on confirmed my long held belief that group travel, entailing community singing and perpetual jolly bawling from one group to another, was awful. I liked it when I was a Girl Guide in my teens but it seemed desecration in such surroundings as Khumbu. Pemba told me that this party was going to Dingboche next morning and as groups, or anyone for that matter, go faster than I do I should then see more birds, for none could stay in the region of this brassy clamour.

While I was drinking my coffee I heard English voices. They belonged to the two doctors I'd met before. I gave them cups of coffee too and found that one of them had been to school with my cousin. We talked for hours until I went to have dinner in the small Sherpa 'hotel' nearby in which Pemba's aunt, uncle and many others were also feeding.

I was warmly welcomed and put near the fire for the first time for a long while and as the room, which measured about ten feet by eight, had a minute window as well as an open door the atmosphere was less smoky than usual. It was crammed with people of all nationalities, some eating round the fire, some still cooking and others reclining on the floor in their sleeping bags. Uncle sat opposite to me and auntie, ragged and not too clean with hair that had never encountered a brush, beamed at me from the surroundings of her magnificent Tibetan necklace, so large and opulent that beside it Pemba's wife's 6,500 rupee trophy looked like cracker jewellery.

'They are very rich,' said Pemba, 'and they own this hotel.'

We all sat and talked for some time although we did not understand each other but Pemba did a fragmentary job of interpreting and there was ample goodwill all round. And we were warm and happy.

Pemba suddenly announced to all who were ready to listen that we were short of sugar. As he had bought sixteen *mannas*, — a *manna* equals roughly a pound — in Namche and another three *mannas* at Lobuje just before we left for Gorakshep, I could not believe my ears for I took sugar only in tea and coffee. Pemba insisted that neither he nor the porters used any, preferring to drink their tea with salt. I wondered what had happened to such a staggering amount of sugar for I could not possibly have used more than nineteen pounds in sixteen days. Pemba couldn't tell me.

The two doctors left next morning for Kala Pattar and we told them to follow our backdoor route. I took a last look at Lobuje before we started down and, as we reached the top of the rise from which we were to begin the steep descent to Pheriche, turned for a final fascinated scrutiny of Pumori. Through my binoculars I clearly saw two pairs of roped climbers slowly inching their way up the last few hundred snowy feet of the mountain. Pemba, shaking with excitement, was absolutely certain that they would get there. It was then Wednesday and we had watched them leave early on Monday. We watched for twenty minutes before descending most reluctantly.

'They *will* get there, sure, *sure, SURE!*' said Pemba exultantly.

When we reached Pheriche there was Mingma making tea on our camp fire which was exactly opposite the hotel on the site where, said Mingma, they always stayed. I became very unpopular for insisting on having my tent put elsewhere, well away from the noisy hotel in a little ploughed field from which I could look into the yak-filled valley and towards the place from which the snow leopards were alleged to have come.

Pemba immediately dived into the hotel and came back saying that it was full of people from my country discussing whether or not they could manage Kala Pattar and he had said to them all,

'My Mummy is sixty-six and *she* has been up Kala Pattar!'

That night he told me that the three *mannas* of sugar bought the previous day at Lobuje were already finished and that he, Mingma and the porters hadn't had any. I asked who had and he replied seriously that it all went into the cups of tea I kept giving to visitors. He did not seem to appreciate that during the twenty-four hours in which three *mannas* of sugar had disappeared I had not had any visitors.

The doctors caught us up later, full of the beauty of Kala Pattar and bringing news that the four members of the French expedition to Pumori had all reached the summit safely just before lunchtime on Wednesday, a superb achievement by Monsieur and Madame, the young man who had talked to me and taken care of the dog and a Sherpa, whether Pemba's brother or not they didn't know. I also met a man from Rover Treks who had been to the British Army Expedition's base camp on Nuptse. He said they had established five camps and were all set to try for the summit next week.

Next day we walked with the doctors and instead of going right on to Thyang Boche, which had become increasingly crowded of late, we all stayed together in a field solid with *Primula denticulata,* near the Devuche nunnery. I shocked Pemba by again inviting the two doctors to take a cup of tea but I told him that I would buy one *manna* of sugar, *and no more,* when we got to Thyang Boche next morning.

The two men wanted to do another walk before leaving and we suggested that they should retrace their steps to Pangboche and take the high path to Phortse, going down the Gokyo valley, coming out at Khumjung and so down to Namche.

We ourselves intended to go on to Thyang Boche and then down in the ordinary way but I could not be prised away from our camp next morning and incurred Pemba's wrath by keeping him waiting because he wanted to get to his home in Khumjung.

It was the height of spring and the fields and bushes were full of blue-fronted redstarts, red-flanked bush robins, red-headed bullfinches, a golden bush robin, pink-browed rosefinches, nutcrackers, grosbeaks and many, many other entrancing species. I simply had to stay with my telephoto lens at the ready to see what pictures I could get. It really needed days of careful lying in wait to get the right pictures which could not be achieved with an hour or so's hopeful snapping but it was irresistible and I had to try. The golden bush robin, after all, is supposed to be a skulker that seldom comes out and there it was standing in full view in the spangled meadow, bright as a marsh marigold with a black eye patch like Moshe Dayan. It was a magical site and it was with the greatest regret that I left it and went on to Thyang Boche.

Pemba bought a *manna* of sugar there for an exorbitant sum and I suggested that I should keep it in my tent for as nobody else wanted any it might be as well for me to look after it. I kept it for the next three days and there was still a half-pound left when we had finished the trek.

It was a long, long day's walk from Thyang Boche to Namche, but the pervasive cerise rhododendrons, mauve irises and lemon-gold spurge spurred me on. Pemba left us at the Khumjung turn-off to spend the night with his wife, promising to rejoin us in the morning, and Mingma, the porters and I went on to Namche and camped on the old site. The weather, which had been so wonderful, suddenly worsened and grew grey, a terrific wind sprang up and there was a thunderstorm in the night.

On the way down from Thyang Boche I met a bearded man who asked if I were Miss Forster and handed me a letter sent by Rover Treks. He was a doctor in charge of a small high-altitude clinic at Pheriche and he had just been down to Kathmandu with a party of five very ill people from the Mountain Travel Group I had met at Gorakshep, three of whom had apparently escaped death by inches, two having cerebral oedema and one pulmonary oedema.

It was, it appeared, useless to tell over-eager tourists that they must take things slowly; they had only a fortnight and they wanted to see everything and go everywhere. They tried, their bodies rebelled and they passed out. Down below, at 10,000 feet, he had been treating a young girl who had been very ill. She had insisted on going up another 2,500 feet to Thyang Boche and would surely be ill again, but she had refused to listen to his warnings and had merely hired a yak to take her up instead of trying to walk. He fully expected that when he himself reached Thyang Boche he would find her there in a very bad condition.

After a thundery night, with the wind stronger than ever and blowing clouds of dust about, Mingma took me to the office to have my trekking permit checked. There was a little difficulty for someone had locked the office door and lost the key so that the staff could not get in. They did not seem to mind this at all and were sitting in the sunshine outside playing draughts. I produced my permit and they gave it a few casual glances between moves. When he reached the page giving my age the officer looked hard, raised his eyes to mine and said, '*Very* old man!'

I informed him that my sex was female and he laughed so much that he was unable to make the next move on the draught board for some time.

On the way to visit Namdo, pausing first to buy sweets for her string of daughters, we fell in with an American re-visiting Namche after ten years and noting considerable differences, and a middle-aged Swede called Leonard who came up to me and asked if I were the lady of over sixty who went as fast and far as young people and who had been trekking for eight months, the lady everyone was talking about who was so marvellous? I said yes to all of it, of course, except that it was eight weeks and not months.

Namdo was as delightful as usual and at once made us large glasses of European tea and also offered an omelet and well-preserved yak cheese which I tasted but wasn't able to appreciate. We sat beaming at each other but Mingma was not well equipped to translate though I did gather that the two eldest daughters were now at school in Kathmandu. She asked us to do her a favour, which we gladly did, by taking a small leg of smoked mutton, unwrapped, and a plastic bag of yak cheese squares, two special delicacies, to give to Pasang who was then in Kathmandu.

By this time Pemba had arrived at Namdo's house accompanied by his wife, dressed in all her finery, wearing the necklace and also an enormous gold hair slide costing £160 (everything is priced in Khumbu), which gleamed richly in her oiled black hair. She and Pemba made a handsome couple and I could well understand why he was loth to leave her.

Time was getting on and we had to go to the big market before we left. I had twice been on the road with porters seething towards the Namche Saturday market and I was resolved to attend it this time without fail. Namdo and I bade each other a fond farewell and she hung a *kata* round my neck.

Mingma and I and a porter or so stepped into a narrow street brimming with Sherpas, Rais and tourists and tried to make our way to the market but every street was packed with people, their high spirits whipped almost to a frenzy by the dust-filled wind which was tearing through the street.

Quite early in this progress we met Pasang's mother and great embracings and greetings took place; everyone in Namche seemed to be embracing someone and the general air of bonhomie was inescapably infectious.

When we finally battled our way to the market site, it was packed with people selling small quantities of all kinds of goods but, thank heaven, as yet no tourist tat. There were hundreds of Asian versions of Dickensian characters including one wonderful man with long hair in a plait, turquoise earrings and a big wrapover coat tied round him with thick string, the whole topped by a sky blue plastic hat with a large undulant brim.

There was nothing I wanted or needed to buy but I can never resist markets and this was refreshingly different from any other I had seen. Almost every Sherpa in Namche and many more from other villages were there and large numbers of Rais who, having sold their rice, were already making their way down to the lowlands to fetch more. Mingma and I found our porters at last, nestling against a high rock and grey with dust and we were in exactly the same powdered condition. Pemba was not to be found and we decided to go without him, hoping that he would join us eventually.

We made our way down remarkably quickly for me, slithering in thick dust for much of the time, and then sat down to lunch a little way along the river. The porters and Mingma cooked by the path but I, true to form, made my way through the bushes to the river's edge and sat on the bank to watch a little forktail, a tiny, black and white, very short-tailed relative of the much bigger forktails with their long, trembling tails. This diminutive creature was happily walking *up* a waterfall which was running down a rock face from about fifty feet above. This water was not more than an inch deep but the bird behaved as though it weren't there, except for the fact that it contained tasty titbits which it was eating with relish.

I felt a touch on my shoulder and there were my two medical friends to tell me how much they had enjoyed the Pangboche-Phortse walk. Later on we saw them happily settled in camp further down and this time they invited me to take a cup of their tea before going on later to our own camp of three weeks ago. This, so nice before, was now black and dirty.

Next day was the last of the trek when we *had* to get to Lukla. We left camp at seven and made good time but soon after lunch it began to rain. We reached Lukla in a very cold and damp condition. In the airport office were fourteen letters for me and I read them blissfully. I then paid the remainder of our fares and was told that we would certainly be flying tomorrow.

Lukla was full and there seemed to be nowhere to camp. Pemba, needless to say, soon found a room in a house for himself, Mingma and the porters put up my tent halfway down the runway but safely at the side. He told me that the Sherpa Co-operative, something of which I had not heard before, had a chartered plane to Lukla every Monday and Thursday and as tomorrow was Monday we would surely get seats when it went back. A number of planes also flew up to Lukla carrying salt and there were already hordes of porters waiting to run away with this at high speed. If the Sherpa Co-operative planes were full there should be room on a salt plane.

Lukla had altered out of all recognition since I first saw it in 1970 and pretty considerably even since 1973. Now it was full of wide boys making a splendid killing out of chartered planes and little favours from those people who badly needed seats. Foreigners pay the full fare, of course, while Sherpas in 1975 flew for only 80 rupees; but the foreigner has to pay his Sherpa's fare in addition to his own.

Pemba was lucky in that he had the entree to the cooking fire in the house where he and the porters were staying so I asked him to cook all the curry, dried peas and dried apple that I had left and invited my two doctors to help me finish it. We had quite a feast and they pronounced it excellent and a wonderful change. I knew it was excellent but after 49 nights it was beginning to lose its capacity to tickle my palate.

The rain stopped and we walked about a little in the evening light before taking a cup of tea, and also getting warm, in the Sherpa hotel/restaurant where a very pretty young woman with a baby was eternally cooking noodles and rice and frying cabbage, carrot and onion, piling them on to waiting plates.

We went to bed early as the plane left Kathmandu at 7 a.m. and took only about half an hour to get to Lukla, and it was imperative to be packed, ready and waiting when it arrived. It was a beautiful morning and Pemba and Mingma brought all my luggage on to the airstrip. I sat down beside it, chatting to the two doctors and the Swede, all of us happy in the knowledge that we had guaranteed seats to Kathmandu.

At 7.30 we heard an engine. It was not our plane but a helicopter which flew in and almost immediately flew out again, returning a few minutes later and again taking off almost at once. Every time it came in or out the waiting passengers and everyone else were enveloped in clouds of dust, flying paper and everything else that normally lay about on the airstrip.

I asked what was the matter and the Swede said that the chopper had come to look for the French. What French? He told us that, as we already knew, four members of the French expedition to Pumori had reached the summit on the preceding Wednesday. On the following day, two more, a Frenchman and a Sherpa, had started up in their turn and nothing had been heard of them since. I remembered the worsening weather, the violent thunderstorm and the constant tearing wind of Friday and Saturday and was filled with apprehension. The helicopter returned later and the pilot reported that he could see no sign of life anywhere but as Pumori is well above the altitude limit for helicopters, he could not be certain. But one thing was certain: people could not live at that altitude in those conditions and the climbers must be badly injured or probably dead. The most dreadful thing was that the missing Sherpa was very likely to be Pemba's brother, father of five children. Pemba, whose wife had lost her brother on an expedition only recently, was desperately anxious.

A little later on two planes went over on the way to Thyang Boche but none came to Lukla although the weather was flawless. If no plane came by 11 o'clock there wouldn't be one at all, said the office. And there wasn't. No reason was ever given to the waiting throng.

Richard, one of the two doctors, was frantic with worry for he was due back in the hospital at Kathmandu to take over from a colleague who was going on holiday and there was no spare doctor available. I, too, was upset for I was booked on a plane to Delhi on Wednesday and had to pick up my ticket, see to manifold odds and ends and check over my bird list with the Flemings before leaving, all of which took time. I hoped that a plane would come: I should have known better.

I asked Pemba to re-erect my tent but at 1 o'clock I was still sitting on the runway guarding my luggage and waiting for either Pemba or Mingma to take some action. I wondered what to do for I had eaten all my food and paid off my porters and supposed there was nothing for it but to take lunch and dinner in the Sherpa hotel. The Swede was very angry that my Sherpas had left me to shift for myself in the middle of the runway, and when at last Pemba appeared abused him roundly for leaving 'that poor old woman' in such a predicament. This provoked an extremely hostile reaction from Pemba who picked up a large stone with which he threatened the Swede most menacingly. The Swede, brave man, ignored it.

The second doctor, Tim, departed just before lunch for a solo trek to Okhaldhunga and after a plate of noodles and cabbage Richard and I went birding, neither of us able to concentrate very well due to worrying over our departure. If planes did not come in perfect weather what chance had we of getting out if the weather broke?

It broke half an hour later and in heavy rain we went back to the Sherpa hotel to have some tea and there heard the news we most feared, that it was Pemba's brother who was lost on Pumori. Pemba himself was nowhere to be found but another Sherpa who knew him said that he was attempting to drown his sorrows in *chang*. This was very understandable for the loss of a brother with five children was not only a grievous emotional blow but would also involve him in greater responsibilities and financial commitments.

Richard and I decided to amalgamate tea and supper and while we sat waiting for it to cook watched the Sherpa girl who seemed never to stir from her seat by the fire. She was then feeding the baby with *tsampa* which she first put into her own mouth to test and/or soften, and then hooked it out with her little finger and pressed it into the baby's mouth. She ensured the liquid content of the baby's diet by breast feeding it from time to time. When it had had enough of both she held it out to pee over the sooty floor, then laid it on a piece of cloth on a shelf nearby and began the night's cooking of noodles and vegetables. I saw no water of any kind used on either food or baby but happily we all survived.

The rain became more violent and poor Richard's tent leaked so copiously that he asked if he could share mine. Mine was a tent for two so I offered hospitality but neither of us could sleep for the singing and dancing, accompanied by rhythmic stamping, which continued without abatement until 5.30 in the morning when we went to get tea from the young woman who was still *in situ*. We thought that all the noise was probably the Sherpa version of a wake for Pemba's brother but it turned out to be a ceremony in honour of two Sherpas who were pledging themselves to be friends for life.

We had a very early breakfast, the tent was struck and the luggage again taken to the runway. A plane came at 7 o'clock. Who should get on it but a party of Japanese who had arrived twenty-five hours after we did! The plane was a chartered machine and nothing could be done to offend the big travel agencies.

Richard and I waited more than apprehensively till 10 o'clock when two planes came at once, landing safely on the tiny uphill runway. They were soon followed by a salt plane so it was sure that all anxious passengers would be able to get away.

We crowded in and flew off to Kathmandu and at the airport I said goodbye to Mingma, noisy, tiresome but fundamentally excellent Mingma, and Pemba, so marvellous in some ways, so unutterably awful in others.

This latest trek, though dreadful in some respects, had included three golden days, Gokyo, Chukhung and Kala Pattar, that would be enshrined in my memory for ever.

The Rough and the Smooth

The spring of 1977 saw me back in Nepal once again. The place had changed greatly in two years and the airport was thick with people, well-heeled tourists rubbing shoulders with hippies and hikers.

Before starting my eight weeks of roughing it, I gratefully accepted an invitation to be the guest of the management of Tiger Tops. This is the Jungle lodge where the moneyed can rough it with satin smoothness.

We flew from Kathmandu in a small, nineteen-seater aeroplane to Meghauly airfield where the children and buffalo moved away just in time for us to land safely.

The taxis there to meet us had a short, thin tail at the back and a trunk and tusks in front but, like all good taxis, each could take four passengers. They knelt down one by one in front of a little flight of portable stairs. We climbed up and then stepped down on to the elephant's back where a thickly padded seat was surrounded by a stout wooden railing at elbow height with an upright post at each corner. It was an ideal arrangement, for you could lean on the bar or rest your binoculars on it and could also suspend your camera from the post.

During two hours of hypnotic swaying through jungle I noted that the rhythm of the elephants' slow progress was exactly that of the scherzo of Beethoven's violin concerto. Now I can never encounter one without thinking of the other.

From our lofty viewpoint we had magnificent views of the rare one-horned Indian rhinoceros, chital or spotted deer, hog deer and peacocks; it gave me intense joy to watch those lovely metallic blue-green creatures stalking royally through the forest, their wings showing rich tomato when they were forced to take unwilling flight.

My companion in the taxi was an American travel agent, a portly man who inadvertently pressed me into my corner of the seat by means of a wall of solid fat. His safari jacket was covered with embroidered badges showing where he had been, the collection of which had been, he assured me, 'a whole bundle of fun'.

I was eager to see what bird and animal life there was around and pointed out everything I saw, imagining that he had come to Tiger Tops with the same idea in mind. I was quite mistaken. He was not a traveller but a travel *agent*, casing the joint to which he would later send clients at vast expense. He didn't care a button for natural history and preferred conversation on the lines of 'And what is a lovely girl like you doing travelling alone like this?' to which I turned a deaf ear. And when a jungle fowl, splendidly gold and red and with a fine, arched tail, crept out of the high grass near to our elephant's foot: 'Rooster hen!' said my companion proudly.

At the end of the journey we came to the wide, shallow river opposite Tiger Tops. There were several little waders at the edge of it and I badly wanted to see them as I thought that one was a Temminck's stint. My companion said 'WHOOSH!', waved his arms and all the birds flew up in alarm.

I was so angry that I hit him, almost breaking my wrist when my furious hand struck his rock-hard back. I was ashamed of myself and apologised profusely, which he acknowledged, but from that time we could not speak, he from a sense of affront and I from acute embarrassment. I could find no excuse for my outrageous behaviour even under such extreme provocation.

Our elephants crossed the river and climbed the bank to the lodge, a very cleverly designed building, mostly of wood, which blended almost imperceptibly into the landscape. The bedrooms looked either over the river or into the jungle which backed it, a thick jungle of tall trees which housed — tigers? monkeys? leopards? Soon we would know.

The focal point of this complex was a large round dining-room with a conical, shingled roof, a beautiful room with a central open fireplace to keep us warm when darkness fell. We had tea or coffee and were afterwards taken to our rooms, each with its own bathroom. A torch and a flask of boiled and filtered drinking water stood by the bed together with a little oil lamp that was lit later. There was another lamp in the bathroom. Roughing it?

Before dinner the resident naturalist, Chuck McDougall, gave us a highly informative recorded talk illustrated with slides to show us what we could see during our stay. Afterwards he replied to questions from the erudite and the nit-witted and was never at a loss for an answer.

Drinks were obtainable at the bar and a magnificent dinner was served from 7 onwards. As they ate everyone discussed the possibility of seeing a tiger or leopard. Bait is staked out every night and a watcher is left in a hide (or blind) until 10 o'clock. As soon as the animal arrives and has killed the bait the watcher runs to the lodge to tell the guests. They immediately leave their meal and are led, creeping silently through the forest in a state of suppressed excitement, to the hide to see the tiger. The watcher goes home at 10 and after this the tiger can kill and eat in peace and the guests see nothing.

That night after dinner some fifty people of many different nationalities sat, hoping, hoping, that the tiger would come and that they would just for once see this most magnificient of wild animals prowling through its natural habitat. Nothing happened and, dreadfully disappointed, we all went to bed. The room was clear by 10.05.

The varied and unfamiliar bird song calls coming from the river and the jungle from dawn onwards were most tantalising and by 7.30 we had had breakfast and were boarding the elephants for another ride. This time we took a totally different route and fortunately I had a totally different companion, a doctor who was also deeply interested in natural history. We saw a lot of mammals and a host of different birds.

In the afternoon there was a chance to see the elephants being bathed and fed, the feeding, tending and driving requiring three men to each beast.

Next day half of us went to the tented camp further down the river, a boat trip of bewitching beauty. There were sandbanks at intervals on which stood odd waders, occasional little pratincoles and Brahminy ducks, known in Europe as ruddy shelducks. These creamy-headed, deep orange ducks with large white patches on their wings are a magnificent sight even in ones and twos and when a flock of more than 200 flew past us, honking sonorously, I was spellbound. An osprey plunged into the river and caught a fish and a wavering black line of cormorants flew upstream followed by a pair of great black-headed gulls, enormous and much lovelier versions of the smaller black-headed gull that I knew so well at home.

We landed and walked through thin jungle for half an hour to reach the tented camp on a big island and we were told that with any reasonable luck we should certainly see tigers. The previous week a party had seen four tigers on the bait at once. I should have loved dearly to have seen four tigers at once but I wasn't greedy: one would do. The chances were apparently good as there were known to be four or five tigers on the island which had a lot of good cover and an abundance of natural prey as well as the prepared bait.

The tented camp was in a clearing at the edge of the jungle overlooking the river from a height of about 20 feet. The situation was ideal and the view magnificent. The tents were arranged in a semi-circle and meals were taken under the trees at one or two tables or on our knees. There was a bar for those who wanted it and for those who did not there was boiled and filtered water.

It was very hot in the afternoon and we retired to our tents, each with four netted windows to keep them airy, and with torches, water and soap in a box by the bed, which was a down sleeping bag with a large mummylike hood placed on top of a thick Dunlopillo pad. The wash-houses and loos were in another smaller clearing below, and had lights at night. Even hot water was available. This was the nearest we came to roughing it and a picnic to my usual experience.

After tea the resident naturalist took us on an instructive and interesting jungle walk around the island. One of the tigers had recently been there, big pugmarks and the remains of half a chital showing his route clearly. I was very nervous as we went on this circuit for although it was unlikely that a tiger would spring from the undergrowth on to one of these succulent tourists, he just might. He didn't and we reached home safely having seen much other wildlife instead.

I was enjoying my steak under the black velvet, moonless sky when I noticed a camp guard coming up the path to speak to the naturalist. He came to us at once. 'The tiger has come!' he said.

Leaving our delicious dinners without a moment's hesitation, we all rushed to our tents for torches and jackets. We were enjoined to walk quickly and not to speak. We followed our guide in the sooty blackness, those sensible enough to have brought torches lighting the way. My heart beat so quickly that I could hardly breathe, my ears were cocked to hear the slightest sound. Shivering with excitement and apprehension we sped on as fast as we could until, some 200 yards from the hide, we were told to take our shoes off and NOT TO SPEAK ON ANY ACCOUNT.

We walked on and reached the hide, some 20 minutes from the camp. Somebody took my arm and pushed me into a place from which I could look through a tiny square in the wall. The spotlight shone on the bait some 100 yards away and there I saw a huge, golden tiger, just leaving it, his enormous paws stepping gently down as, with serpentine grace, he wove his way out of sight behind a clump of long grass. We waited for ten minutes but he did not return and we were shepherded outside to where the rest of the party was waiting to know what had happened.

'You didn't miss much', I said, I hoped comfortingly. 'I only saw him for about five seconds.' 'But *I* didn't see him *at all!*' said a little boy accusingly.

We walked back more slowly, the stars twinkled, the silence was absolute. Our dinners were now congealed and we went quickly to bed, finding a lovely comforting hot-water bottle in the sleeping bag.

Next morning, immediately after breakfast, we left camp, climbed into long boats and were paddled down the river. Terns and gulls fished around us, three species of kingfisher plunged headfirst for their breakfast, herons, egrets and ducks stood by the banks and an occasional eagle and a few vultures quartered the sky.

All too soon we reached disembarkation point and were packed into a jeep and driven over a sandy track to the lodge. We had coffee and heard from a Belgian lady that on the previous day she and her husband had been walking in the jungle with a guide when a tiger had crossed the path unhurriedly in front of them.

Our elephant taxis arrived and after an hour's rhythmic plod we reached the airfield and were seen off by a member of the staff who made every single guest feel special.

I thought over those lovely days and decided that although the cost was high this included, besides food and accommodation, elephant taxis to and from the airfield, morning elephant rides, jungle walks, boat and jeep rides and leopard and tiger viewing when they chose to come.

If you want a smooth and painless introduction to the wonders of Nepal then Tiger Tops is for you.

*　*　*　*

I spent the next few days with the Flemings planning my next trek to east Nepal. They thought that I should go first to Ilam and the forests bordering India, and then to the Mai Valley. This was an area that was not yet fully documented ornithologically and which was known to be full of good birds. I was to finish by going to Dharan, town of horrid memory, and so to the Kosi barrage, a new structure across the Kosi river which was said to be the best place in all Nepal for seeing quantities of birds, particularly water fowl.

My companions for the trip were to be the Flemings' man Tule and three porters. They set off very early one morning to go by bus to Itahari, where I was to meet them at 2 p.m. on the following day.

I flew to Biratnagar and took a bus to Itahari, arriving there on the very stroke of 2. I descended at the crossroads, as ordered, but there was no sign of Tule and the porters. I looked carefully down all four roads and after twenty minutes began to feel apprehensive for in this small, scruffy town there seemed little chance of finding anyone who spoke English and would be able to help me out of my difficulty.

After half an hour I could stand no longer and managed to make one of the many youths who were staring at me understand that I wanted somewhere to sit down. Surely there must be a bus station?

A kindly boy took me to a three-sided shelter with a table and a bench on which I collapsed gratefully. I tried hard to retain some composure and began to write up my diary to keep my thoughts from straying. Relief came suddenly in the shape of a portly Indian who spoke impeccable English and asked if he could help me.

I explained that I was supposed to meet four men who were coming from Kathmandu by the bus which arrived at 2. He said that the bus came at *10* and there wasn't another until 5. There was a bus stop further down the road he said. Maybe the men were there?

I thought it unlikely that they would sit immovably by the roadside from 10 until 3.30, but agreed that it would be both kind and sensible if he sent a man to look.

Five minutes later the man returned with Tule and the porters who had indeed been waiting patiently since 10 and were as relieved as I was that we were reunited.

Refusing to allow me to accept the proffered tea, which I badly needed, they at once took me to the Birthe bus which was due to leave at 4. In a remarkably short time the porters had nipped up and down the spindly iron stairs to the roof, deposited all our baggage and settled down inside.

The journey to Birthe was only about 30 miles but it took three hours, stopping, so it seemed, at every mile, sometimes for as long as 20 minutes, while people ate, gossipped, shopped or watched other people dancing. I grew hungrier and hungrier for I had had almost nothing since breakfast.

It was quite dark when we reached Birthe and Tule led us to a field on the edge of the town where he said we could camp. He pitched my tent by the light of my torch, a tricky and laborious procedure, and as we had no wood for a fire I retired to bed at once after a supper of a few ginger nuts and a drink from my water bottle. It was an inauspicious start to the trek.

Next morning I hired a jeep to take us to Sunischari where we were to start walking. We trudged off through thick dust till we reached sandy fields interlaced with many small streams, over which Tule insisted on carrying me.

We stopped for lunch at 10 and by the time we were ready to move off at 12 it was so hot that I sat down in the lee of a shed till 2. We plodded off along a road thick with loose sand, numerous tree stumps indicating that this had once been forest, until at last we came to real forest.

The men all stayed for a drink at the tea-house but I went ahead to look for forest birds. They were immediately evident. Gold-fronted chloropses, grass-green birds with black throats and golden foreheads, were in the trees, together with several kinds of bulbuls, black-headed orioles, grey-headed and other mynas and hair-crested drongos, their long tails curling roguishly upwards at the tips. To my intense delight, a crested tree swift flew over, unmistakable and immeasurably delicate in design, its very long, swept-back wings slicing through the air like tiny scimitars when it flew and crossing over its tail when perched, at which time its little crest stood up from its forehead, a feathered tiara.

Near at hand was a splendid contrast in the shape of a large racquet-tailed drongo, a big, blue-black bird with a large, rather untidy crest that curled back over its head and two long outer tail feathers that terminated in flat, oval racquets.

Standing entranced in this marvellous area where all the birds of the tropics seemed to be congregating, I heard a sound like heavy breathing and waited to see what caused it. I soon found the source of the sonorous sound was a flock of about a dozen necklaced laughing thrushes, great big birds of a species that I had never seen before. They were lovely creatures, earth-brown above with a white throat and peachy-apricot breast crossed by a thick black necklace, their wedge-shaped tails terminating in conspicuous white spots which showed only when they flew.

The damp, gravelly path widened and at the sides were areas of sand sometimes containing flashes of water. In one of these, just below a little bluff, a pair of black-backed forktails flew off as soon as they saw me, their white-spotted banners trailing behind them.

Best of all these wonders was a trio of pied hornbills, large black and white birds with totally mad faces, swinging about on a tall evergreen bush like children on a climbing frame as they stared with lunatic incomprehension at the strange creature invading their terrain.

By this time I was in a bird-happy daze and was delighted when Tule suggested spending the night where we were. He chose a site for my tent on a little hill in the middle of the trees. As dusk fell the daylight noises ceased and night-time ones began, most of them unknown with the exception of the long-tailed nightjar whose 'Tock-tock-tock' went on for many hours in sequences of monotonous monosyllables.

The morning was even better, warm and bright with orioles, fairy bluebirds and various species of thrushes thronging the trees and bushes. On the path before us was an emerald dove, its head the palest French grey, its body and wings of the clearest emerald green with a tinge of bronze. This lovely bird had an ineffably mournful call that carried for a long way. And then, as if this were not enough, five pied hornbills, now looking quite sane, flew in echelon across the bright blue sky.

The great excitement of this wonderful day was the moment when Tule froze and in a hoarse whisper said 'Memsahib!'

I looked up to where he pointed and saw a slim black animal with a

Top: *The summit of Everest.*

Bottom: *Bringing in fresh food for cattle.*

Top: *Tule supervising cauliflower weighing in Ilam market.*

Bottom: *Icy mountains on the way to Chukhkung look like accordian pleating.*

creamy-yellow face and chest and thick black tail about two feet long. It went at high speed from one tree to another and then relaxed and lay along a branch like a leopard, its little legs hanging down on either side, its head turned sideways to rest on the branch, its thick furry plume depending like a bell pull. It slept at once but two minutes later, as a lot of rowdy boys came by, it sprang to life and motion simultaneously. It soon settled down again a few trees away until something else disturbed it and we watched entranced as it bounded from one slender branch to another, hardly touching them as it went. I discovered later that it was a Malayan giant squirrel, *Ratufa bicolor.*

We were on the main road between Sunischari and Ilam, with a great deal of pedestrian traffic, ponies carrying rice and wheat to and from Ilam and a few carts. One of these terrified me as I stood at the bottom of a fairly steep incline. A man was driving a very low cart on which were strapped long, long bamboos that trailed for many feet over the end. The cart was pulled by two bullocks which tore down the slope as though bears were after them, urged on by the driver, the noise of the cart and the rattling and swishing bamboos. I cowered at the roadside as they flashed past but was assured that this unnerving progress was quite normal.

That night we slept at the forest edge and there heard the Indian nightjar instead of its long-tailed relative. This one said 'Chunk-chunk-chunk' interminably, monotony of utterance being the badge of this family.

Two days later, after a long walk through mostly cultivated country with very little forest, we came to the Mai Khola, a beautiful, fast-running river in which the porters, true to type, washed themselves and everything they possessed. It was a beautiful place to stop for lunch for a giant Himalayan kingfisher flew up and down from time to time, both river redstarts were in evidence and an occasional goosander flew by. There was a good modern suspension bridge and also a strange, very low bridge a little further down the river. This was made of thin poles lashed together and to my amazement was the bridge used by wheeled traffic. Tule said yes, of course, this was the main road to Ilam. This 'main road' had now broadened from a mere track in the sand to a pebble-packed and sometimes gravelled surface that at times became almost like an ordinary American dirt road.

As all this was being explained to me I heard the unmistakable sound of an engine. 'Car coming!' I said. 'No car,' said Tule, 'Line over.'

Line over turned out to be Land Rover, the inside packed to suffocation point, the outside festooned with last-minute passengers, proving once again, if proof were needed, the road-worthiness and carrying capacity of this remarkable vehicle.

As we scrambled out of the river valley through forest and later cultivation we met a number of students from Ilam University, anxious to practise their English. I had no choice but to give an endless English lesson. One conversation took a peculiar turn when my companion told me that he had nine brothers, five sisters and three mothers. I queried this but he said no mistake, he *definitely* had *three* mothers. Maybe one was his real mother, another a stepmother and the third a grandmother?

Ilam stood in a wonderful position on a hill commanding extensive views of the surrounding country but the town itself was highly unattractive with the usual wide gutters full of blackish ooze. It was market day and there were a lot of people about but the shops, so far as I could see, all sold the same things: biscuits, cigarettes, Kerosene sold by weight, plastic items, and piece goods in very bright colours. The main foodstuffs appeared to be in the market.

We passed through as soon as we could and on the upper side of the town it was hard to see the road for the dust which arose in clouds from the tramping feet of large parties of people scampering down to market. The women were all arrayed in their best, some in diaphanous saris with gold trimmings, others in more conventional Nepalese dress of long-sleeved blouse under black sleeveless crossover bodice and long black skirt. All wore nose rings or ornaments, many bracelets, at least one necklace, several pairs of earrings and rings as well. It was disproportionally festive attire for such a dirty, fly-blown town but they looked delightfully gay in the real, old-fashioned sense of the word.

As we walked on and up above Ilam I saw several goldsmiths in front of their houses making delicately wrought gold nose ornaments. Other men were machining both old and new clothes, women were winnowing rice in large flat trays and I stopped again and again to take photographs, all with the courteous agreement of the subjects, importunate tourists with cameras being apparently rare in the area. I was still impeded by the crowd of students, one particularly assiduous conversationalist being a teacher of English there who walked with me for more than two hours, talking all the time. Subjects of discussion were limited and his accent deplorable but it would have been unthinkably churlish to refuse to chat. I freed myself at about 4 only by pointing out that if he didn't turn round then it would be dark before he reached home. He agreed and departed, accompanied by about 20 other students and friends who had joined in the talk from time to time.

Instead of the expected forest the countryside above Ilam turned out to be hillsides of terraced cultivation. We had no map as I thought that Tule was familiar with the route, but after careful prodding I discovered he had never been in this area before. Although he did not know anything about the country he was, like Lobsang, endlessly resourceful. Tule was my constant companion. He was serious, responsible and conversational, and would never accompany me without wearing his cap.

I was getting to know the other porters as well. Bodri was the nicest, a great extrovert, tall for a Nepalese, slim, handsome and immeasurably active. If we stopped near a tree that was even remotely climbable Bodri was instantly among the branches and whenever I stopped to take a photograph he was in it whenever possible. On every trek there is one porter who gradually emerges from the rest, the one who brings tea, helps with making the *chapattis* and does any little extra job; this year it was Bodri. He spent most of his spare time with Naini Lal, also helpful and pleasant but lacking Bodri's ebullient vitality.

The third man, Ganza, was something of a mystery who did his duty uncomplainingly but was seldom to be seen after we reached our destination. I solved this mystery after a few days. He was occupied with an old book, so well read that its pages had become a deep orange through which a spidery black script showed with some difficulty. This was obviously a hymn or prayer book to which he was deeply attached and, holding his book, he would sit with his back to the rest of us, singing or intoning softly or else praying quietly. He seldom talked but when he did the other porters were, so I gathered, subjected to harangues on the virtues of godly life.

The road from Sunischari to Ilam had been unbearably hot at times but above Ilam the temperature dropped considerably at night and I was grateful for my hot-water bottle.

The day we reached Mai Pokhari began with the sight of the first verditer flycatcher of the trip, a chaffinch-sized gem of total turquoise except for a black mark from eye to bill.

Mai Pokhari was a small village by a fair-sized lake. The scrubby hillside held so many birds that I decided we would camp there, which delighted the porters, as a family were having a *puja* by the lake which would mean conversation and food.

We still found no forest at Mai Pokhari and after we had left I swept the horizon with my binoculars and, seeing trees in the distance, said firmly to Tule that we would go there and off we went.

We walked for many hours along a high path above a beautiful valley, the pleasure of the excursion marred by a talkative young couple with two children who insisted on coming with us. I stopped politely for them to go by but they also stopped to chat with us as we rested. When we went on I quickened my pace to outdistance them, a stupid thing to do for I should have remembered that the Nepalese can outdistance any Westerner when walking. I lagged behind to watch birds and they waited for me patiently. It was two hours before we separated.

At last we came to the upper reaches of what I thought was the Mai Khola but which turned out to be the Puwar Khola. There, by this delightfully purling river, well peopled with whistling thrushes, redstarts, dippers and kingfishers, we spent the night.

Next morning was almost unnaturally brilliant and we climbed up to the edge of the forest. There were birds everywhere, scarlet minivets, a little pied flycatcher that obligingly stayed put just long enough for me to take his photograph, bulbuls, blue flycatchers, everything that I wanted. We pressed on to another stream at the opposite side of the forest belt and there had lunch. Birds called from every tree but to my surprise and distress not one was visible; this is the chief drawback to tropical trees: their leaves are far too big for ornithologists to achieve satisfaction.

After lunch Tule was all set to go uphill through the dusty potato fields that bordered the forest but I insisted on finding a path through it. This narrow path grew rapidly narrower as we ascended and finally disappeared altogether. We had no alternative but to struggle upwards where we could.

The forest was magnificent, composed of towering trees enveloped by various epiphytes. Orchids hung from the trees and on the ground were large stones masked with a spidery moss. But even in this comparatively remote forest we came upon traces of man in the form of cut bushes and occasional felled trees. After clambering almost vertically for far too long we came to a place where a large bite had been taken out of the forest and turned into a couple of potato fields with five shacks. Several magnificent hardwoods lay rotting on the ground, one in particular being at least three and a half feet in diameter and not less than 60 feet high. It was a heartbreaking example of what wreckage one or two families can bring to a primeval forest.

I had been told by the forest officials in Kathmandu that the department was doing all in its power to protect the forests and the village *panchayats,* comparable to our parish councils, were all deeply concerned about preservation. Maybe they are having effect in some parts of the country but in the hill districts wherever there is forest there are men with axes and children with *kukris.*

Apart from this disturbing evidence of man's destructive powers the situation was exquisite. We camped at the forest edge and when I had recovered from my climb with the aid of lemon tea sweetened with enormous spoonfuls of sugar I went for a short exploratory walk and found a great many new birds, including a lovely striated bulbul, fluting away from the topmost twig of a tall conifer, its yellow-green plumage enhanced by a heavily streaked breast, bright yellow throat and a high crest.

After supper Tule said that we ought to have a camp fire as there was much spare wood about. After so many treks in which the porters sat around the fire and Memsahib had a tiny warm beside it before eating and then went shivering to bed I thought that this was a fine idea. Tule, Bodri, Naini Lal and even Ganza scoured the forest and came back with a rich harvest of decayed trunks which they built into a huge pile. Tule supervised the lighting and maintenance of this splendid edifice with expertise and the heap of rotting logs was soon transformed into a blaze of warmth and light, diminishing the solid blackness of the forest which lay behind.

At 6 p.m. a collared pygmy owlet said peremptorily 'Pooh, poo-poo, pooh!' and continued this scornful observation throughout the evening. It was still expostulating when I fell asleep and when Tule brought my washing water at 6 a.m. the first sound I heard came from the owlet.

Besides the owlet's last remarks the air was ringing with the cries of great Himalayan barbets, the melodious whistles of many orioles and countless other calls. It was a superb dawn chorus but, alas, transient.

We went down after breakfast on the opposite side of the thick dark forest. There was a good wide path and the trees were full of birds that I now knew, as well as little phylloscopus warblers, which I have always found insufferably difficult to distinguish, and unknown cuckoos that disappeared almost as soon as sighted.

This was March and the season of weddings and just before reaching Ilam we passed two wedding processions. One was that of a thin little girl in a rather poor quality red sari who, seated on a drooping pony, was being dragged uphill accompanied by her friends. In another we saw the bridegroom, a very young boy dressed in a mixture of Nepalese and Western clothing and wearing as his wedding finery a thick garland of tarnished gold made of what was in my youth called mermaid's hair. He was followed by a group of excited friends blowing tinny trumpets and banging drums and one of them, aged about 11, impressed me greatly with the originality of his ceremonial attire for he was wearing on his closely cropped head a metal colander, the handles hanging down over his ears.

We went back to Ilam by a slightly different route and one morning at about 7.30 after Tule and I had spent some time in tracking down hidden laughing thrushes, we left the undergrowth to walk along a high hillside. Winging high and very fast across the sky came a skein of 13 pale grey bar-headed geese bound for their nesting grounds further north. It is always lovely to watch geese in flight but to see them going so purposefully towards their summer quarters had a magic all of its own.

On the way up to Ilam I had noticed that outside every house and shop were little twisted bamboo stools topped with cowhide, with the hair left on. These were very comfortable and I wanted to buy one to take home for my indulged cat to sit on beside the fire. I had found out that these stools, called *mooras,* were made by the inmates of the Ilam prison.

When we got there Tule and I went to the prison, which looked like an ordinary, rather large house and asked for *mooras.* After a trifling delay a couple were brought with the tops embellished with geometrical designs in sisal, dyed magenta, royal, canary and emerald. These were quite hideous and I asked for the hairy cowhide type. We came away with two *mooras* for 20 rupees which at present prices is about 50p or less than a dollar each, a very good bargain indeed.

This time we spent the night at the Mai Khola, camping at the river's edge on a wide sandy stretch which was almost certainly covered in the monsoon. There were birds of every kind around, and in the morning, near our camp I had at the same time a close view of the scarlet-breasted sunbird, fiery and bright as a guardsman's tunic, and in sharp contrast a white-bellied yuhina, a name that does no justice to this lovely little bird, gentle lime green above and bright white below with a forward-tilted, full, green crest.

We climbed up through the forest, meeting dozens of birds on the way and then pressed on to a tea estate behind which lay the descent to the Mai valley which Tule called My Belly. I was most anxious to see this place about which both Flemings had spoken so glowingly and in the late afternoon we trudged down, on a good, solid road which twisted through untouched forest. Tree swifts floated above us, assorted bulbuls and barbets called from the trees and small birds without number were all around.

By the time we reached the bottom at 5.15 I was so tired that my legs would hardly take me another step but I managed to drive them forward till we reached camp where the wholly admirable Tule had tea ready brewed and *makai* on the fire. *Makai* is the Nepalese popcorn which I had enjoyed at Chomrong. With a mug of sweet tea after a long day it is one of the very best aspects of trekking in Nepal. The grain, like its growers, is very tough and I could not eat the hard kernels that had failed to pop; not so my porters, whose teeth were strong as bulldozers.

After this reviving snack I looked around. Our camp was on a rice paddy in the very middle of a flat, flat valley down which a broad river had obviously once flowed. Birds were thick both on the ground and in the sky. In the forest I heard woodpeckers, bulbuls, bee-eaters, barbets and nuthatches, egrets in quantity flew over and in every little splash of water there was a sandpiper, stint, greenshank or perhaps a common kingfisher while a red-winged bush lark pecked nearby. As dusk fell grey partridges began to call, a musical, insistent piping.

It was almost completely dark when I heard a loud, imperious 'Tweet!' This was repeated again and again. To me tweet is the kind of sound made by a small, perhaps rather hesistant bird but this had a note of command.

I looked and looked and then at last I saw it, a large nightjar with big, rounded wings. It was Franklin's nightjar and it looked enormous but the Flemings, and who would dispute with them, said in their book that it was merely 10 inches long. I sat there in the hot, velvet darkness and watched entranced as it flew in wide circles on silent wings.

Next morning we started off early to go down the fabled valley which was filled with flocks of egrets, various migrating waders, odd storks, eagles and kites and when we reached the forest at the other side there were tropical forest birds of countless varieties, all those I had already seen and many, many more.

And then, close by the side of the path, Tule and I saw another of the wonderful squirrels that we had seen earlier, 'breakfast catching' as Tule put it. It sprang from tree to tree, launching itself from apparently nothing and alighting on some invisible landing stage and leaping off again immediately We were extremely lucky to see it once more, so beautiful, so marvellously agile and such a master of its habitat.

After lunch the road became an open tunnel through the forest, hemmed in closely on either side by thick bushes. It was like walking though a long, hot oven, and I sat down to rest. Through my semi-coma I saw a bright green bird fly across the road and perch in a small tree, unfortunately with its back to me. It wasn't any of the green chloropses and I began to hope that it might be a long-tailed broadbill which I had never seen. Size, shape and colour fitted but the book showed that the broadbill had a black cap and my bird had not. And then it turned its head to show a longish black bill, thin at the tip. I wondered about bee-eaters? It was not chestnut-backed and was too large to be the little green. Could it possibly be the blue-bearded? I could not tell from the back view and then, by tremendous good fortune, a second bird flew in and immediately copulated with the first one. After this one of them turned to face me and showed the longed-for confimation of my diagnosis, a 'beard' of blue feathers, cascading down its green breast. This really made my day.

165

It began to get a little cooler and we walked into real forest and then on to a settlement overlooking the Mai Khola itself, much wider than it had been where we had camped far above on the way from Ilam.

Here we camped, overlooking a small stream. My tent was on the edge of a bluff some 50 feet high in a spot romantic to the point of disbelief with thick forest behind and in front, grass and rice paddies studded with egrets, little houses nestling in trees nearby and the measureless, unknown valley disappearing into the distance.

I took my tea and *makai* in that haze of utter contentment that comes so frequently when on trek in Nepal, induced by the contemplation of unspoilt natural beauty, the proximity of snow mountains, the sight of beautiful birds and animals, in the company of kind and simple people who do all they can to make enjoyment keener. All but the high mountains were there then and I lay in the sun, grateful, contented and uplifted.

After tea my feet itched to explore the rice paddies and sandy flats near the river with their many little flashes of water, doubtless the home of luscious insects which, with cattle to stir them up, made it certain that there would be plenty of birds about.

The other porters were busy so I set off with our religious porter Ganza. At once a flock of black ibis flew up, making an odd honking noise, the white patch on their wings identifying them. Nearby was a lesser adjutant stork, large and lovely in flight and extraordinarily hideous on the ground, with bare head and neck and huge, gross bill.

We made our way gingerly over the rice paddies, each about the size of my small walled garden at home and separated from each other by a mud wall about 6 inches high. There were little creeks and gullies to be negotiated and from them we flushed wood, green and common sandpipers. Snipe were everywhere and so were cattle egrets, bush larks and pipits, wagtails, little ringed plovers, greenshank, the list was endless.

A beautiful black-bellied tern, its rose-red bill glowing a deeper red in the evening sun, flew down the river but what I had my eye on above all else was something that crouched motionless on a big sandbank, an almost shapeless creature of a creamy-pinky-pearly shade with no real distinguishing marks that I could discern. As we crept slowly nearer my suspicions were confirmed and I found myself gazing at two great stone plovers with their strange, meaningless face pattern and in the centre of it those two large, demented eyes that stared fixedly back at me. The birds neither ran nor flew but one squatted in a sexually inviting position while the other ignored both her and me. I could not get really close to them for the river ran between the sandbank and me but I saw them well. Very few birds have this quality of absolute strangeness, potoos, nightjars and stone curlews for example, but none that I have seen so far is quite the equal of this extraordinary creature with its unwieldy bill, peculiar patterning and wild eye from which all intelligence seems to have departed. This is an obviously anthropomorphic reaction for the bird is perfectly well able to take care of itself.

After this climax we went slowly back to camp, flushing more new birds on the way, more than satisfied with a day that had afforded me the sight of a giant squirrel, two blue-bearded bee-eaters and two great stone plovers.

There was even more to come for as I ate my supper I heard three different kinds of owl, one that I could not place, another whose call sounded like 'tic-TOC-tic' and a third which said what the Flemings described as 'bu-ku' but which I thought sounded more like 'thank-you'. This was apparently the tawny fish owl. To lie in my tent with three new owls lulling me to sleep was all that I could desire.

The luck of the previous day continued next morning for we flushed a chestnut bittern from a ditch as we set off down the valley. We walked along the forest edge with the narrowing valley and the river on our right. There were spur-winged lapwings on every sand-bank, a honey buzzard flew by, an osprey came over to fish and both black-bellied and river terns, the last with a big orange-yellow bill, were fishing.

We stopped for lunch in the shade of some trees, many of them erythrinas, thick with brilliant scarlet, tubular flowers that held the nectar beloved by many species. They were covered with bulbuls, mynas and drongos and as I watched a flock of unknown birds flew in, some with black heads and white-centred, orange-red breasts, others, presumably females, were more dully dressed. They were very beautiful, very greedy and rather excitable, hopping about and feeding rapidly. They looked like rather beautiful starlings and a search through the invaluable book showed them to be a relative, the spot-winged stare.

When we went on after lunch we had to take to the jungle again. A previous upheaval of the land had produced many small cliffs with intervening depressions and sometimes the river flowed right at the foot of these cliffs, so that people walking had to turn into the jungle, climb to the top of the cliff and down again before regaining the riverside.

This cliff-top jungle was full of enormous fallen leaves. All tropical leaves seem big to me but these were of fantastic size. One seemed almost circular but when I picked it up I discovered that it had folded in half and when opened it had the quite unexpected but certain shape of a human behind. Another was even bigger, rather in the shape of a long beech leaf. When measured against my skirt, which was 25 inches, it projected a further 2 inches, without the stalk. Scuffling through fallen leaves is always a joy but scuffling through these monsters produced a rustle of enormous proportions. Tule and I shuffled through them with abandon and to hell with dignity and thoughts of age. Their beautiful colouring contained something of all the rotting, mouldy shades so popular nowadays, from silvery grey with a mauvish tinge through every nuance of exquisite decay.

When we left this delightful plateau to descend to river level we had to find a place to camp. There was a high wind blowing by then and I discovered a sheltered bay which seemed fine. Unhappily there was a dead dog there already and no vultures had yet discovered it.

Tule then found another good site on the shore where the river bent sharply right, past a most splendid example of geological upheaval where the ground had been folded so steeply that the strata were almost upright. This toothed example of nature's force was thickly forested above. The river ran swiftly at its foot with sandbars in the centre and on them were several pairs of spur-winged lapwings and little ringed plovers. The Flemings had not exaggerated when they told me that the Mai valley was good for birds.

As I sat eating supper two young men appeared carrying between them a long pole on which three bundles were strung. There were few houses in this very remote district but these two were travelling salesmen flogging plastic belts and other Western junk for which Nepalese peasants could surely have little use. On the other hand the men would surely not have made so long a journey without any hope of reward.

In the morning several youths with guns over their shoulders, to my sorrow, waded across the river. It did not appear to be very deep and I decided that I would like to go over too as I badly wanted to see what lay round the bend. The porters were surprised but agreed to humour the sporting old thing and Tule, as usual, offered to carry me but I said that I preferred to wade.

He and I and Bodri put on our plimsolls and launched into the stream. I was in the middle in case of accident. We splashed on in wonderfully warm water which never came to more than 3 inches above my knees, only stopping momentarily when I was overcome by giggles realising that I was engaged in a rather ridiculous ploy.

It was magically lovely round the bend with fold upon fold of jungle-encrusted rock opposite the white sandy beach on which we sat. There were no houses or clearings or felled trees visible and no sign of human beings. And then, suddenly, 12 young women appeared, all wearing saris or long skirts and some carrying large pots on their heads. They waded into the river and across with total unconcern.

I left Tule and Bodri sitting on the sand and went to explore what would obviously be a small watercourse in the monsoon. Now it was a high-sided cleft in the forest, twisting backwards and forwards and beckoning me on irresistibly. I saw forktails, maroon orioles, blue rock thrushes and sunbirds of several kinds and still could not bring myself to go back for nothing is more seductive than a path that bends as frequently as unravelled knitting wool.

After about half an hour of this delectable exploration I heard Tule coming up behind me and prepared to go back with him but he said no, we should go on for this little path would obviously come out on the river bank just opposite our camp. It did end there but not at ground level and we found ourselves on top of a 50-foot cliff from which we looked down at our tents on the opposite side of the river. Tule urged me on but I was a trifle fearful of trying to scramble down a 50-foot cliff with my stiff knees. He looked resigned but when Memsahib said well, she'd try if he could help her a great deal, he brightened visibly and began to find or construct steps where none had been before. Eventually, by dint of much skilful manoeuvring on his part and a lot of trusting to luck on mine, I stumbled and slithered down the 50-foot drop and so waded over to camp and lunch that Bodri had already prepared.

Just after we had started back up My Belly, a small avian fragment darted past my head and alighted on the very top of a nearby tree. I was breathless with excitement as so frequently on this trip for it was a red-thighed falconet, only 7 inches long, black and white with a rusty throat and trousers, a ferocious midget that I had hoped so much to see. I brought out my telephoto lens in an attempt to photograph it but such good luck was not to be and in a few seconds the piebald arrow had sped on its way.

We walked on steadily throughout the day, still finding new birds every so often, until we returned to our lovely camp in the forest. I was very tired after the day's exertions and flopped down to rest but not before I saw in the dimming light a lone spoonbill flying past. It was 'very scarce' according to the Flemings.

I had seldom visited a more beguiling place than this enchanting Mai valley which contained so many birds and I left next day with profound regret. We returned to Sunischari by a different route which Tule was unable to explain to me in English, but we joined a road in the forest about half a mile beyond where we had camped on our first night. We reached there between 3 and 4 in the afternoon, the best time of day for seeing birds, and the place was almost choked with them. Within 10 minutes I saw three sights as lovely as any that had gone before. The first bird sat high in a bush surveying the landscape, a tall, slim creature, elegant as a Vogue model, its plumage grey, black and white and its breast a soft, pale rose pink. My very first rosy minivet looked quite disinterested and left far too soon.

Before I had time to repine at the brevity of the encounter my attention was taken by a small bird that was attacking a bamboo stem with great assiduity and undisguised impatience. It was a spotted piculet, a tiny woodpecker only $3\frac{1}{2}$ inches long but, like so many small people, assertive to a degree. It had a rather disproportionately large head and was yellowish-green with a black-spotted creamy breast. When I inspected the bamboo after the bird had left I could see no trace of the hammerings to which it had just been subjected.

And then Tule drew my attention to yet another new and lovely bird. This was a rufous-breasted blue flycatcher, not much bigger than the piculet. It was brilliant blue, almost royal, with an orange-red breast and very short, very thick white eyebrows which gave it a rather enquiring expression. It zipped in and out of the foliage in almost perpetual motion and occasionally flew down to peck in the damp ground under the bushes.

Next morning necessitated a very early start as we had to walk to Sunischari and then go by public transport to Dharan. Before 1 o'clock we had managed the walk that had taken all our first day. I hired a jeep that was in a most dangerously dilapidated state and in it we jolted to Birthe just in time to catch the bus to Dharan. This bus was very ill and needed a long drink of water at every mile or so to enable it to jerk along. When there was a longer distance between villages the conductor took on further cans of water which slopped all over the bus and the passengers before it was used.

We managed to reach the bus station where I enquired as to the whereabouts of the British Army cantonment. The superintendent provided me with a chair, tea and the use of his telephone with which to ask my compatriots if I could camp in the cantonment grounds, mentioning diffidently that I was a friend or Dr. Fleming's. This worked like a charm and I was told to come over at once. It was a long walk but we made it just before dusk and presented ourselves at the main gate, a distinctly grubby Memsahib, Tule and three porters, all rather the worse for wear.

I was told to speak on the telephone to the duty officer who said yes, of course I could camp in the cantonment if I liked but wouldn't I prefer to come and take pot luck with him and his wife? I thought then, and still think now, that this was the most amazingly spontaneous offer of hospitality that I had ever had. I accepted with alacrity and the duty officer soon arrived, gave orders for the porters to be shown to their quarters, and took me home to his luxurious bungalow. Here I received a welcome as warm as if I had been a long lost friend, and my first bath for three and a half weeks.

Next day, after a tour of the cantonment, the Army sent us by Land Rover to the Kosi barrage, of which I had heard so much. This large barrage, built across the Kosi river to control excessive flooding in the monsoon, resulted in a build-up of water in the hinterland which has created marshes and damp areas, splendid habitat for duck, waders and water birds of all kinds. I found the barrage terrifying, rearing its ugly head high above the river which swirled in evil eddies behind it. As it gave this sinister impression in the dry season whatever would it be like in the monsoon?

A road led in behind it to a little observatory some three-quarters of a mile away and there we were to camp. I noticed a large number of sandbanks in the river and on them great numbers of ducks. When the fierce heat of the sun subsided Tule and I walked back towards the main road, looking to the right for birds of scrubby grassland and marsh and to the left for those of the river and sandbanks.

I could hardly credit the wealth of bird life that was all around us. Apart from the thousands of duck on the sandbanks, too far off for definite identification with the exception of the obvious orange Brahminy, the white-patched widgeon and the easily recognisable pintail, there were five different terns, the two that I had seen in the Mai Valley, plus the gull-billed tern, the tiny, acrobatic little tern and the enormous Caspian with its punishing pillar-box-red bill.

There were flocks of openbill storks, a great many egrets and herons of various species, a flock of more than 100 curlew, whose wild whistles took me straight back to Norfolk, and as evening drew on little pratincoles by the dozen, the score and then in hundreds, never flying in close formation but each one performing its own complicated convolutions above the river, a wonderful whirling and plaiting with never a collision.

There were greenshanks in numbers which I found hard to credit, many different sandpipers and plovers and one great stone plover, looking saner than its counterpart in the Mai valley, bee-eaters and shrikes on the telephone wires and eagles and harriers beating over the marshes; further on there were many odd passerines such as wrynecks and bluethroats. It was indeed an *embarras de richesse*.

Next morning, soon after dawn, I went out again before the heat built up and saw a great many more birds that had not been there on the previous day, the best of all being two greater black-headed gulls.

By the end of the afternoon a terrific wind had risen and I could see little as the air was full of dust. This, together with the intense heat, made me grateful for the shelter of the Land Rover that had been sent to fetch me. I reached the Butlers' bungalow filthy, sweaty, dishevelled and aching for the comfort of their large warm bath. I was in it within a few seconds of my arrival but as I lay down to soak I felt an obstruction on my back that prevented me from lying down flat. I found to my horror that I had plunged in wearing the money belt containing my passport, travellers cheques and money. I sprang out with creditable swiftness, called to my hostess and handed her the not quite sodden mass to dry out as best she could.

Next morning I was taken to the airport and seen off, never before having received such kindness. My bird list for the trip was 256. Bob Fleming, Jnr. had told me before I left that with luck it might reach 160. It just shows what you can do if you go to the right places with a good book.

When I reached Kathmandu I had to ring the British Embassy to ask if a rather crinkled passport and slightly smudged visa and travellers cheques would still be acceptable as I had got into the bath whilst wearing my money belt. I was asked to bring them to the embassy for inspection where the models of British impassivity who handled them neither laughed nor expressed surprise but merely examined the questionable articles carefully and said that they thought all would be well.

After three days in Kathmandu I was ready to start on my second trek: a two-part affair specially planned by Bob Fleming, Jnr.

He was sending me first to an area which he guarded jealously as it was remote and almost unvisited and contained many of Nepal's rarest birds. He had drawn little maps showing me just where to find the desirable creatures.

He told me that this part of the country was largely composed of thick, untouched forest in which there were leopards and as this was the breeding season they would be calling with a kind of unmistakable coughing. If I heard this it would be wisest to retreat.

There were also, he assured me, a number of bears and as these were savage and prone to attack it would be better not to go out alone but always to take one of the men with me. He may have been teasing me, but he was a kind and responsible man and I was prone to believe him.

For the second half of this trek I was to go to another kind of forest which held different types of birds and from there was to press onwards and upwards until I reached a height of about 15,000 feet, where there was beautiful country, a spectacular lake and great numbers of birds. He knew of only one party that had been there and they had seen Hodgson's grandalas, those wonderful violet-blue birds that I had seen only in bad light near the Hinko cave in 1971, plus snow partridges and many other high-altitude goodies.

Tule and the porters left very early by bus and I went by plane with orders to await their arrival. The bus was badly delayed and I waited for many hours while the bright sky grew grey and murky and finally became a vicious, dirty purple. At the same time a strong wind blew up.

I felt rather apprehensive but when Tule arrived at 4 p.m. all seemed to be well. We took a jeep to the top of the town from which we were to walk to our camp but by then the wind had become almost a gale, dust and debris blew in every direction and suddenly it began to hail, great stones almost half an inch in diameter. This was not a very jolly start to the new trek but the hail did not last very long and we were able to make camp in dry weather although growling thunder and sheet lightning continued for many hours.

Next morning was fine and sunny and the mountains showed clearly at first. The path was full of trekkers bound for higher altitudes but we left them after an hour or so and took a route through rice paddies. We lunched by a river where giant kingfishers, which I can watch happily for hours on end, zoomed up and down.

After crossing a rather wobbly bridge we climbed to a beautiful upland path and swung along it happily. The weather, which should have improved after the thunderstorm of the previous day, deteriorated rapidly and the sky became thick with menacing clouds. We hurried on towards a village where Tule, who suspected the worst from the weather, was anxious to camp in the school. Suddenly thunder began, followed a few minutes later by torrential rain, like stair rods.

Tule, with the rest of us in tow, made for the nearest house. We were given shelter and sat on straw mats in the gathering gloom waiting for the storm to blow over. It showed no intention of doing so and the rain grew heavier and heavier until it turned to hail even bigger than that of the night before.

After an hour Tule disappeared, coming back to tell me that the school was far away but that we could stay for the night in a house very near at hand. He led me out to the path, which was by then a running stream, and into a house thick with dust and crammed with people and, pointing to a wide shelf about two feet above the floor, said that I could sleep there.

The windowless room was full of men, mostly smoking and coughing, but I had no choice. I had a cold coming and felt rather poorly and was not really enjoying the new trek. At about 6 p.m. the rain eased off for a few minutes and the men departed but this still left the porters, Tule, a mass of staring children and odd people coming and going continually.

Suddenly there was a terrific clap of thunder and the rain began again, even more violently than before. Little drowned girls ran in and out bringing bundles of wood for the fire, which produced smoke

173

of a peculiarly pungent kind that made my eyes run and increased the coughing all round.

I could not talk, as nobody spoke English and my Nepali was non-existent, and as there was no light available I could not read, crochet or do anything at all. There was nothing to do but sleep though as my little hutch had only a half door between it and the main room the coughing, spitting and snoring made this almost impossible. The atmosphere was very thick, as with no windows and a closed front door no fresh air could enter. It was a far cry from Tiger Tops.

The morning was dry but obviously destined to become wet fairly soon. We thanked our host and hostess and trotted off as soon as possible to our next stop. To my suprise the sky cleared, the sun came out, birds appeared and all was well.

We again lunched by a stream and then climbed to a lovely stone-built village. We were not allowed to camp there and had to go beyond to an as yet unplanted terrace which commanded an extensive view. This seemed fine but at 5 p.m. the sky blackened and the usual thunderstorm took over.

I did not feel happy for my cold was worsening. The colds one catches in Nepal are not the ordinary English kind, but incapacitating afflictions that make one feel fit for nothing. I stayed in bed next day, my sleeping pad and bag being taken outside in the sun and put where I could enjoy the best view. Apparently nobody noticed that they had been placed between two large heaps of dung that were destined to be spread before planting began.

Soon after breakfast I saw a small party go up a nearby hill, some of them beating drums and blowing tinny trumpets and with them was a small child, dragging a little buffalo calf. Tule said that this was a *puja,* and the calf was to be sacrificed. Fortunately this occurred out of sight and earshot for I am not tough enough to watch with equanimity while animals are sacrificed.

By evening my temperature had gone down and I felt better. Thunder rumbled in the distance but there was no rain and I decided that, all being well, we would push on in the morning. This dawned fine and clear and I hoped that normal Nepalese spring weather would now begin.

We started fairly early and crossed a corner of thin forest. Within ten minutes I had the reviving sight of a blue-headed rock thrush with its pale blue head, darker blue wings with a white shoulder spot and tomato breast and rump. This smart and sprightly bird was followed almost immediately by an orange-headed ground thrush, which so many others had seen but I had never found before. Some laughing thrushes plunged into the undergrowth before I could check their indentity, yellow-cheeked tits performed prodigies of acrobatics amongst the branches, the first verditer flycatcher flew past and I had a magnificent view of a rusty-cheeked scimitar babbler, a rather angry looking bird which was grubbing among the roots of the trees for its breakfast. There were so many birds about that I could not look at everything properly.

We came out of the forest on to a path that went up the hillside and I soon realised that far from feeling better I was feeling much worse, both faint and giddy. I knew that I could not climb for a couple of thousand feet; all I could hope for was to remain upright until Tule could find a place to camp which he quickly did in a little dell that looked in to the forest. I lay down once more, furious, for nothing is more maddening than to waste good birding time by being taken ill on trek. I lay there, learning *The Birds of Nepal* almost by heart and staring hopefully into the second-growth forest where some mature trees had been left, many with a froth of *Coelogyne cristata* pouring down their moss-grown trunks.

Although I could not take anything but tea and fruit juice my interest in birds was fully maintained and in the afternoon I noticed a green shape disappearing behind a leaf, one of those over-large leaves of Asia. A little bit of red showed from time to time which indicated that the bird was neither a bee-eater nor a chloropsis. When the bird emerged at last I found that it was a golden-throated barbet which the book described as 'fairly common but rather difficult to see': very difficult indeed if this bird were a true sample of the species.

It was nice to add another to my life list but barbets are not a family that appeals to me. Their heavy beaks and rather hunched, thick-necked appearance reminds me inescapably of over-fed, under-exercised business men who are not very attractive as a group. Their voices, with the exception of the wild, shrill call of the great Himalayan barbet, are on the whole monotonous to the point of desperation, mostly single notes, penetrating aural hammering that goes on and on, seemingly for ever.

In the late afternoon I was looking at a rather odd, grey thrush when my eye again caught something green, which is not unusual in mid-forest. This was not a moving leaf but a portion of some living thing. It was quite small and when it came out of the concealing foliage presented only a rear view, a back of brilliant, polished green, shining and gay as a Christmas-tree bauble. Its head shone too but more darkly and I could not decide if it were a deeper green, dark royal blue or even black.

I had a flash of intuition which only a front view could confirm but would the provoking creature turn? When it deigned to look slightly to one side I caught a glimpse of a vivid, orange-yellow bill. When I was almost in despair it turned, disclosing a white breast and under-parts closely barred with fine black lines. I was so excited that I was trembling for I knew then that I was looking at an emerald cuckoo, described as 'very scarce'. This beautiful little parasite had, so I found out later, been seen only once before in Nepal and it left me as unobtrusively as it had arrived.

I spent nearly two days recovering in this forest camp but never saw anything to equal the emerald cuckoo. Every morning and evening I heard all around me the mournful, carrying call of the satyr tragopan. This was the third time that I had camped where it had been close at hand and yet I had never managed to see it, even though the male should have been easy to see in his white-spotted, scarlet plumage.

We set off again in good spirits through scrubby hillside and forest, which became wilder and thicker as we climbd. There were birds in quantity and I enjoyed myself and felt much better and when we reached the top of the slope there was a lovely glade with a good view to one side and an inviting path through tall deep forest on the other.

Tule and Bodri set off to get water for lunch and I stayed to see what I could find. Suddenly it began to rain, harder and harder. Eskay, one of the new porters, was gathering wood and the other one, Asa, was sitting in the open, watching the baggage get wet. As the rain soaked through the bag containing my down jacket, he just sat there in the middle of the downpour. I put a bit of plastic over my precious down jacket and retired to shelter under a thick tree, motioning to Asa to move too. He chose not to understand me and remained in the open, stoically soaking up the rain.

Tule returned shortly and set about Asa verbally and the luggage physically. Both were quickly moved to shelter and Asa was made to work, something to which he never took kindly. He did not have a religious fixation, as Ganza had had, merely an allergy towards any kind of effort. He was doing very nicely on this trek being paid 15 rupees a day for carrying and having spent three of them sitting immovably. He seemed to be convinced that his function was to be the life and soul of the party and to keep up the others' spirits by singing tuneless songs and banging out a noisy rhythm on anything that came to hand, from a plate to a piece of wood. Poor Asa, he irritated me profoundly for, while all the others could interpret signs and gestures, he did not choose to and remained unmoved and uncomprehending, try as I might to communicate.

After lunch in the shelter of the big trees we climbed up through steep forest. Suddenly the rain began again, heavy rain alternating with even heavier hail. Tule motioned me towards the overhang of a large rock and I climbed under it as best I could and so did Bodri but the poor porters were in a bad way for, as usual, none had any change of clothing and they were drenched and shivering.

The resourceful Tule dashed here and there looking for dry leaves and twigs and although the wind was quite strong managed to light a fire round which the porters huddled gratefully.

In between storms we struggled up until we reached our camp site, a damp, rushy area which buffalo had been churning up but which contained a few drier spots where we could put tents.

By this time Asa had managed to get my down jacket really wet by putting it on top of his load. One of my sleeping bags was also wet. My tent leaked in the middle and I had to sleep to one side of it. Altogether I felt rather a misery. I went through one of the phases of wondering why on earth I undertook treks which were at times so very hard and unhappy.

Next morning was bright, sunny and exquisitely beautiful. Behind us a magnificent snow mountain gleamed blue-white and cold and I reached for my camera. Last night's discomforts seemed like a bad dream and I took heart.

Tule and I went out to explore the sort of country we were now in. The forest, dense and wonderful, held many splendid old trees but few rhododendrons. Some of the trees looked rather like sweet chestnuts and there were many others that I did not know at all. Some had one huge solid trunk, others had a clustered growth of many smaller uprights but all trunks of whatever size, and every branch and twig as well, were covered with a heavy moss, like thick green cream. Some types had what looked to me like little leaves, spurs and tendrils and some had long streamers that hung towards the ground. The whole effect was of a damp, mysterious gloom, in which everything was covered in living, olive plush.

The forest floor was a thick carpet of dead leaves and more moss, so spongy and wet that it was all too easy to slip. The stones were moss-covered too and when I trod on them the moss slipped aside and I had to struggle to retain my balance.

The forest was gorgeous and fascinating and on the edge of it lay another, this time of fine bamboo, the leaves thin and small and the stems never exceeding half an inch in diameter. They grew close together and all kinds of birds patronised them, as we heard but could not see.

Beyond the forest there was a large upland area, a wide gully of rush, sedge and coarse grass, with a few clumps of bamboo and berberis sticking up here and there. This grassy gully, which rose a thousand or so feet above us, was where we might expect to find the goral, the Nepalese chamois. Tule's X-ray eyes picked one out almost at once, leaping upwards at high speed until it vanished from view. I was quite happy to spend several days in this wonderful place as Bob had advised.

Tule and I tried hard to see the tragopans that were very near and calling persistently but we failed and after lunch I went with Bodri to look again. Ten minutes after we started it began to rain and we had to go back for it was not the sort of Scotch mist that could be braved by the uncaring but a real downpour such as we had come to know only too well.

At 6 o'clock the sky grew even darker but this time it was dusk and not an intensification of cloud cover. And still the rain went on and heavy thunder cracked and rumbled all around. I could not help thinking of the charming old lady I knew in Norfolk who used to insist on getting up, together with her family, dressing and going downstairs immediately a thunderstorm began. She would have had a very tiring time on this trek. When the thunder gave a very loud roll like heavy drums that culminated in a resounding thwack it was as impressive as a climax of percussion in the vastness of the Albert Hall but this constant banging was more in the nature of a pop festival to which one was compelled to listen with no avenue of escape. And to cap it all the brain-fever bird shrieked insistently at intervals.

Next day it seemed that the weather might stay fine for there was no longer the almost feverish brilliance of recent mornings. Tule and I decided to take our lunch and go down to the lower area which Bob had said was so full of good birds. When taking lunch I usually put a little something in a rucksack but Tule collected an enormous amount of food and all manner of cooking utensils, enough to make a back-breaking load. We trotted down in lovely weather enjoying good but not unusual birding, had an excellent and large lunch and started back.

The sun was still shining and I was changing the film in my camera when there was a great clattering and a fairly large bird broke cover and flew off. Tule immediately went to hunt for it and in about 10 minutes crept back and beckoned me to follow. I stole after him till we came to a very tall tree and there, right on top of it, sat a pigeon, an exceptionally well nourished member of this never skinny family. It had a pale grey head, a wide black and buff collar and its grey breast was decorated with beautiful dark spots at the perimeter. The rest of it was dark and it sat there surveying us in a rather comatose way, so lethargic that I thought I could safely try for a photograph. I was mistaken for it took off immediately. It was an ashy wood pigeon, listed as 'occasional'. Tule, rightly, was rather pleased with himself.

We flushed several flocks of large necklaced laughing thrushes and as they flew they uttered a rather grizzling small mew which I found surprising. I heard another more genuinely cat-like mew nearby and this time it turned out to be a maroon oriole with a black head, maroon back and shoulders and a bright red tail, more scarlet than maroon, which it fanned as it alighted. This fine bird frequents high altitudes and has the typical mellow oriole whistle. I never expected it to be author of the mew that I both saw and heard it utter.

Tule was on his mettle that day finding birds that I never even glimpsed before he pointed them out. One of the best was a large niltava, a big dark-blue flycatcher that looks almost black in a poor light, his sombre suiting relieved by a much paler blue crown, blue flashes at the side of his neck and a blue rump. It sat very calmly, occasionally opening and shutting its fairly large black beak, from which came a tiny bat-like squeak. Almost next door to it was another much smaller flycatcher, tiny and navy blue, the blue extending in what looked like lapels on either side of its white breast. It had a long, thin, white eyebrow and, like so many small flycatchers, could not keep still for a moment.

Rain held off until we reached camp but then it began to drizzle and later settled in to the usual heavy downpour.

I retired to bed and was woken at 1 a.m. and again at 5 by the brain-fever bird calling ever more insistently. I heard the rain still pattering on my tent and when I opened the door I looked out on to a new misfortune: the whole area was wrapped in obliterating fog.

After breakfast I drew out my crochet yet again. I could write a monograph on the therapeutic effect of crochet, for it had helped me to withstand the ravages of dysentery in Brazil, long bus journeys over washed-out roads in Ecuador, a three-day wait for engine repair on a Costa Rican river, twelve-hour journeys in the dust of Indian trains and many other tiresome troubles. Not only does it help to pass the time and distract the mind but I have something to show for my trouble when all is over. How I longed for something to read, someone to talk to or something else to do. This mountain was my desert island and I had no discs.

Next day it was not actually raining although Tule looked at the sky and said 'No good, water coming!' I asked Tule if he thought it would be all right to go down, which meant 500 feet of ascent first, as four days in rain and cloud had been more than enough and we had seen nothing of what I had come so far to see. He said all should be well so we started off.

We had first to cross the grassy gully where the goral lived. Normally there was a wonderful and extensive view over miles of untouched forest down to the valley below but all we could see in the mist was a trifle of sedge and bamboo emerging from time to time. The path, which led straight across the very steep hillside, was not more than a foot wide and in places only six inches. It was sometimes muddy, sometimes stoney and often almost worn away so that I had to keep a close watch on where I put my feet. The porters, younger and more sure-footed, went ahead and Tule and I made slower progress, catching them up when they were resting and Asa doing his usual 'Oh I am such a funny man!' act.

At 11 o'clock we completed the crossing of the gully and Tule, Bodri and I sat down to rest, Eskay and Asa having already gone ahead. In five minutes I decided that it was high time for us to start the descent. All around us men had been cutting the thin bamboos, leaving the small ends lying about and as I got up I trod on some of these and fell heavily, striking my right ribs on a large, sharply pointed stone. The pain was frightful and I screamed loudly. I am not brave, and we were 10,000 feet up in thick forest in swirling mist and at least two days' walk from a village.

The pain was so intense that I felt sure I had broken my ribs but Tule and Bodri prodded me everywhere and pronounced me whole. There was one consolation, both arms and legs were all right so I could walk down when I had recovered slightly, whereas a broken leg would have immobilised me.

I realised, though not immediately, how lucky I had been. The medicine box which I had carried on so many treks was now put to good use. I swallowed a couple of pain killers, Tule massaged my agonisingly painful ribs with Tiger Balm from Singapore and then wrapped my three-inch crepe bandage tightly round my rib cage. This done he suggested walking down but I did not feel I could manage that quite so soon and suggested coffee.

'No water here!' said Tule. And then his resourcefulness again came to the rescue. Water, except that which fell unasked for from the sky, had been in short supply and a long way off at the last camp, and Tule had used my rubber hot-water bottle as an extra utensil when fetching it. He had not emptied the bottle that morning so now he made a fire, emptied the bottle into a pan and presented me with some rubber-flecked coffee, liberally laced with sugar to give me energy. He then scrambled two eggs and made some *chapattis*, not mentioning that as there was no water in the vicinity the porters, who must have been ravenous, would have no rice.

And so we started down, a laborious crawl which became easier as my pain killers started to work. 'How wonderfully brave you were!' said all my friends when I told them of this experience. I was not brave at all. There was nowhere to pitch a tent and no water and, to survive, I had to go down.

Tule, ably assisted by Bodri, behaved angelically. He held my left hand and led me down every inch of the way while I supported my other side with a strong stick. The path was difficult by any standards, sometimes covered with slippery leaves and moss, sometimes a mere muddy slope, an additional hazard being provided by plaited tree roots of varying thicknesses which wound malevolently over the path.

We went down very slowly through this thick dark forest. I heard birds from time to time but could not see them, firstly because of the mist and secondly because my hands were no longer free to hold my binoculars. Sometimes Bodri walked with the other two porters, but often dumped his load with them and then came back to help Tule and me, a kindly gesture that we both appreciated. There was one point at which he was more than useful when we came to what appeared to be a solid wall of rock in which a dozen steps had been cut. With Bodri above and Tule below I managed to get down, only to find that a notched tree trunk led from the ledge on which I stood to the one below. Balanced on these small notches I had to descend the trunk, which my two companions held firmly, and after this came 16 steps down another rock wall.

Added to all the other troubles of this dreadful day there were leeches in profusion. I had not met them in any numbers before and was surprised and disgusted at their pertinacity and skill in getting to a good blood supply. Tule was for ever knocking them off me but, even so, I had bites on hands and legs and another inside the collar of my sweater, where the mess it made was revolting.

After a short rest and another hour's walk we came to a large, flat, grassy field, hemmed in on three sides by forest and with a good stream running through it. It had taken three and a half hours to reach this camp. It was fine and almost sunny by then and I lay down quietly to recover and to reflect on how lucky I was to have Tule and Bodri looking after me with such wonderful care. After all, I had had six previous treks without an accident so, perhaps, I was due for one.

Next morning was still fine but Tule's gloomy prognosis was, as before, 'Water coming!', and I knew that it surely would. He brought my breakfast, massaged my ribs with Tiger Balm and replaced the crepe bandage. As soon as we could, we set off down a replica of yesterday's path, even more profusely decorated with mosses, lichens and liverworts which made me resolve to buy a book on them as soon as I reached home, being now convinced that I would get home and not be left to die in the wilderness.

We struggled on in mist and then torrential rain set in. Luck was with us once more for within a hundred yards was a building, half house and half cattle shed, where the owners, an elderly couple who had passed through our camp the night before, welcomed us warmly. Within a few minutes Tule had taken over their fire, which was housed in a hole, and had made tea for everybody, after which the old woman smoked first a cigarette, then a water pipe and finally what I took to be hash. Tule cooked my lunch and the porters' rice, talking volubly meanwhile to the many callers who appeared from nowhere and settled down for conversation. I brought out my crochet once more during all this, the fineness of the wool and the complexity of the pattern creating enormous interest, particularly among the women.

The rain, which had looked at one time as though it might stop, began again in earnest and there was no shelter of any kind to be had. At 4 o'clock, drenched to the skin, we reached the village school, only to find that the pupils were engaged in some sort of performance until 5. The headmaster was found and was kind and charming and said that certainly we could camp in his school.

'I am afraid,' he said in halting English, 'that it is not very elegant but I hope you will not mind!'

I was extremely grateful and did not mind at all, even though it was filthy. I settled in thankfully and my sleeping pad was placed on two adjacent forms in a windowless classroom. Every child in the school stayed behind to have a look at this extraordinary sight, an English memsahib, very old, soaking wet, with rough hair and covered in leech bites. They only stopped gazing at this fascinating specimen when darkness fell.

They were all there again at 6 the next morning to watch me get up and dress. Wonders of wonders it was fine and warm and the sun was shining. My ribs were not quite so painful and I began to feel a little better. We left early, waved away by about 30 little well-wishers all crying 'Namaste!'.

Excepting one and a half hours spent at lunch we walked and walked and walked until we reached our very first camp site. It was here that I realised what I had not admitted earlier, that I was in no shape to go to 15,000 feet the very next day. I still had horrible pains from time to time, just as though some unkind person were digging amongst my ribs with a screw driver. During the evening, as thunder rolled and rumbled and more rain washed over and around the tent, I decided that I would go to the airport next day to see if I could get a seat on the plane for Kathmandu.

I was lucky again and, leaving Tule and the porters to the bus, I took to the air, full of sorrow at missing the last half of the trek but quite unable to tackle it.

Bob, Snr. was at the airport to meet me, full of concern at my plight. He took me home and Bob, Jnr. and his wife tucked me up in bed, where I stayed for a few days. A visit to the hospital for X-rays showed that my injuries were merely bad bruises and that no bones were broken, a diagnosis which confirmed what I had been told by several people, that bruised ribs were as painful as broken ones.

It was a sad end to what had promised to be a super trek but the weather in 1977 was even worse than it had been when I went to the Annapurna sanctuary in 1971. It would seem that central Nepal is not for me.

Appendix I:
A Word About Nepal

When I first went to Nepal in 1964 I was enchanted by this little-known country ringed by wonderful snowy mountains that glowed pink in the setting sun. It seemed to be almost 200 years behind the times, strange and romantic, though in parts utterly filthy. It was full of temples, many of them pagoda-shaped, some decorated with gold, and others embellished by wooden carvings which were often decidedly erotic. These temples provided plenty of spiritual nourishment but physical nourishment in the shape of hotels and restaurants was hard to find and not very good when available.

There were few roads and cars were conspicuous by their absence. I saw quite a lot of bicycles but transport of goods was mostly on the inhabitants' backs - still the case in the roadless areas - and people walked everywhere. Living conditions were usually extremely primitive but, although unused to visitors, most Nepalis were very friendly with wide, welcoming smiles.

Today, only eighteen years later, the country has changed to an astonishing degree. Many big, modern hotels have been built, quite out of keeping with old Kathmandu. Tourism has now become Nepal's chief source of foreign currency and hotels are full nearly all the time. Less pretentious establishments catering for people with medium and lower incomes have sprung up throughout Kathmandu, most of them staffed by coveys of keen, obliging youths who are desperately anxious to make a success of the job.

There are now a great many small restaurants and also pie shops, the later stuffed to bursting point with Western youth stocking up with enormous slices of chocolate or carrot cake, brownies and apple pie before starting out on trek. Those who have just returned are there too, trying to fill up the empty spaces that seem bottomless, for although trekking doesn't make one inordinately hungry when on the trail nothing seems able to assuage one's hunger when one gets back. (An excellent point in favour of trekking is that it appears to be an infallible method of losing weight: I always manage to discard some 10 to 15 pounds and this is very comforting).

In early days the winding lanes of the bazaar and other streets contained small, open-fronted shops filled with the merchandise that every household needs. Most of these have now gone from the centre where all streets cater for tourists in a big way. They sell everything from rugs, made by the many Tibetan refugees who now live in Nepal, to rings and pendants, bracelets and earrings, for the Nepalese are very good jewellers who charge comparatively low prices. There is an intriguing selection of traditional necklaces to be found in the bead market though this is difficult to locate. There are also holy figures of all kinds, genuine relics - many of them newly made - and an abundance of attractive clothing.

The thing that most men and women buy is a heavy sweater, loosely hand-knitted in thick, local wool and bearing a Nepalese or Tibetan pattern on the front. This can be topped by a woolly hat with a patterned border, both sweater and hat made in natural-coloured wool with the pattern in a darker brown. Almost equally popular are woven jackets in varying stripes and patterns, made in every colour of the rainbow. I never saw a Nepalese wearing one but there is hardly a tourist - and not one under 30 years old - who doesn't buy something of this kind and peacock about in it. Some of them who are over 30 - including one of 70 plus - buy such things too, although it is difficult to discover garments in larger sizes as the Nepalese find it hard to realize that other people are both taller and wider than they are.

Now that there are a few roads in the Kathmandu Valley, and more are being built elsewhere in a valiant effort to modernize this land-locked mountain kingdom, buses go daily to Patan and Bhadgaon, the other two cities of the valley, and to all the big temples nearby. There is also a trolley bus to Bhadgaon and daily services to some other parts of the country.

There was little need for cars in the virtually roadless country of 1964 but Nepal now has a traffic problem. The Chinese have built a road from their border at Kodari to Kathmandu, a fine, metalled highway along which curious visitors can go by bus to look into China. Another road goes from Kathmandu to Pokhara and there is a bus for travellers who cannot afford the air fare for the spectacular trip over the mountains.

The aeroplane is now the most popular means of transport in Nepal and there are daily flights to most of the principal cities and less frequent services to smaller places, with at least one flight a week to more remote regions. Kathmandu airport, which used to accomodate only small planes, has been considerably enlarged and big jets scream in several times a day. Many of the international airlines have offices in the centre of Kathmandu and eager travellers besiege the desks from morning till night.

185

The favourite trip is the Royal Nepalese Airline's flight to the Everest region which takes off every morning between 7 and 8 a.m., depending on the weather. During this hour-long flight over the fabled area the passengers, each one with camera at the ready, can see for themselves, and with little effort or danger, the majesty of the high Himalayas. From this unparalleled vantage point they have a view more extensive than any the humble trekkers can ever see but, having done both, I can assure you that the rapture of seeing at last those sublimely beautiful mountains, after having slogged laboriously towards them for weeks on end, far surpassed anything that I felt when flying over them. This is not to decry the flight by any means, for it is a breath-taking and unforgettable excursion, but getting there under one's own steam and being able to sit down and enjoy the prospect for some considerable time, absorbing the matchless beauty all around is, to my mind, the most wonderful experience in the world.

So much for the good side of Nepalese progress. There are disadvantages too; there always are. While the changes in Kathmandu and its valley are enormous there are marked changes in the countryside too.

On my first, idyllic trek there were very few foreigners about and Nepal was an unspoilt paradise. On my mid-winter trek in 1970 I still saw very few visitors but in 1971 there were a lot of tourists on the Jomson trek and there I saw the first signs of litter and over-use of camp sites. It was on my fourth trek, in the spring of 1973, that I realized how popular trekking had now become, as evidenced by the distressingly obvious litter that had been left behind. It lay all around, great piles of repulsive Western rubbish. And everywhere was toilet paper, short scraps and long ribbons of it, blowing in the wind and defiling the landscape as far as the eye could see. The problem was at its worst from the Thyang Boche monastery to Everest. Litter is revolting, depressing and quite unnecessary wherever it may be left but in Khumbu, and particularly around Thyang Boche, which is a holy area to Buddhists, litter is not only unsightly and distasteful but also a desecration. As all trekkers have a fire to cook and warm themselves at night they can easily burn their day's rubbish then. Dedicated bands of volunteers do go up to clear the trails out of season but it is a Herculean task and one which shouldn't need to be done. Nepal has very few natural resources, the main one being the possession of regions of unique beauty containing many of the world's highest mountains that foreigners come thousands of miles to see. It is a poor reward to the country if its visitors pollute the lovely land that lies all around them by scattering their rubbish over it so freely.

This unpleasant habit may be broken in some measure now that the Everest region has become one of Nepal's national parks, of which there are five: Everest in the northeast, Lake Rara in the northwest, Dolpo and Langtang in the centre, and Chitawan in the south. The charge for entering each park is 60 rupees.

National parks are still a fairly new feature of Nepal's efforts to accommodate their many tourists and when everything is as they wish there will be scheduled camping areas in every park with attendant facilities and also tourist centres, the big one recently built at Namche Bazar making an excellent start. The use of wood as fuel will be forbidden in the parks, for Nepal is lamentably short of wood, particularly in the high areas such as Khumbu. It is likely that trekkers will be allowed to use only kerosene, obtainable at specified depots to which containers must be returned, but the transport of kerosene to remote areas is a complex problem that has not yet been solved.

The usual regulations regarding the picking of flowers, digging up plants and shooting birds and animals also obtain and it is hoped that the establishment of national parks will effectively safeguard the wildlife and scenic beauty of the areas, for mountain habitat, though tough to live in, is of itself fragile and must be carefully safeguarded and respected. To ensure this the parks will be patrolled by men under control of the Nepalese army and transgressors who do not observe the rules will be heavily fined.

All these changes have not yet been enforced in every park. It is hoped that they soon will be but such fundamental alterations take time and cannot be hurried.

The park in the south of Nepal, Chitawan, which is reached by air, is part of the very large forest at the foot of the Churia hills (or should I say mountains?), formerly the hunting region of the King of Nepal, a staunch conservationist who realizes to the full the responsibility his country has for maintaining and preserving its unique quality and its wildlife, a view held by other members of the royal family as well.

In Chitawan tourists can stay at Tiger Tops Jungle Lodge, plushy and expensive, where they can be moderately sure of seeing tiger or leopard on the baits put out each night. They can be quite certain of viewing the rare one-horned Indian rhinoceros on the daily elephant rides which take place in the early morning and in the afternoon. Trekkers can go to either the Elephant Camp or Gaida in a different part of the park for cheaper accommodation and a chance of seeing the same animals but in less luxurious conditions.

As many tourists now come to Nepal to trek as those who arrive for a less arduous visit. The trekkers bring a great deal of money into the country and it is sad to see that a few Nepalese - intrinsically such willing, delightful and infinitely lovable people - are being adversely affected by its impact. They see hordes of apparently rich visitors, hung with cameras, interchangeable lenses, telescopes, binoculars and who knows what else, coming into their beautiful country, many of them wearing expensive new clothing and boots. They cannot be blamed for realizing that the distribution of all this wealth is unequal and asking why they shouldn't have their share. Such an attitude is understandable for the average Nepali outside the main centres — and often inside them — is desperately poor and probably lives in a very simple house with no gas, electricity or plumbing, subsisting on very scanty rations.

Nepal's population is increasing at a prodigious rate — family planning has a long way to go — and there is little industry to absorb it and insufficient land to grow enough food. In this small, crimped country, which would be quite sizeable if ironed flat, the amount of cultivable land is sadly restricted and although the farmers terrace it up to 10,000 feet, and sometimes more, there is a limit to their ingenuity. In many places forests are being rapidly cut down to clear more ground for planting with grain and potatoes. This is not always a wise move for many forests lie on steep slopes and their removal can cause landslides which constitute a great danger to people living below. Erosion is yet another big problem for when the monsoon comes earth that was formerly held in place by trees is washed down from higher altitudes by the turbulent streams. The good soil is then lost and the silt raises the level of river beds on the plains below and intensifies risk of flooding. And still the babies come and the trees go.

Nepal possesses no coal or oil and is dependant on wood for heating, cooking and building material. To meet these needs forests are being cleared with frightening speed in the vicinity of places such as Namche Bazar, where many of the hillsides are already bare. What Nepal will do in even twenty years, when ample wood is no longer available, is a disturbing thought, for people in high regions such as Khumbu cannot live without fuel. There is re-afforestation, of course, but this is small compared with the rate of cutting that is still going on, particularly in hill districts far removed from supervision. Around nearly every village the biggest trees have already gone and smaller trees and bushes are all that remain.

Felling trees is forbidden in Nepal but when the family is cold and there is no fuel to cook their food it is not surprising to find that this rule is often ignored. There is much fine timber in the Terai, the low-lying area near the Indian border, and this is being ruthlessly exploited. Unfortunately there is also a lot of tree poaching, despite precautions, and although the forestry department has guards on duty at all times they are no match for the gangs of armed men with bullock carts who go to the forest at night, cut down a tree, take it quickly over the border and sell it at a good price.

A further anxiety is the provision of food for livestock. There are numberless cattle in Nepal, a predominantly Hindu kingdom whose religion forbids their slaughter. There is little grass available for animals and the substitute is leaves. These are ruthlessly cut from trees and bushes as soon as they appear, a custom which kills them in time.

Despite the rapid modernization and increasing population of Nepal, both of which make one look back regretfully to some of the picturesque features of the country that are no more, there is still much that one can both love and admire. No one with an atom of sensitivity can fail to be moved by the incomparable beauty of the country in all its different aspects and by the widely different cultures of its many races. All of them have abundant charm, great friendliness and a wish to please, three very endearing qualities. Small, mostly slim and exceedingly strong, the Nepalis remain good-humoured and cheerful in almost any situation, regardless of their poverty. To me the Nepalese are not merely pleasant people who form a picturesque background to a Himalayan trip. After so many visits to their country they are men and women whom I know well and for whom I have a deep love and concern. They so much deserve an easier life than they lead at present.

Nepal has managed to achieve an enormous amount in a very short time. It still has a long way to go and many intractable problems to solve, not the least of them financial.

Political differences have also emerged in the past year or so and Nepal's individual form of government has recently changed in some measure. More modern and sophisticated development cannot be ruled out for the future but this formerly backward and rapidly developing Hindu kingdom remains under the rule of its young monarch, H.M. King Birendra.

Nepal has received a great deal of help and advice from many organisations such as the World Bank, the United Nations Development Programme and other international bodies such as the OPEC Fund. Bilateral aid is also received, the largest contributors being Britain, China, India, Japan, the United States and West Germany. The Nepalese, having profited by the expertise so generously provided, are now beginning many projects on their own. They make mistakes: they will surely make more but their feet are, it is hoped, pointing in the right direction and many of their rough paths are being turned into paved roads.

Appendix II:
Useful Hints for a Trek

Trekking may be just the thing for you if you are reasonably healthy and accustomed to walking long distances, but remember that it is arduous, can be exhausting and may be dangerous. If you are made of the same stuff as I am, however, and long to walk in Nepal more than anything else in the world, whatever hardships it may entail, then off you go and good luck.

The first thing to decide is whether to go on a package tour, with a small party of friends or completely on your own.

You don't have to think for yourself on a package tour but you have to go when and as your leader decides for the requisite number of miles per day and there is no time for lingering. On the credit side you will have a leader who knows the country and the route, competent Sherpas and porters and plenty of people to help you should anything go wrong.

The second alternative is to make up your party and go to a recognized trekking organization which will provide equipment, plot your route, engage Sherpas and porters and tell you what supplies to buy. You have more freedom but also more responsibility and you must take enough to pay porters and Sherpas and to buy food and fuel on the way. You can, however, go at your own pace and stop when and where you like, always bearing in mind that in certain areas camping is impossible because there is no water. A good supply of water is essential and you must trust your Sherpa over this. You may be unwilling to stop at three o'clock when you are quite able to go further but if there is no good water for another five miles, it is better to stay where you are and to set off a little earlier than usual next morning.

The way in which I have done all my own treks is the solo trip. I find it splendid and most rewarding. 'Solo', of course, refers to the tourist; I always took a Sherpa and porters. In 1968 porters cost 10 rupees a day and the Sherpa sirdar was 15; in 1977 the prices had risen to 18 to 20 and 30 rupees respectively. They will surely be more by the time you read this.

The cheapest way of all and the best, if you are young, healthy and tough, is to go with one or two friends, carrying your own pack containing a sleeping bag, change of clothing and a few personal effects. If you carry a light tent you can sleep where you wish. In the last few years conditions have altered in some measure and now it is unwise to go alone and pitch a solitary tent. People doing this have been attacked and killed and robbery, sometimes with violence, is not unknown. This is a sad and most unpleasant development but don't let it discourage you: the average Nepali is fine. If you don't camp you must stay in a house or a Sherpa hotel. A Sherpa hotel is really a one-roomed house, sometimes fitted with a wooden shelf about 18 inches from the floor, sometimes not. You lie in your sleeping bag in the closest proximity to your neighbour. If you are cold the crowding makes for warmth; if you are a light sleeper and some people snore you don't do so well.

Washing and sanitary accommodation are alike non-existent and you must wait till you get to the nearest stream, lake or bush for such necessary facilities.

Have a medical check-up before you go and be sure that your feet can be trusted to carry you comfortably for long periods. If you are wearing climbing boots for the first time it is wise to buy them long before you leave and break them in to good effect. You won't need them for the whole time but they are absolutely necessary at high altitude and on snow or ice. Good walking shoes are all right lower down and I have found that strong plimsolls are the best wear in the valleys for though they are tough they are light. Many Sherpas and porters wear them in preference to anything else.

When you have been passed fit by your doctor it is best to have injections. I always have TABT and cholera, and also smallpox, although this is not now considered obligatory. It's a good thing to have a polio preventive too. Check about the incidence of malaria in the district you propose to visit and if in doubt take pills for that as well. The dosage is very simple, one a week while you are there and the same amount for a few weeks before you go and after you return.

Hepatitis is another danger. It is quite prevalent in Nepal and it is wise to have a gamma globulin injection. This is not always easy to arrange and as it doesn't last for very long the best thing to do is to have it when you get to Kathmandu. The Kalamati Clinic there gives these swift and painless jabs every Friday and the last time I had one, in 1977, it cost 65 rupees. Whatever it costs now, the expenditure is worthwhile.

Take a small supply of medicines with you: plasters in various sizes for blisters or cuts, a few bandages of different sizes, a small quantity of reliable disinfectant and, very definitely, pills for the almost inevitable stomach upsets. A few indigestion tablets are a good thing, too, as Nepali food doesn't suit everyone at first. People are inclined to get bad throats at high altitude so take some antiseptic throat tablets and cough lozenges. Pack a plentiful supply of aspirin or paracetamol, for women are apt to come up to you, especially if you are travelling alone, clasping an ailing baby and asking for something for a fever. An aspirin — or a piece of one for a small child — does no harm and the giving of it promotes good will. And just in case you do get anything really nasty it is best to carry a course of some broad spectrum antibiotic for most of the time you'll be out of reach of doctors or hospitals. If you are going really high take some sleeping pills. I can't sleep well above 10,000 feet without some slight assistance. This is a widespread experience and I remember the leader of the Italian Mount Everest Expedition telling me that everyone at the Base Camp, including the Sherpas, took a nightly pill.

A little vaseline is helpful for chapped skin or finger tips that crack in deep frost, as they always seem to do, and a good supply of suntan cream or lotion and glacier cream for use above 10,000 feet is vital. A little glacier cream rubbed well in each day prevents swollen, cracked and bleeding lips which are acutely painful.

The most important item of all, for you can't go without it, is your trekking permit. You get it in Kathmandu at the Immigration Office in Raj Path. This took no time at all in 1964 but it is very different now when milling hordes beseige the office thoughout the day. Take with you your passport, two extra photographs and a pen for form filling. You will be given a long form to complete asking for all the usual passport details and a lot more besides, including the name of the place you want to trek to and the details of your route there and back. When you have completed the form, in duplicate, you must leave it, together with your passport and the two photographs, to be collected next day - with luck. Before being given your permit you must show that you have at least $5 a day (or its equivalent in your own currency) for the entire period in which you intend to travel on foot. Carry your permit everywhere and show it on demand. In 1977 these permits cost 15 rupees a week, plus 1 rupee for a stamp, payable once only. Trekkers can walk for as long as their vistas are valid.

Visas, obtainable at Nepalese embassies in foreign countries or in emergency at Kathmandu airport, used to be issued for short periods only but now they can be had for 30 days and can be renewed in Kathmandu for not more than two further 30-day periods, making 90 days in all. This is as much as the most dedicated trekker will need, I think, for I found that after 50 days I was thinking far oftener than I had thought possible of a real bed, succulent food and a deep, hot bath. The cost of visas works out at an averge of about 11 rupees a week which is quite reasonable.

Clothes are a very personal affair but there are certain basic garments that everyone needs: strong trousers — I found corduroy good for most of the way but took a thicker pair for higher up — an anorak, some kind of waterproof jacket and leggings, a down jacket, thick gloves, sweaters (one light and one heavy) with polo collars, and woollen underwear, including long johns. And plenty of good, thick socks.

In the lowland valleys on the long approach to Everest it is very hot. Men can wear shorts but it is impolite for women to do this as it offends Nepalese susceptibilities. I know that when in Rome you should do as the Romans do but this is a bit much to ask in Nepal where all the women wear ankle-length skirts, long sleeves and plenty of jewellery. I wore a knee length cotton skirt and cotton sleeveless blouse in the lowlands and sweater and cords higher up, adding further layers as the temperature dictated. At Gorakshep and the Base Camp I wore everything I possessed all at once and took very, very little off at night.

You need a plastic bottle to carry water which has been boiled on the previous night, because you get very thirsty when trekking. You also need a rubber hot-water bottle for high altitude; it makes all the difference between comfort and misery. Take scissors, needles and thread for emergency mending as these are all unobtainable on the way. A torch with lots of spare batteries, *lots,* is very necessary for on dark nights it is all the illumination you will have if you wish to leave your tent. Take matches for cigarettes if you smoke and for your candles if you don't. Dark glasses are essential particularly at higher altitudes.

You will need paperbacks, particularly if you are going alone. If you are a birdwatcher take *The Birds of Nepal* by the two Flemings. I would have enjoyed my first five treks even more if this indispensable book had been in existence then.

Other pastimes could include a pack of cards or a pocket chess set. I have found myself, though this may sound ridiculous, that a little knitting or crochet is invaluable for on all long travels times occur, sometimes of a few hours' duration, sometimes even a few days, when there is nothing at all to do but wait, often in uncomfortable circumstances. A little handwork helps to occupy the mind and body and saves you from either bursting into tears or screaming; neither does any good and both make you lose face.

A few boiled sweeties are a good thing on trek, particularly at altitude. Chocolate is the thing you want most of all - you simply long for it - but it is only too apt to melt in the hot valleys and when you come to eat the precious stuff in celebration at the highest point you reach it has become beige and brittle with a dull surface. Do without it, as you have to do without so many things on trek, and remember that while people at home can have chocolate, roast beef, ice cream, fresh fruit, salad and hot baths only you can have that exhilarating air, those uniquely lovely mountains and the delightful people who live among them.

List of Birds
mentioned in the Text

PHALACROCORACIDAE: Cormorants
Large Cormorant *(Phalacrocorax carbo)*

ARDEIDAE: Herons
Cattle Egret *(Bubulcus ibis)*
Little Egret *(Egretta garzetta)*
Chestnut Bittern *(Ixobrychus cinnamomeus)*

CICONIIDAE: Storks
Open-billed Stork *(Anastomus oscitans)*
Black Stork *(Ciconia nigra)*
Lesser Adjutant Stork *(Leptoptilus javanicus)*

THRESKIORNITHIDAE: Ibises and Spoonbills
Black Ibis *(Pseudibis papillosa)*
Eurasian Spoonbill *(Platalea leucorodia)*

ANATIDAE: Ducks, Geese, Swans
Bar-headed Goose *(Anser indicus)*
Ruddy Shelduck or Brahminy Duck *(Tadorna ferruginea)*
Pintail *(Anas acuta)*
Eurasian Widgeon *(Anas penelope)*
Common Pochard *(Aythya ferina)*
Tufted Duck *(Aythya fuligula)*
Goosander *(Mergus merganser)*

ACCIPITRIDAE: Hawks, Eagles, etc.
Honey Buzzard *(Pernis ptilorhynchus)*
Black Kite *(Milvus migrans)*
Goshawk *(Accipiter gentilis)*
Crested Serpent Eagle *(Spilornis cheela)*
Golden Eagle *(Aquila chrysaetos)*
Steppe Eagle *(Aquila nipalensis)*
Black Eagle *(Ictinaetus malayensis)*
Osprey *(Pandion haliaetus)*
Himalayan Griffon Vulture *(Gyps himalayensis)*

Bearded Vulture or Lammergeier *(Gyps barbatus)*
King Vulture *(Torgos calvus)*
Egyptian Vulture *(Neophron percnopterus)*
Hen Harrier *(Circus cyaneus)*
Marsh Harrier *(Circus aeruginosus)*

FALCONIDAE: Falcons
Red-thighed Falconet *(Microhierax caerulescens)*
Peregrine Falcon *(Falco peregrinus)*
Lesser Kestrel *(Falco naumanni)*
Eurasian Kestrel *(Falco tinnunculus)*

PHASIANIDAE: Pheasants, Partridges, Quails, etc.
Tibetan Snowcock *(Tetraogallus tibetanus)*
Snow Partridge *(Lerwa lerwa)*
Grey Partridge *(Francolinus pondicerianus)*
Blood Pheasant *(Ithaginis cruentus)*
Crimson Horned Pheasant *(Tragopan satyra)*
Impeyan or Himalayan Monal Pheasant (Nepalese Danphe)
(Lophophorus impejanus)
Kaleej Pheasant *(Lophura leucomelana)*
Red Jungle Fowl *(Gallus gallus)*

GRUIDAE: Cranes
Common Crane *(Grus grus)*

CHARADRIIDAE: Plovers, Sandpipers, Snipe
Red-wattled Lapwing *(Vanellus indicus)*
Spur-winged Lapwing *(Vanellus spinosus)*
Little Ringed Plover *(Charadrius dubius)*
Curlew *(Numenius arquata)*
Greenshank *(Tringa nebularia)*
Wood Sandpiper *(Tringa glareola)*
Green Sandpiper *(Tringa ochropus)*
Common Sandpiper *(Tringa hypoleucos)*
Fantail Snipe *(Capella gallinago)*
Woodcock *(Scolopax rusticola)*

RECURVIROSTRIDAE: Stilts, Avocets, Ibisbills
Ibisbill *(Ibidorhyncha struthersii)*

BURHINIDAE: Stone Curlews, Thick-knees
Stone Curlew *(Burhinus oedicnemus)*
Great Stone Plover *(Esacus magnirostris)*

GLAREOLIDAE: Coursers
Small Pratincole *(Glareola lactea)*

LARIDAE: Gulls, Terns
Great Black-headed Gull *(Larus ichthyaetus)*
Caspian Tern *(Hydroprogne caspia)*
Gull-billed Tern *(Gelochelidon nilotica)*
Indian River Tern *(Sterna aurantia)*
Black-bellied Tern *(Sterna acuticauda)*
Little Tern *(Sterna albifrons)*

COLUMBIDAE: Pigeons, Doves
Snow Pigeon *(Columba leuconota)*
Ashy Wood Pigeon *(Columba pulchricollis)*
Emerald Dove *(Chalcophaps indica)*

PSITTACIDAE: Parrots
Rose-ringed Parakeet *(Psittacula krameri)*
Blossom-headed Parakeet *(Psittacula cyanocephala)*
Slaty-headed Parakeet *(Psittacula himalayana)*

CUCULIDAE: Cuckoos
Common Hawk Cuckoo (Brain-fever Bird) *(Cuculus varius)*
Eurasian Cuckoo *(Cuculus canorus)*
Indian Cuckoo *(Cuculus micropterus)*
Himalayan Cuckoo *(Cuculus saturatus)*
Emerald Cuckoo *(Chalcites maculatus)*

STRIGIDAE: Owls
Tawny Fish Owl *(Bubo flavipes)*
Barred Owlet *(Glaucidium cuculoides)*
Collared Pygmy Owlet *(Glaucidium brodiei)*

CAPRIMULGIDAE: Nightjars
Long-tailed Nightjar *(Caprimulgus macrurus)*
Jungle Nightjar *(Caprimulgus indicus)*
Franklin's Nightjar *(Caprimulgus affinis)*

APODIDAE: Swifts
Crested Swift *(Hemiprocne longipennis)*
Alpine Swift *(Apus melba)*

ALCEDINIDAE: Kingfishers
Large Pied Kingfisher *(Ceryle lugubris)*
Small Pied Kingfisher *(Ceryle rudis)*
Eurasian Kingfisher *(Alcedo atthis)*
Stork-billed Kingfisher *(Pelargopsis capensis)*
White-breasted Kingfisher *(Halcyon smyrnensis)*

MEROPIDAE: Bee-eaters
Blue-bearded Bee-Eater *(Nyctyornis athertoni)*

BUCEROTIDAE: Hornbills
Pied Hornbill *(Anthracoceros malabaricus)*

CAPITONIDAE: Barbets
Great Barbet *(Megalaima virens)*
Golden-throated Barbet *(Megalaima franklinii)*

PICIDAE: Woodpeckers
Wryneck *(Jynx torquilla)*
Spotted Piculet *(Picumnus innominatus)*
Large Golden-backed Woodpecker *(Chrsyolaptes lucidus)*
Fulvous-breasted Pied Woodpecker *(Dendrocopus macei)*
Black-naped Woodpecker *(Picus canus)*
Rufous-bellied Sapsucker *(Hypopicus hyperythrus)*

ALAUDIDAE: Larks
Bush Lark *(Mirafra assamica)*
Horned Lark or Shore Lark *(Eremophila alpestris)*

HIRUNDINIDAE: Swallows, Martins
Crag Martin *(Hirundo rupestris)*
Nepalese House Martin *(Delichon nipalensis)*

ORIOLIDAE: Orioles
Golden Oriole *(Oriolus oriolus)*
Black-headed Oriole *(Oriolus xanthornus)*
Maroon Oriole *(Oriolus traillii)*

DICRURIDAE: Drongos
Large Racquet-tailed Drongo *(Dicrurus paradiseus)*
Hair-crested Drongo *(Dicrurus hottentottus)*

STURNIDAE: Starlings
Spot-winged Stare *(Saraglossa spiloptera)*
Grey-headed Myna *(Sturnus malabaricus)*
Common Myna *(Acridotheres tristis)*

CORVIDAE: Crows, Magpies, Jays
Eurasian Jay *(Garrulus glandarius)*
Red-billed Blue Magpie *(Cissa erythrorhynchus)*
Yellow-billed Blue Magpie *(Cissa flavirostris)*
Nutcracker *(Nucifraga caryocatactes)*
Raven *(Corvus corax)*

CAMPEPHAGIDAE: Cuckoo Shrikes, Minivets
Large Cuckoo Shrike *(Coracina novaehollandiae)*
Scarlet Minivet *(Pericrocotus flammeus)*
Rosy Minivet *(Pericrocotus roseus)*
Little Minivet *(Pericrocotus cinnamomeus)*

IRENIDAE: Fairy Bluebirds, Ioras, Leafbirds
Golden-fronted Leafbird *(Chloropsis aurifrons)*
Orange-bellied Leafbird *(Chloropsis hardwickii)*
Fairy Bluebird *(Irene puella)*

PYCNONOTIDAE: Bulbuls
White-cheeked Bulbul *(Pycnonotus leucogenys)*
Striated Green Bulbul *(Pycnonotus striatus)*
Red-vented Bulbul *(Pycnonotus cafer)*
Grey Bulbul *(Hypsipetes madagascariensis)*

MUSCICAPIDAE:

SUB-FAMILY TIMALIINAE: Babblers
Slaty-bellied Scimitar Babbler *(Pomatorhinus schisticeps)*
Rusty-cheeked Scimitar Babbler *(Pomatorhinus erythrogenys)*
Slender-billed Scimitar Babbler *(Xiphirhynchus superciliaris)*
Nepal Parrotbill *(Paradoxornis nipalensis)*
White-throated Laughing-Thrush *(Garrulax albogularis)*
Large Necklaced Laughing-Thrush *(Garrulax pectoralis)*
White-spotted Laughing-Thrush *(Garrulax ocellatus)*
Black-faced Laughing-Thrush *(Garrulax affinis)*
Red-billed Leiothrix (Pekin Robin) *(Leiothrix lutea)*
Nepal Cutia *(Cutia nipalensis)*
Hoary Barwing *(Actinodura nipalensis)*
Red-tailed Minla *(Minla ignotincta)*
Bar-throated Minla *(Minla strigula)*
Yellow-naped Yuhina *(Yuhina flavicollis)*
Stripe-throated Yuhina *(Yuhina gularis)*
Rufous-vented Yuhina *(Yuhina occipitalis)*
White-bellied Yuhina *(Yuhina xantholeuca)*
Black-capped Sibia *(Heterophasia capistrata)*

SUB-FAMILY MUSCICAPINAE: Flycatchers
Orange-gorgetted Flycatcher *(Muscicapa strophiata)*
Little Pied Flycatcher *(Muscicapa westermanni)*
White-browed Blue Flycatcher *(Muscicapa superciliaris)*
Slaty Blue Flycatcher *(Muscicapa leucomelanura)*
Rufous-breasted Blue Flycatcher *(Muscicapa hyperythra)*
Sapphire-headed Flycatcher *(Muscicapa sapphira)*
Large Niltava *(Muscicapa grandis)*
Beautiful Niltava *(Muscicapa sundara)*
Verditer Flycatcher *(Muscicapa thalassina)*
Paradise Flycatcher *(Terpsiphone paradisi)*
Yellow-bellied Fantail Flycatcher *(Rhipidura hypoxantha)*
White-throated Fantail Flycatcher *(Rhipidura albicollis)*

SUB-FAMILY SYLVIINAE: Warblers
Black-faced Flycatcher-Warbler *(Abroscopus schisticeps)*

SUB-FAMILY TURDINAE: Thrushes, Robins and Chats
Eurasian Rubythroat *(Erithacus calliope)*
Bluethroat *(Erithacus svecicus)*
Orange-flanked Bush Robin *(Erithacus cyanurus)*
Golden Bush Robin *(Erithacus chrysaeus)*
Grandala *(Grandala coelicolor)*
Black Redstart *(Phoenicurus ochruros)*
Hodgson's Redstart *(Phoenicurus hodgsoni)*
Blue-fronted Redstart *(Phoenicurus frontalis)*
Güldenstadt's Redstart *(Phoenicurus erythrogaster)*
White-capped River Chat *(Chaimarrornis leucocephalus)*
White-throated Redstart *(Phoenicurus schisticeps)*
Plumbeous Redstart *(Rhyacornis fuliginosus)*
Little Forktail *(Enicurus scouleri)*
Black-backed Forktail *(Enicurus immaculatus)*
Dark Grey Bush Chat *(Saxicola ferrea)*
Blue-headed Rock Thrush *(Monticola cinclorhynchus)*
Chestnut-bellied Rock Thrush *(Monticola rufiventris)*
Blue Rock Thrush *(Monticola solitarius)*
Orange-headed Ground Thrush *(Zoothera citrina)*
Long-tailed Mountain Thrush *(Zoothera dixoni)*
Speckled Mountain Thrush *(Zoothera dauma)*
White-collared Blackbird *(Turdus albocinctus)*
Grey-winged Blackbird *(Turdus boulboul)*
Whistling Thrush *(Myiophoneus caeruleus)*
Tickell's Thrush *(Turdus unicolor)*
Grey-headed Thrush *(Turdus rubrocanus)*
Black/Red-throated Thrush *(Turdus ruficollis)*
Missel Thrush *(Turdus viscivorus)*

TROGLODYTIDAE: Wrens
Wren *(Troglodytes troglodytes)*

CINCLIDAE: Dippers
Brown Dipper *(Cinclus pallasii)*

PRUNELLIDAE: Accentors
Alpine Accentor *(Prunella collaris)*
Robin Accentor *(Prunella rubeculoides)*

PARIDAE: Tits
Grey Tit *(Parus major)*
Green-backed Tit *(Parus monticolus)*
Yellow-cheeked Tit *(Parus xanthogenys)*
Spot-winged Black Tit or Crested Black Tit *(Parus melanolophus)*
Rufous-breasted Black Tit *(Parus rubidiventris)*
Crested Brown Tit *(Parus dichrous)*
Red-headed Long-tailed Tit *(Aegithalos concinnus)*

SITTIDAE: Nuthatches, Wall Creepers
Chestnut-bellied Nuthatch *(Sitta castanea)*
White-tailed Nuthatch *(Sitta himalayensis)*
Wall Creeper *(Tichodroma muraria)*

CERTHIIDAE: Tree Creepers
Nepal Tree Creeper *(Certhia nipalensis)*

MOTACILLIDAE: Pipits, Wagtails
Rose-breasted Pipit *(Anthus roseatus)*
Eurasian Tree Pipit *(Anthus trivialis)*
Grey Wagtail *(Motacilla caspica)*
Yellow-headed or Citrine Wagtail *(Motacilla citreola)*
White Wagtail *(Motacilla alba)*

DICAEIDAE: Flowerpeckers
Fire-breasted Flowerpecker *(Dicaeum ignipectus)*

NECTARINIIDAE: Sunbirds
Fire-tailed Yellow-backed Sunbird *(Aethopyga ignicauda)*
Scarlet-breasted Sundbird *(Aethopyga siparaja)*

ZOSTEROPIDAE: White-eyes
White-eye *(Zosterops palpebrosa)*

PLOCEIDAE: Weavers, Sparrows
House Sparrow *(Passer domesticus)*
Tree Sparrow *(Passer montanus)*
Cinnamon Tree Sparrow *(Passer rutilans)*

FRINGILLIDAE: Finches, Grosbeaks
Allied Grosbeak *(Mycerobas affinis)*
White-winged Grosbeak *(Mycerobas carnipes)*
Himalayan Goldfinch *(Carduelis spinoides)*
Tibetan Siskin *(Carduelis tibetana)*
Hodgson's Mountain Finch *(Leucosticte nemoricola)*
Brandt's Mountain Finch *(Leucosticte brandti)*
Common Rose Finch *(Carpodacus erythrinus)*
Pink-browed Rose Finch *(Carpodacus rhodopeplus)*

Great Rose Finch *(Carpodacus rubicilla)*
White-browed Rose Finch *(Carpodacus thura)*
Crossbill *(Loxia curvirostra)*
Scarlet Finch *(Haematospiza sipahi)*
Red-headed Bullfinch *(Pyrrhula erythrocephala)*

EMBERIZIDAE: Buntings
Little Bunting *(Emberiza pusilla)*

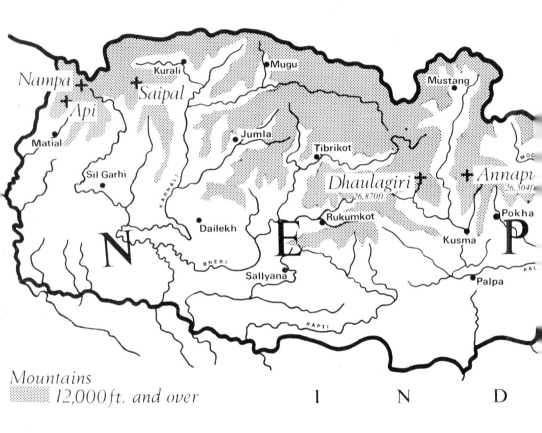

Mampa

Api

Matial

Kurali

Saipal

Sil Garhi

Mugu

Jumla

Dailekh

Tibrikot

Mustang

Dhaulagiri
26,870ft.

Annapı
26,504f

Pokha

Kusma

Palpa

Rukumkot

Sallyana

N E P

MOD

KARNALI

BHERI

RAPTI

KAL

I N D

Mountains
12,000 ft. and over